P9-BAV-182

SABR

THE
National Pastime
A REVIEW OF BASEBALL HISTORY

Our covers this month emphasize the gently bucolic element of our sport. In these ugly and frustrating times, I thought we could all use an afternoon lolling about on the soft spring grass listening to the crack of the bat, the pop of the mitt, and the chatter from the infield. (Maybe we could even step in and take a few cuts ourselves, amazing everyone with line shots into the alleys before modestly returning to the sidelines.)

I'm not very big on nostalgia. It is, after all, a kind of lie, excluding as it does all but the good memories (or worse, turning ugly times and circumstances golden). But there's nothing wrong with good history that also makes us smile. During this awful period for baseball, such history can bring us to a place where the Brattleboro Islanders take on the Twin State League in their picturesque ballpark, or where 14-year-old Dutch Doyle sells "cold drinks"—never lemonade—in the stands at Baker Bowl, or where Billy Loes overmatches the opposition in his first minor league season, or where Roy Face throws his forkball and simply can't lose, or where the big guns are guys named Goslin, Manush, Mayer, Foxx, and Vosmik, not Reinsdorf, Selig, and Fehr. I suspect we all feel a little better just picturing Richie Ashburn and Wally Berger and Swish Nicholson and Mort Cooper. This year, thanks to Geoff LaCasse, we can even glimpse the marvelously talented Hal Chase—before The Fall.

In this issue, there are also important articles by Norman Macht, who sets the record straight on the financial relationship between Ty Cobb and Mickey Cochrane (virtually none); by Tom Nawrocki, who discusses Cap Anson's early experiments with platooning; by Jerry Malloy, who gives us a history of baseball in the black 25th Infantry Regiment, and by others who cover SABR's typically huge range of interests and eras. This is by far the largest issue of *The National Pastime* that we've ever produced, and it is the result of a vastly increased number of good manuscripts flowing into the publications office.

—M.A.

THE NATIONAL PASTIME (ISSN 0734-6905, ISBN 0-910137-62-5), Number 15. Published by The Society for American Baseball Research, Inc., P.O. Box 93183, Cleveland, OH 44101. Postage paid at Birmingham, AL. Printed by EBSCO Media, Birmingham, AL.

Contents

NEWS AND NOTES

Society for American Baseball Research
PO Box 93183
Cleveland OH 44101
216-575-0500, 216-575-0502 fax

SABR Membership Open to All

SABR was founded August 10, 1971, to facilitate the dissemination of baseball research information and to establish an accurate account of the history of baseball.

Today, nearly 25 years later, SABR members number over 6,500 worldwide and share in the enjoyment of reading about, talking about, writing about, and learning more about the game of baseball.

You can join SABR and help continue a long tradition of producing and sharing new and interesting baseball information. You can take advantage of any or all of SABR's research resources, even if your research is limited to reading SABR publications and other baseball literature. If your objective is more information about, appreciation of, and enjoyment of baseball, give SABR a try.

Membership for the 1995 calendar year is only $35 (materials already produced in 1995 will be mailed to you with your new member packet, so you're not missing anything by joining in August or September) and gets you ***Baseball Research Journal, More Nineteenth Century Stars***, *The SABR Bulletin, the SABR Membership Directory* and ***The National Pastime #15***.

If you've bought this book and don't want a second copy of it, just notify us and we'll send you a $5 gift certificate for purchase of other fine SABR publications. Combined with all the discounts on SABR materials and commercially published books, you'll more than get your money's worth.

What Some SABR Members Are Saying...

"SABR handles large projects through cooperative efforts. But even if you're just a fan, you get your money's worth in publications."

Pete Palmer, author

"SABR brings the fun of finding new friends, new facts. I'm researching top players' high-school careers. Mickey Mantle's 41 classmates did not vote him Most Athletic."

Jim Kreuz, Chemical Engineer

"SABR is fun--and essential for anyone who writes baseball. SABRites are knowledgeable and helpful."

Paul Dickson, author

"I can't imagine any baseball enthusiast not belonging to SABR. Some SABRites know everything--and they'll share it.

Jack Carlson, retired Aerospace Engineer

SABR 1995 MEMBERSHIP FORM

Name ____________________

Address ____________________

City ____________ State______ ZIP__________

(use ZIP+4, if possible)

Home Ph. ____________ Wk Ph. ____________

E-Mail (or fax) Address ____________ Birthdate ____________

Occupation/Title: ____________________

1995 Dues payable by check, money order, Visa, Master or Discover Card

US: $35 ($99-3 year) $20 Senior (65+)
Canada/Mexico: $45 *($129-3 year)*; $30 Senior (US funds or equivalent)
Overseas: $50 *($144-3 year)*; $35 Senior (US funds or equivalent)
Family: $10 extra per family member at same address

FAX THIS FORM TO 216-575-0502 WITH VISA, MASTER OR DISCOVER CARD PAYMENT FOR FASTEST SERVICE!

Interest Codes (please circle)

01 Minor Leagues
02 Negro Leagues
03 Baseball Records
04 Biographical Research
05 Statistical Analysis
06 Ballparks
07 Hall Of Fame
08 19th Century
09 Socio-Economic Aspects
11 Bibliography
12 Book Collecting
13 Collegiate Baseball
14 Latin America
15 Umpire/Rules
16 Computerization
17 Women in Bball
18 Box Scores
19 Baseball Education
A1 Baltimore Orioles
A2 Boston Red Sox
A3 California Angels
A4 Chicago White Sox
A5 Cleveland Indians
A6 Detroit Tigers
A7 Kansas City Royals
A8 Milwaukee Brewers
A9 Minnesota Twins
B1 NY Yankees
B2 Oakland A's
B3 Seattle Mariners
B4 Texas Rangers
B5 Toronto Blue Jays
B6 St. Louis Browns
B7 Phil Athletics
B8 Wash Senators
C2 Seattle Pilots
N1 Atlanta Braves
N2 Chicago Cubs
B9 KC Athletics
N3 Cincinnati Reds
N4 Houston Astros
N5 LA Dodgers
N6 Montreal Expos
N7 New York Mets
N8 Phil Phillies
N9 Pittsburgh Pirates
O1 St. Louis Cards
O2 San Diego Padres
O3 SF Giants
O4 Boston Braves
O5 Brooklyn Dodgers
O6 New York Giants
O7 Milwaukee Braves
O8 Providence Grays
O9 Troy Haymakers/Trojans
P1 All-Star Games
P2 Japanese Baseball
P3 European Baseball
P4 Amateur B'ball, Semi-Pro
P5 Colorado Rockies
P6 Florida Marlins
P7 Photos, Pictorial History
P8 Scouts

DISC/MC/VISA# ____________________

Exp Date________ Amount Authorized $____________

Signature ____________________

The Brattleboro Islanders

Seamus Kearney

An euphoric wave of civic pride and boosterism swept through Brattleboro, Vermont in 1911 like a panacea for communal ills. Rarely does a community earn the benefits that the bustling Vermont village reaped for that year. Expecting a dance hall with an outdoor grandstand for summer fun, Brattleboro gained that plus a new baseball team playing in a pioneering league featuring a pennant race meant for the ages.

Two Brattleboro businessmen, George Fox and Michael Moran, built their Island Park on the island in the Connecticut River opposite the village. The amusement pavilion was meant to add spice to the lives of Brattleborans. But their multipurpose facility became a centerpiece of progress when the Brattleboro Islanders of the Twin State League provided New England with a zesty baseball season culminating in a championship game worthy of a Thanksgiving repast.

The Islanders' creation stemmed from Moran's and Fox's disclosure in October, 1910 that a baseball grandstand would adjoin their planned amusement pavilion. The promise of the construction of a 1,200-seat grandstand without a team posed too seductive a lure for baseball fans in Brattleboro. Hardly had the ground been broken in November than baseball fever broke out in the town. Acting with passion and pride, Brattleboro's fans pledged to support a team and founded a baseball committee in December. A subscription drive gathered over $1,000. But, not satisfied with just a team, the villagers puffed out their chests and began clamoring for a league.

Fortunately for them, Island Park's construction spread baseball fever throughout the Connecticut River Valley. Two other towns succumbed in December when Keene in New Hampshire and Bellows Falls in Vermont formed committees. Other towns in the region were urged to catch the frenzy, but, after the initial outbreak, baseball fever incubated in the Connecticut Valley winter, waiting—it seemed—for the breakout of warm weather in the spring.

But people did not lose interest, as the paradigm, "If you build it, they will come," spoke for the reality of Island Park. Hundreds of curious onlookers visited the island site to see the work in progress every Sunday after building began in February, 1911. Such voting with their feet encouraged the baseball associations to do likewise. At the Rockingham Hotel in Bellows Falls on March 12, 1911, the associations founded the Twin State Baseball League.

Unlike previous amateur leagues in the Valley during the 1890's and 1900's, the Twin State Baseball League featured paid players, umpires and officials. Created to take advantage of the rivalry of the mill and factory towns of the Connecticut Valley, the league included Brattleboro, Bellows Falls, Keene and a Springfield, Vermont-Charlestown, New Hampshire hybrid (quickly dubbed the Hyphens by area wags). The league scheduled a season of 36 games, with the first game to be played at the new Island Park.

As work on the ballpark progressed, construction of a team to play there built up steam. Most players were local or regional and the associations competed

Seamus Kearney is an independent researcher and writer. On deck are projects on baseball and the Internet and futher work on the Twin State League. This article is based on his presentation at the 1994 SABR Convention.

fiercely to build teams from scratch. On the same day the Twin State League was formed, the Brattleboro Baseball Association hired E. L. Breckinridge to gather a team and manage the local entry.

"Home Run" Breckinridge was a renowned minor league star known for his slugging. He hit 120 homers during his career and led *all* minor league players in four-baggers during two of his twelve seasons. After his playing days, he entered the umpiring ranks in the New England League before turning to managing. He had been the baseball coach at Amherst College in Massachusetts from 1905 to 1910 and for three summers had been the manager of the South Manchester, Connecticut professional team. He also had coaching stints at Williams and at Dartmouth. At 42 years of age, savoring the new opportunity, he immediately launched a fervent search for a team. By June, he had his Brattleboro Islanders ready to initiate the new Island Park Amusement Company's grandstand.

Island Park—But baseball was not to inaugurate the opening of the new facility. It was not built for just baseball. Two days before the start of the Twin State League opener at Island Park, George Fox and Michael Moran presided over the official opening of the facility to the public with over 2,000 people in attendance. The pavilion was crowded all evening and hundreds lined up on the bridge leading to the island, waiting to gain entrance.

The new amusement pavilion was worth the wait. Painted in various shades of green, elaborately lit with 400 incandescent bulbs, Island Park sparkled alluringly on its island setting. Inside, a beautiful dance floor of rock maple measuring 84 by 48 feet nestled under an overhanging balcony seating 250. A wide veranda flanked the ballroom on the west, river side, while the baseball grandstand abutted on the east, accessible by doors leading to a wide walk-around. Open windows on all sides attracted cooling breezes, while a soda fountain provided cooling refreshment. Under the ballroom were the new bowling alleys.

Island Park was without equal in the Valley. The Brattleboro *Reformer* reported to those who were not there:

> Brattleboro people who have awaited the opening before visiting the park will be astonished at the outlay of money and ingenuity upon the equipment for this amusement enterprise which promises to be the recreation spot par excellence in this part of New England.

On Saturday, July 1, baseball debuted at Island Park. Country balderdash spiced the heralding of league-style baseball returning to the town. The *Reformer* boasted:

> And let it be said right here and now, a few flail-handlers to the contrary notwithstanding, that the boys who are to wear the Brattleboro uniform are a likely looking lot—clean, manly young fellows, full of pepper and anxious to represent well a town which they seem to think is a pretty good place in which to summer.

The Vermont *Phoenix* informed its readers about the new baseball in town a little less effusively:

> "Play bawl"
> "Strike One"
> Then the resounding smack of wood meeting leather, the chortling of hundreds of lovers of the national game and the Twin State baseball season will be in full blast on the Island park tomorrow....

The season begins—"Breck's" team was ready. He had assembled a group of young professionals and collegians from New England—twelve in all, including one local pitcher, J. J. Clune. The opening day lineup had:

F.J. Kelley CF	N. Attleboro, Mass.
J.J. Slattery 2b	Marlborough, Mass.
Horan 3b	S. Manchester, Conn.
Charles Ivers 1b	Middletown, Conn.
Thomas McLeod C	Torrington, Conn.
Gus Flynn LF	N. Attleboro, Mass.
Charles McDonnell RF	–
Hollis Cobb SS	East Putney, Vermont
John J. Bennett P	Plymouth, Mass.

Reserves included pitchers Clune and "Slats" Atwood of Tufts University, and J.F. Meehan, 2b, who was recovering from an injury.

Opening day was a hoot. The two teams, Bellows Falls and the Islanders, assembled at 2 PM on Saturday at Brattleboro's Town Hall and paraded down Main Street and across the bridge to the Park. Brattleboro's own First Regiment Band led the parade and regaled the fans during practice.

"It was a corking opener," trumpeted the *Reformer*. 1,200 fans crowded the new grandstand and cheered as their team took its and the league's opener, 8-3. Ivers went 4 for 4 and "Reds" Bennett was the winning pitcher, striking out 10, giving up six hits and six walks. The park, agreed both teams and fans, was magnificent.

The joy and expectation at the opener evaporated on July 4. Brattleboro dropped both ends of a morning-afternoon, home-away doubleheader to its chief rival, Keene of New Hampshire. Cobb had three errors in each game. Bennett yielded six walks and 11 hits (plus six wild pitches) in the morning's 12-3 loss seen by "a throng of spectators" at Island Park, said the *Reformer*.

The misery continued in the afternoon at Keene before a large crowd as Clune lost big. He and Atwood yielded 10 runs in an 11-5 loss. A rarely seen assist was earned by the Keene rightfielder when he threw Flynn out at first after the latter had "singled."

After the loss, Breckinridge went to work. He dropped Cobb, Clune and Atwood, and brought in two pitchers, Paul Wachtel and Bill Conroy. The move characterized the rest of the Islanders' season as Breck wheeled and dealt, going through nine roster changes in search of a winning combination. By the season's end, 27 players had worn the blue and gray colors of Brattleboro and only two players remained from opening day—Horan and McLeod.

Initially, Breck's changes did little to alter results and at the end of the fourth week the Islanders were 7-7, three games back of Keene. The outlook was not bright for the team. Keene had taken the measure of Brattleboro, winning four of five games between the two. In addition, the Islanders lost their captain and batting leader, Ivers, on July 22 when he fractured his leg.

But prospects improved the very next game. With Ivers on the bench sporting cast and cane, the Islanders notched their first win over Keene before a wild midweek crowd of 800 at Island Park. Unfortunately, that rousing win was followed the next day, July 26, by a heart-rending 1-0 loss at Keene—decided by a fluke hit in the 11th inning.

Things look up—But "Breck" had found effective pitchers in Wachtel and Jackson (added on July 14) in addition to Conroy. The Islanders pulled together behind these three and Brattleboro ran off four straight wins following the July 26 shutout loss at Keene.

Conroy won two, but the real lift was Jackson's two hit shutout of the league-leaders at Island Park before another ecstatic crowd on August 1. The team's confidence increased when Conroy pitched a victory at Keene the next day. The four game win streak ended with Brattleboro in first place and Keene a half game behind.

Keene regained the lead on August 8 with a gutsy extra-inning win at Island Park. Nine-hundred fans could not prevent sloppy play by the Islanders (seven errors) as Keene rallied for five runs in the 11th, taking a formerly tight game 8-3.

From then to the end of the season it was a race between Brattleboro and Keene, with Bellows Falls and the Springfield-Charlestown contingent trailing far behind. Keene and Brattleboro were longtime commercial, industrial and cultural rivals in the Connecticut Valley community and it was appropriate that the two towns vied for the first Twin State League flag.

Other attractions—Island Park was part of that rivalry. There was nothing like it in all of New England. Praise was pouring in for the new facility. A Boston visitor wrote to the *Reformer*, calling Island Park "...a fine baseball park, beautifully and conveniently located." A group of excursionists from outside Vermont "...were loud in their praise of the park with its various attractions."

But rival's praise was more pleasing. The Keene *Cheshire Republican* said of the pavilion:

> "A visit to the pavilion and grandstand at the riverbank will make a man gasp...Fox and Moran have surely done their share in providing a proper...setting for baseball, and if Brattleboriens do not appreciate their efforts every man, woman, and child in that beautiful burg should be sentenced to 60 days in some less favored locale."

Though an exciting pennant race was drawing hundreds of fans to Island Park's grandstand, hundreds more attended the casino's other attractions. The pavilion's location was ideal. Access to the island was a couple hundred yards walk from the Brattleboro railroad station and downtown area, over a road bridge linking the island and the town. Two railroads brought patrons from all over the Connecticut Valley and many places beyond.

Over 1,000 attended a concert by the First Regiment Band on the 24th of July and this attendance was duplicated at another concert a month later. Nightly dancing on the marvelous floor and motion pictures projected from the grandstand onto a screen set up on the ballfield were popular attractions. The casino's management ordered two more bowling alleys added to the four on the bottom floor "to take care of demand.".Low admission prices for most events, generally 10 or 15 cents for adults and a nickel for kids, kept attendance high. Baseball games were a quarter for grandstand and a half-dollar for reserved seats.

Area residents and visitors could enjoy multiple entertainment choices with which to spend leisure time at the pavilion. An advertisement in the Vermont *Phoenix* presented one typical Saturday offering for August 19:

Baseball at 3 pm: Islanders vs Keene for 1st place

Movies at 7:45 pm: *Wanted—A Wife*, "a rattling farce"

Vaudeville acts between the movies

Dancing at 10 pm, from "our regular orchestra"

Pennant race—Two friends who attended that August 19 game against Keene, would have seen a Brattleboro team fresh from a victory over Bellows Falls at Island Park on Friday that enabled the Islanders to recapture the League's lead. Saturday's crowd, said the *Phoenix*, "...taxed the capacity of the grandstand and filled the bleachers...." With first place on the line, the fans rooted for their heroes' chances against Keene.

The friends would also be privileged to tell their neighbors that they witnessed a dominating performance by the winning Islander pitcher that afternoon. Jackson faced only 29 batters as he threw a masterful, one-hit shutout. The win lengthened Brattleboro's lead to a game and a half.

The Islanders were in the midst of a winning streak that would top at five making their record at the end of the eighth week of play 18-10. They were playing good ball, compiling an 11-3 record since the 1-0 loss at Keene on July 26.

Brattleboro retained its place atop the Twin State League with two shutout wins at Island Park on August 28 and 29. The shutouts stretched a remarkable scoreless streak for Islander opponents there to 37 innings. The 1-0 victory against Bellows Falls on August 29 was described as one of the most exciting games ever played at Island Park. But Brattleboro could not lengthen its margin, as Keene kept pace and narrowed the lead at week's end with a come-from-behind victory over the Islanders at Keene on August 30. Keene won it by scoring four runs in the bottom of the seventh.

At the end of August, Brattleboro's lead remained one game over Keene. They needed to win two of the last four games to cop the pennant and, after a September-opening victory over Bellows Falls, they required only one.

In the next two games, Brattleboro could not capitalize on opportunities to clinch the pennant against the weaker teams in the Twin State League. They lost to a strong-finishing "Hyphens" club and to an underdog Bellows Falls nine, previously vanquished eight straight times by the Islanders. But Keene also had faltered and the Islanders clung to a shaky one-game lead.

The Bellows Falls loss was the morning affair of a Labor Day away-home doubleheader. Swelled by Islander fans hoping to celebrate a pennant, the largest crowd of Bellows Falls' season witnessed the loss. Though denied, Brattleboro supporters hoped for another chance for celebration in Monday's afternoon game. Breck herded his Islanders aboard a train and headed south toward home and Island Park and Keene, and maybe the pennant in the last game of the season.

Aboard the train, Breck rallied their spirits, no doubt urging his charges to focus on the task at hand—the afternoon game on which all of their season's aspirations rode.

The clinching game—When the Islanders strode across the bridge to the park, they had every expectation of victory. They were 13-4 on home ground, and had beaten Keene four games out of seven since July 26. What's more, they had a recent, strong addition slated to pitch for them—John Bosk, winner of fifteen games for the Bennington, Vermont team. Breck had snatched up Bosk when his club's season ended. Bosk had pitched well, winning one game for the Islanders since joining on August 24. He was rested and ready.

On September 4, 1911, 3,500 baseball enthusiasts from all over the valley packed the grandstand at Island Park, spilled onto the field, crowded both foul lines and circled the outfield. The Vermont *Phoenix* said:

> "More than 500 Keene supporters came to see the game in automobiles and on a special train and Bellows Falls sent a delegation of more than 200. The large crowd was handled without a hitch, there was not the semblance of rowdyism on anybody's part and it was a fitting climax to the two month's race for the leadership of the league."

"It was the game of a lifetime," said the *Phoenix*, "...not settled until the last man was out in the last inning of the last game." Both the *Reformer* and the *Phoenix* called the throng at Island Park the largest crowd ever to witness a baseball game in southern Vermont. The *Phoenix* said they saw, "...virtually a perfect game, full of the thrills and uncertainties which makes baseball the greatest popular sport in America...."

"The gonfalon is ours!," crowed the paper. It said the "...home team was cheered on to victory by a crowd of howling fans which did valiant work at every opportunity."

John Bosk pitched a marvelous game that was matched in every way but the outcome by the Keene pitcher, Smith. Bosk shutout the Keene batters, 2-0, giving up only three hits while striking out four. Smith went eight innings and struck out 10, giving up only four hits and surrendering the two runs on sacrifice flies. Each pitcher walked only one batter.

The game was conspicuous for great plays and great catches on both sides. The crowd was reported to be delirious during the sixth inning, which featured spectacular catches by right fielder Wachtel and center fielder Vance. The Islanders themselves were retired in the seventh inning on a reported "difficult try of a catch" by McCarthy, the Keene center fielder, a stunt that the *Phoenix* said, "...necessitated his lifting his hat as he came to the bench."

One of the most intense parts of the game happened in the fourth, when Keene loaded the bases with one out. A close collision play at the plate forced out the Keene team's player-manager, Leonard. An unpopular player with Island Park fans, Leonard was booed loudly when the crowd interpreted his collision as an attempt to impede the catcher's try for a double play at second.

"Bedlam was let loose for several minutes," said the *Phoenix*, but calm was restored and the threat ended with a foul pop to third.

The game was so exciting that one fan almost literally lost his shirt. The *Phoenix* reported that a Keene man bet "...every cent he had with him..., and then because the Brattleboro betters were yelling for more of his cash and calling him a 'quitter' he bet his coat and hat, losing both his money and his clothing."

Another interesting sidelight to this obviously riveting game: the vast throng barely had time to display its delight. The game lasted a mere one hour and thirty-eight minutes.

There are no accounts of the crowd's reaction at the end, but who could imagine such an excited mass of fans simply walking away, savoring—or ruing—the climactic victory. There must have been a celebration, perhaps too wild for family newspapers to report on, that kept Brattleborans buzzing for days.

Even though the pennant was in hand, there was more baseball at Island Park that season, but it was clearly anticlimactic. Bennington had challenged Brattleboro for the so-called Vermont championship and, only a day after beating Keene, the Islanders dropped the first game to Bennington in a three-game series. Attendance was sparse. In no way did the game match the excitement of the Twin State championship contest, and, after Brattleboro lost again the next day, the series stopped when the third game was rained out. Another challenge series with a Turners Falls, Mass. team also failed to entice fans to Island Park.

The Twin State League race over, proud Islander fans were smug and satisfied with the pennant residing in Brattleboro. They were content to stay at home, preparing for the cold winter months, by gloating over the warm memory of the pennant copped by Breck's boys at the unforgettable championship game—dreaming, perhaps, of a repeat performance in 1912.

NOTES ON SOURCES

The bulk of my baseball research emanates from two sources: the Brattleboro *Reformer* and the Vermont *Phoenix*. Descriptions of the Island Park pavilion come from the same sources and from interviews of two area residents: Bernie Harris, who danced there, and Burt Baldwin, who played music there.

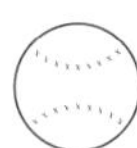

"Rubes" on the Mound, 1901—1919

1. *Adams*
2. *Benton*
3. *Bressler*
4. *Dessau*
5. *Foster*
6. *Geyer*
7. *Hartranft*
8. *Kinsella*
9. *Kisinger*
10. *Kroh*
11. *Manning*
12. *Marion*
13. *Marquard*
14. *Marshall*
15. *Parnham*
16. *Peters*
17. *Robinson*
18. *Suter*
19. *Taylor*
20. *Vickers*
21. *Waddell*

—Cappy Gagnon

"Boy, this looks like Simmons."

An Afternoon with Bill Chamberlain

Dick Thompson

It was late in the summer of 1993 and I was headed for Cape Cod to interview Bill Chamberlain of the 1932 Chicago White Sox. I was pretty excited, for gathering biographical data on New England-born major leaguers is my chief interest, and Chamberlain had been on my "want" list for a long time.

Do you want to hear a great Babe Ruth story? Or maybe read another Ted Williams interview? Well, not me. Give me a player who made just a brief big league appearance: they are the people with real stories to tell. I will always remember the afternoon I spent with 97-year-old Joe Burns shortly after the 1986 World Series. Burns had a minor league career that lasted close to twenty years, but he played in just five major league games. Burns' recollections ranged from Hugh Duffy to Dwight Evans. His first big league hit came off Mordecai Brown on June 19, 1910. (Burns batted for Slow Joe Doyle, the pitcher, in the ninth inning of a 10-3 loss to Chicago at Cincinnati. Brown went the route for Chicago.) And Ty Cobb gave him tips on outfield play. Visiting with Burns was a great experience, and I was hoping for repeat performance with Chamberlain. I wasn't disappointed.

Bill met me at the door of his daughter's home in Mattapoisett, Massachusetts. He had recently been released from a long hospitalization following an automobile accident. I found him quite frail and very modest. He didn't think he had anything of importance to say. I told him SABR thought otherwise.

Chamberlain was born in Stoughton, Massachusetts, in 1909, and grew up in the nearby town of Milton, which was also the hometown of two other 1930s major leaguers, Elbie Fletcher and Charlie Devens. Devens came from money and took the private-school road to Harvard, the Yankees, and then Wall Street. It seems odd that two players from the same small town, debuting the same season in the major leagues, would not know each other, but Chamberlain said he never met Devens. Fletcher, who was seven years younger than Chamberlain, was a different story. "I can still see Elbie coming through the gate of the Milton Town Field," recalled Chamberlain. "He was just a little kid then, with his glove tied to his belt. We always let him play a couple of innings. I never thought he'd grow up to be as big as he was."

Following his graduation from high school, Bill attended the Dean Academy (now Dean Junior College) in Franklin, a local hotbed of baseball activity that both Mickey Cochrane and Gabby Hartnett had earlier attended, and St. Anselm's College in New Hampshire. He played semipro baseball in Canada, and with the Neponset Wanderers of the Boston Twilight League.

The summer of 1932 found Chamberlain in the amateur Cape Cod League. "I had just pitched a game against Falmouth. I was pitching for Harwich. A fellow [scout] came up to me. He asked me if I would like to try out for the Chicago White Sox. I agreed to meet the White Sox in New York, where they were playing the Yankees. I bummed rides from Harwich up to Milton Village, where I had two brothers who were cops. I borrowed 20 dollars from my sister and was off to New York. The next morning I worked out with the White Sox. Then we went up to Montreal, where I beat the

Dick Thompson is a member of SABR's Biographical Committee. He would like to thank Ray Nemec, Bob Richardson, Bill Ruiz, and Dave Vincent for assistance with this article.

Dick Thompson

Bill Chamberlain

Montreal club [of the International League] in an exhibition game. From there I went to Chicago. The club kept me there awhile, you know, kind of working out with the batters. They signed me to a contract and all of a sudden I'm in the big leagues."

The White Sox were an awful team in 1932, finishing the season with a 49-102 record. Only the Red Sox prevented them from finishing in last place. Chamberlain made his major league debut on August 2. He started and pitched eight innings against the Washington Senators, allowing just four hits but losing the game, 4-1, as his teammates made three errors. His next start was against the St. Louis Browns. He gave up just two hits through the first six innings, and left the game trailing 2-0 after eight innings. The White Sox, who gave him no run support, lost the game 5-0.

Such was the pattern of Chamberlain's luck as a major league pitcher. He appeared in 12 games for the White Sox that summer. He started five and lost all of them. But despite the fact that

Chamberlain never won a big league game, he has plenty of big league memories.

These guys play real good—On August 23 Chamberlain pitched in a game against the Philadelphia Athletics. He came into the game in the second inning, after the Athletics had knocked out the White Sox starter. "I'm looking at the first hitter coming up. I said to myself, 'Boy, this looks like Simmons.' My catcher called for a curveball. I made the pitch. The ball was about three quarters of the way to the plate and I'm still thinking that this had to be Al Simmons. The ball broke down low and inside, a good pitch. I saw him shove his foot in the bucket and swing. The next thing I knew the ball was out in the stands. I started to laugh; I just knew it was Simmons. Luke Appling, our shortstop, yelled over to me. He said, 'Billy, turn your head, don't let the guys in the dugout see you laughing.' I yelled back, 'Gee, Luke, did you see him hit that ball?' All I could think of was a Fourth of July bomb. You could hear it screeching out to the stands." Chamberlain also gave up two home runs to Mickey Cochrane in that game. These were the only major league homers he allowed. No banjo hitters for Bill. When he gave up a homer, he did it with style. Simmons's home run was the 200th of his career.

On August 29 Chamberlain lost a 4-3 game to Red Ruffing and the New York Yankees at Yankee Stadium. He held Babe Ruth, Lou Gehrig, Tony Lazzeri, Joe Sewell, and Earle Combs all hitless, and in the process, notched his only major league hit off Ruffing. Not too shabby for a man who started the season pitching in the Cape Cod League.

"Do I remember my hit off Ruffing? It was a line drive over the shortstop. I remember getting thrown out at the plate later. I went to score, and Dickey had his foot just in front of the plate, and he gave me a kick along with it. He turned me around and tagged me out. I said to myself, 'Boy, these guys play real good here in New York.' I also struck out Lou Gehrig. He came up to me between innings and said I got him on a good pitch.

"I made a lot of good friends that year. I had a room at Appling's place that summer. I went to the track with Red Faber and Eddie Collins; they were good friends and hung around together. My salary was $300 a month. They gave us six dollars a day for meal money and we dropped most of that on the horses.

"There was one game that ruined me. It was the last game of the year. I had pretty good luck up until that time. The game was in Cleveland. They got five hits and five runs off me and I didn't get anyone out.

"As I look back at it, there was no reason that I couldn't of made it. I had good control. Some guys were faster, but I had good control. Ted Lyons gave me the best advice, 'Don't let them hit the ball they want to hit. Make them hit your pitch.' I should have listened closer."

Nineteen thirty-two was Chamberlain's only year in the major leagues. He played in the minors until the end of the 1938 season, making stops in the International, Texas, Eastern, New York-Pennsylvania, Northeastern, and Cape Breton Colliery leagues. He remembers playing for Rabbit Maranville in the minors. "When you wanted to throw a spitter, the ball went around the infield and when it came back from Maranville it was all loaded up. He loaded it up naturally. Then you hold the ball between the seams and let it go."

Chamberlain quit baseball when he had the opportunity to join the Boston police force. "I stayed there for 30 years. I got a few commendations, and a couple of weeks off at different times for pinches I made. I was fairly good at getting information. The police force was a good job." He retired in 1970.

Bill's health started to worsen soon after our afternoon together. By the middle of autumn he had been admitted to a local hospital. I stopped in to see him when I got the chance, and no matter how bad he was feeling, he was always happy to talk baseball.

Just before Christmas I called Elbie Fletcher. I had some questions on some local minor leaguers from the 1920s and 1930s that I thought he could help me on. We had a nice talk, Elbie said we discussed players he hadn't thought of in 30 years. I brought up Chamberlain's name during our conversation and filled Elbie in on Bill's health. Fletcher started to reminisce about baseball in Milton during the 1920s, and what a great high school pitcher Chamberlain had been. He laughed when I passed on Chamberlain's recollection of Fletcher showing up at the local field with his glove tied to his belt, hoping the older kids would let him play in their game. "True," he said, "all true."

Bill Chamberlain passed away on February 6, 1994, Elbie Fletcher just over a month later. You can keep those Hall of Famers. Give me an afternoon with gentlemen like these any day.

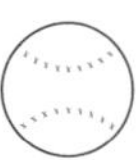

A Forgotten Boston Pennant Race

Dick Beverage

Certainly the most dismal era in the history of Boston baseball is the period from 1919 to 1945. Not only were there no pennants won by the two Boston clubs, but rarely did either the Red Sox or Braves win half of their games. The Red Sox finished last nine times and suffered a hiatus of fifteen years without finishing in the first division of an eight-team league. The Braves enjoyed only three first division finishes, never better than fourth, and suffered through the miserable 1935 season with only 38 wins. Only in 1944 did Red Sox fans have the thrill of seeing their club in contention. The Red Sox were within 1-1/2 games of first place in late August of that year, when calls to military service robbed them of Bobby Doerr, Tex Hughson and Hal Wagner. The club immediately went into a tailspin, losing ten straight games and eventually winding up at .500 in fourth place.

There was one other time during these gloomy years that a Boston club was a legitimate pennant contender, and it is all but forgotten by even the oldest of Boston fans. The year was 1933, and surprisingly, the team was the Braves. They combined a good pitching staff with a steady defense and some timely hitting to give the eventual champion New York Giants a real challenge before losing a crucial series over Labor Day weekend. And then, after slumping badly and falling out of the first division seemingly for good, the Braves rallied and provided one of the most dramatic finishes in Boston history.

Dick Beverage is SABR"s vice-president. His interest in this period was inspired by his long friendship with Wally Berger.

Beantown poverty—The Braves of the '30s were a sad-sack franchise, badly undercapitalized and not especially popular in Boston. The Red Sox had long ago captured the imagination of New England fans, and even during the miserable '20s were drawing more fans than their National League counterparts. The Braves were owned at the time by Judge Emil Fuchs, as they had been since 1923. Fuchs had been a successful attorney in New York. He was not especially wealthy when he bought the ball club, and years of financial losses had dissipated much of what he had. Legalization of Sunday baseball in 1928 had helped somewhat, but the Braves were forced to compete with richer clubs on the open market for players if they were to put a reasonable team on the field; there was no money available for even the beginnings of a farm system.

The onset of the Depression in 1930 and the financial misery that came with it forced Fuchs to borrow heavily from Charles F. Adams, a successful grocery store owner and part owner of the Boston Bruins hockey club. Even though the Braves had begun to play better, they didn't generate enough cash flow to repay the loans. Fuchs' personal habits were not the most frugal either, and by 1933 it was clear that he would soon be in real financial trouble. Adams had indicated that he would no longer provide the operating funds and would demand repayment. A showdown in the near future was inevitable.

The ballpark—The Braves played their home games in Braves Field, on Commonwealth and Gaffney, as they had since 1915. One of the last of the new concrete and steel parks built in the early twentieth century, Braves Field was probably the worst of the lot. A single deck park like Fenway, Braves Field was much larger, seating more than 40,000. It consisted of four sections—a main grandstand extending from just past first base to slightly beyond third, two large pavilion sections in left and right, and a small bleacher section dubbed the "Jury Box," behind the right field wall. With home plate 75 feet from the grandstand even the best seats in the park were a distance away from the action. The usual number of posts made viewing difficult from virtually every seat.

The original playing dimensions were enormous. Distances to left and right field were 402 feet down the line and center field was 550 feet away. Not until 1925, when the park had been open for ten years, did a home run clear these walls.

The prevailing wind usually blew in from left center, which further reduced the opportunities for scoring. In 1928 Fuchs erected fencing in left field to cut down the distances and add some excitement to the game, but since the Braves were such a weak hitting team, the opposition took the greater advantage. It seemed as if there were adjustments to the fences every year after that. In the season of 1933 the distance to left field was a more manageable 359 feet down the line, 417 feet to dead center and 364 to right.

Not a hitter's year—1933 was the third straight season that the subject of the baseballs employed by the National League was controversial. After the slugging that went on in the National League in 1930, when the entire league batted over .300, it was determined that the seams on the baseballs were too low, making it difficult for the pitchers to throw curve balls. This situation was promptly remedied by raising them, and batting averages tumbled by 26 points. Status remained quo in the 1932 season, but during the following winter more production adjustments took place and in the spring it was noted by all that the ball did not seem to travel nearly as far as it had the preceding year. The manufacturer denied that there had been any significant change; the seams were slightly different, that was all. Whatever the reason, batting averages declined another ten points in 1933, and home runs were just over half of what they had been in 1930.

A deader ball was to the advantage of the Braves. Perhaps their greatest asset at this time was their manager, Bill McKechnie. Beginning his fourth year with the Braves, McKechnie had earned a reputation as a pitcher's manager after winning pennants in Pittsburgh in 1925 and with the Cardinals in 1928. His clubs had finished in the second division in each of the previous three years, but they had been competitive because of their pitching. He had made a winning pitcher out of Ed Brandt, previously a big loser in Boston, developed young Bobby Brown, who had won 14 games in 1932, and had resurrected the careers of Tom Zachary, Huck Betts and Socks Seibold as well. Fred Frankhouse had shown promise after coming over from the Cardinals in the Burleigh Grimes deal in 1930, while Ben Cantwell had been effective as a spot starter. All but Brandt relied heavily on the breaking ball, and McKechnie excelled in teaching it.

Preseason—The big excitement in Boston baseball during that spring of 1933 was the purchase of the Red Sox by Tom Yawkey. The American League club had been even more poverty-stricken than the Braves and played in another broken-down ballpark. The promise of Yawkey's millions inspired hope in all Red Sox fans that better days were coming; certainly, they would be better than the horrible season of 1932, when the Red Sox were 43-111 and a solid last. The most significant news from the Braves camp was the loud holdout of first baseman Art Shires. One of the more boisterous players to wear a Braves uniform, Shires complained of unfair treatment, and his battles with Fuchs were described on a daily basis. The Braves, though, had brought up Baxter "Bucky" Jordan from Baltimore when Shires had hurt his knee in 1932 and were quite satisfied with his play. Shires was soon returned to the minors.

The rest of the club was patchwork. Forty-one-year-old Rabbit Maranville was back at second base with Billy Urbanski at shortstop and Wilfred "Fritz" Knothe at third. Maranville had played remarkably well during 1932 but was showing his age. Urbanski was a fair shortstop who didn't really have the arm for the position. He liked to have the ball get to him in a hurry to overcome his shortcomings, so he wanted the grass to be cut short on the left side of the infield. But Maranville liked the right side to be cut long to slow ground balls and make up for his declining range. The groundskeepers at Braves Field had their hands full, trying to satisfy the middle infielders. In addition, McKechnie wanted the home plate area watered down to help the ground ball pitchers on his staff. Knothe, who was one of the finest schoolboy athletes in New Jersey history, was adequate in the field but was never able to hit big league pitching.

The outfield featured the one legitimate star of the team, centerfielder Wally Berger. He'd broken in with the Braves with a bang in 1930, hitting 38 home runs, but that proved to be his major league high. Nevertheless, he remained a constant threat for the long ball and was a very adequate center fielder as well. He was flanked by Red Worthington in left and Wes Schulmerich in right. But Worthington, who had hit .303 in 1932, broke his leg early in April, and Schulmerich soon played his way out of the lineup by failing to hit. McKechnie changed his lineup daily, using Dutch Holland, Earl Clark, Randy Moore and later,

Joe Mowry, who was brought up from Minneapolis.

Catching was adequate, with Shanty Hogan and Al Spohrer sharing the duties. They handled a pitching staff that was caught short as the season opened, when Bobby Brown and Tom Zachary went down with arm trouble. Brown never recovered, pitching only seven innings that season, and his major league career was effectively ended. Zachary missed a month of the season and was relegated to spot starts until August. His absence forced McKechnie to use Cantwell as a regular starter along with Brandt, Frankhouse and Betts, and this turn of events turned out to be fortuitous for the Braves. Cantwell proved to be a workhorse, both starting and relieving, and was off to the best season of his career. The Braves had a small staff that year, using these five regularly, with Leo Mangum the only other pitcher to see significant duty. The five accounted for all but eleven of the team's victories.

National Baseball Library, Cooperstown, NY

Bill McKechnie

A slow start—Boston was picked to finish in sixth place by most observers, and the club did little to prove them wrong during April and May. The Braves were in seventh place by early June with only the Phillies behind them. New York and Pittsburgh were the early leaders with the Cardinals not far behind and the defending champion Cubs, showing the effects of the loss of Kiki Cuyler, a .500 club. Although the Braves' pitching seemed up to expectations, the offense was weak. The club was shut out eight times during April and had to scratch for its runs. Moore had replaced Schulmerich in right field and was enjoying his best season, but left field and third base remained problems while Maranville was barely at .200. Then on June 15, just before the trading deadline, the Braves made a key deal. They traded Schulmerich and Knothe to Philadelphia for third baseman Pinky Whitney and Hal Lee. Whitney was one of the best third basemen in the league, enjoying several .300 plus seasons in Baker Bowl, while Lee showed promise after hitting .303 in 1932. The two became instant regulars, with Lee in left field. Whitney occasionally moved to second to give Maranville some rest, and he was in there on June 21 when the Braves began to turn their season around. Nine games under .500 at the start of the day's play, Boston won a doubleheader from Pittsburgh, and the club was off and running. From that date until the end of August the Braves played the best baseball in the National League.

Streaking into contention—The Braves had a record of 49-49 and were in fifth place on August 1 after beating the Giants at the Polo Grounds behind Huck Betts. During that era clubs tended to have long home stands and road trips. The Braves were coming off a period when they had played 23 straight road games and were looking at an equally long period of home games. Only three games were scheduled on the road for the entire month. The Braves began by taking seven of nine games from Brooklyn and Philadelphia and moved into fourth place for the first time since early in the season.

After winning two of three in Brooklyn, the Braves returned to Boston to entertain the western clubs. They proved to be inhospitable hosts; the Braves took two of three from the Cubs, four straight from Pittsburgh, featuring a game-winning home run by Berger in the 14th inning on August 22, and three straight from St. Louis. Every day there seemed to be a new hero. Berger drove in all four of the runs in a 4-3 win over the Cardinals on August 23; Brandt pitched a gritty 4-3 complete game against St. Louis the next day to put the Braves in second place. And on August 26 Cantwell won his 18th game and fifth of the month with a 3-0, four-hitter over the Redbirds. A crowd of 40,000 turned out the next day to see Zachary extend the Braves winning streak to eight games with a 7-0 gem over Cincinnati in the first game of the doubleheader. The Braves climbed to within four games of the Giants with this win. But in the second game, Frankhouse was hit hard early, and the Reds turned away three late-inning Boston threats with double plays to break the streak. It was a critical loss as subsequent events were to show.

The city of Boston had been indifferent to the Braves during the early season. The weather had been terrible; eight Braves Field games were postponed in April alone, and many games were played in threatening weather. The economic conditions of the nation were at their worst, with almost 25 percent of the work force unemployed and the banking system about to collapse. Weekday crowds seldom exceeded 2,000, although the Braves managed to draw near-capacity crowds to two early doubleheaders with the Giants and Cubs. But as the team's performance improved in July and early August, the fans started coming out. Boston had pennant fever for the first time in 15 years. "McKechnie shares muscle title with Terry as Braves challenge" screamed the lead headline in *The Sporting News* on August 24. "Braves bringing back the memories of Stallings' 1914 team." For two weeks Boston was mesmerized by the success of the Braves.

On August 28 the Braves missed another chance to keep pace with the Giants when they could manage only two hits off Red Lucas, losing to the Reds, 2-0. After a day off they managed to beat the cellar dwellers, 3-2, on Maranville's ninth-inning single. Now the stage was set. A six-game series with New York was to begin on August 31. The Braves were six games behind.

Head to head—The Braves drew first blood in the showdown when they beat the Giants, 7-3, behind Cantwell, who won his 19th game. The game featured Wally Berger's 25th homer which tied him with Chuck Klein for the league lead. Of equal importance was the fact that Randy Moore broke a finger in the fifth inning, an injury that put him out of action for much of the balance of the year. Moore had been hot during August, and his absence in effect left the Braves with one solid hitter, Berger, who could be pitched around.

The next day saw the largest crowd in Boston baseball history engulf Braves Field for the doubleheader, which featured Hubbell and Fitzsimmons of the Giants going up against Frankhouse and Brandt. An estimated 50,000 fans showed up, and the crush was so great that the gates to the park had to be closed at 1:15, 45 minutes before game time. Many spectators did not pay; official paid attendance, according to Phil Lowrey in *Green Cathedrals*, was 40,396, and many who had tickets could not get in. An estimated 15,000 spectators were said to be outside, including most of the newspapermen and club Secretary Ed Cunningham, who eventually found an unlocked gate. The overflow filled the outfield, creating playing conditions that were less than ideal.

The first game was scoreless through nine innings with the Braves missing a chance to break the tie in the bottom of the ninth. In the 10th inning, the Giants scored twice to win with Hubbell driving in the first run, Frankhouse taking the loss. The second game went to the Giants as well, 5-3. This game was tied in the ninth when Fitzsimmons doubled into the crowd to break the deadlock. On the next day, the Giants won again, 5-3, behind Hal Schumacher, putting the Braves eight games behind. The Sunday doubleheader drew another large crowd of 42,000, and the Giants won their fourth straight, 4-3 in 14 innings. In this game another winning run was driven in by a Giant pitcher—relief pitcher Dolf Luque. The nightcap ended in a 4-4 tie, called because of the 6:30 Sunday curfew.

It was so close. The Braves could have won every game with more timely hitting. The absence of Moore was sorely felt, for there were several occasions when his bat in the lineup could have meant victory. The lack of depth in the Braves pitching staff also took its toll. All the starters had seen extensive duty during the weeks before, and were not as fresh as they should have been entering this series. The Braves were praised for making a close fight of it. But all of the Boston papers conceded that the pennant race was over.

The climb back—The exhausting series left the Braves in fourth place as they began a September road trip of 23 games, and they fell to fifth place within a week. McKechnie righted his ship by mid-September, but the Braves were mathematically eliminated from the pennant race on September 16 and were 3-1/2 games out of the first division. With a week to go the club was two games behind the Cardinals, who were in the midst of making a run for second place. Then the Braves won four in a row at New York and Brooklyn while the Cardinals stumbled, and returned home on September 29, only 1/2 game behind St. Louis with two games to go. It looked as if the Braves were out of the running for the first division when Cantwell was beaten by the Phillies, 2-1 in ten innings on Saturday. But the Cardinals lost to the Cubs at home, and the Braves still had a chance.

Berger had caught a serious case of the flu in Pittsburgh and had not played since September 15. He stayed in Pittsburgh until he was well enough to travel and joined the Braves when they returned home. But he was not dressed when the final game of the season began. The Phillies starting pitcher was Reginald Grabowski, who had won 17 games that year for Reading in the New York Penn League and was getting a late season trial. Berger had seen him pitch while he was convalescing in Pittsburgh and noticed that Grabowski had, as Wally called it, "a dinky, little curve. Not much break to it, and it hung up there pretty good ...." He was effective that day. Going into the last of the seventh inning, the Phillies were leading 1-0 and Grabowski had allowed only three hits. Berger decided to suit up around the third inning, but he stayed in the clubhouse for a few innings. He joined the team on the bench when the Braves began a rally. Jordan led off with a single and Moore followed with another hit. After Whitney struck out, Lee's infield out advanced the runners to second and third. The Phillies decided to walk the dangerous Shanty Hogan to get to Rabbit Maranville, who was hitting .218 and had nothing resembling a hit that day. It was McKechnie's move.

"Can you hit?" shouted McKechnie from his third base coaching position to Berger. "I'm ready," Wally shouted back and marched up to the plate. In a conversation with the author many years later Berger remembered that he was looking for that "dinky" curve on the first pitch. But it was a fast ball, and Wally took a wild swing, "not even close...." The next pitch was a ball and then a called strike. Finally, Grabowski threw that "dinky" pitch and Berger pounded it on a line into the left field bleachers for a grand slam home run.

The Braves had a 4-1 lead which Bob Smith was able to protect for the last two innings. Berger jogged slowly around the bases; he was still weak from the flu and was barely able to make it. But the Braves had won. Meanwhile, the Cubs scored six runs in the second inning and went on to beat the Cardinals, 7-1. Boston had reached the first division for the first time in twelve years. Berger's hit meant approximately $400 per man, not an insignificant sum in those years.

It was a dramatic moment for the Braves, one that McKechnie called his most exciting event in all his

National Baseball Library, Cooperstown, NY

Wally Berger

years in baseball. Wally Berger thought so, too, in discussing it over 40 years later. It was fitting that the Braves made the first division. They were not a very good club in reality, but with one more good pitcher—perhaps Bobby Brown, who had looked so good in 1932—and another hitter to back up Berger, the Braves could have won. They were blessed with an outstanding manager, a good defense and some excellent pitching. Pennants have been won with fewer ingredients. It was a one-year phenomenon, however. The Braves finished fourth again in 1934, but were never really close and in 1935 the franchise collapsed. Not until 1946 would a Braves team finish in the first division again, and by that time the 1933 Braves were a footnote in baseball history. But they provided Boston fans with many thrills during that Depression year, and they deserve to be remembered.

The Braves Lineup

		Age	G	AB	HR	RBI	AVG.
1B	Bucky Jordan	26	152	588	4	46	.286
2B	Rabbit Maranville	41	143	478	0	38	.218
SS	Bill Urbanski	30	144	566	0	35	.251
3B	Pinky Whitney	28	100	382	8	49	.246
LF	Red Worthington	27	17	45	0	0	.156
	Joe Mowry	25	86	249	0	20	.221
	Dutch Holland	29	13	31	0	3	.258
	Hal Lee	28	88	312	1	28	.221
CF	Wally Berger	27	137	528	27	106	.313
RF	Randy Moore	28	135	497	8	70	.302
C	Shanty Hogan	27	96	328	3	30	.253

		Age	G	IP	W	L	ERA
P	Ben Cantwell	31	40	255	20	10	2.61
	Ed Brandt	28	41	288	18	14	2.59
	Fred Frankhouse	29	43	245	16	15	3.16
	Huck Betts	36	35	242	11	11	2.79
	Tom Zachary	37	26	125	7	9	3.53
	Leo Mangum	37	25	84	4	3	3.32
	Bob Smith	35	14	59	4	3	3.20

Information You Really Wanted About the 1933 Braves but were Afraid to Ask

1. The Braves batted .252 as a team and scored 552 runs, seventh in both categories. But they finished first in team defense and were second in pitching. They were last in bases on balls received and last in stolen bases. Berger led the league in strikeouts with 77. In discussing this season with Wally he said that he felt "embarrassed" about this feat. He neglected to mention that he finished third behind Chuck Klein and Carl Hubbell in the voting for Most Valuable Player that year and was selected in a poll of the managers as the best regular player of the year.

2. The Braves played 32 doubleheaders, 19 of them at home. This was somewhat more than usual, the New England spring being wetter than normal.

3. Total paid attendance at Braves Field was 517,803. This was a record at the time and far exceeded the Red Sox attendance of 268,715. 1933 was the last time that the Braves outdrew the Red Sox in Boston.

4. The Braves drew over 350,000 in eleven dates, an average of 31,000. For the remaining 47 home dates, they averaged 3,400, a number that was inflated by good weekday crowds during the long August homestand. According to Wally Berger and Joe Mowry, a normal weekday crowd during that era was about 2,000.

5. Although saves were not recorded at that time, a retroactive calculation showed the Braves leading the league with 16. Ed Brandt and Huck Betts had four each. The league leader was Fidgety Phil Collins of the Phillies with six.

6. The Braves hit a total of 54 home runs and Wally Berger had 27 of them. Of the 27 home runs they hit at Braves Field, Berger had 16.

7. The Braves won or tied the season series with every club except Chicago, against whom they were 7-15. They were a reasonably good road team at 38-40, but they were only 1-10 at Wrigley Field.

8. From June 21 to August 31, the Braves were 45-21, the best performance in the league. Unfortunately, they were in seventh place when they began to play well and picked up only six games on the Giants during this stretch.

9. The Braves were shut out 21 times, including two one-hitters thrown by Si Johnson of Cincinnati within two weeks of each other.

10. Rookie pitcher Ed Fallenstin had a 2-1 mark, all against the Giants, and one of his victories was a 3-0 shutout of Carl Hubbell. Yet, he was released to Buffalo in July and never again pitched in the the major leagues.

11. Joe Mowry was the last member of this team to die—in February, 1994. Some died young—Ed Brandt was killed while stepping out of his car at the age of 39; outfielder Earl Clark was killed in an auto accident at the age of 31. Many lived long productive lives—pitcher Bob Smith died at age 92; Huck Betts at 90; Randy Moore at 86; Fred Frankhouse at 85; Wally Berger at 83; Pinky Whitney at 82; Bucky Jordan at 86. The wealthiest member of this club was Moore, who was an early investor in the great oil strike in East Texas in the '30s and subsequently owned several banks in the area.

National League Standings as the 1933 Season Progressed

		W	L		W	L
April 30	Pittsburgh	11	3	Chicago	6	8
	New York	8	4	Cincinnati	5	7
	Brooklyn	7	7	St. Louis	6	9
	Boston	7	7	Phil.	5	11
June 6	New York	26	17	Cincinnati	23	22
	St. Louis	27	18	Brooklyn	18	24
	Pittsburgh	23	18	Boston	20	27
	Chicago	24	22	Phil.	16	31
July 4	New York	44	25	Boston	35	38
	St. Louis	39	32	Brooklyn	33	36
	Pittsburgh	37	34	Cincinnati	32	41
	Chicago	37	37	Phil.	29	43
August 1	New York	57	37	Boston	48	49
	Pittsburgh	56	43	Phil.	41	54
	St. Louis	52	45	Brooklyn	39	54
	Chicago	53	46	Cincinnati	41	59
Sept. 4	New York	77	48	St. Louis	70	63
	Pittsburgh	71	57	Brooklyn	52	73
	Chicago	72	60	Phil.	51	73
	Boston	70	59	Cincinnati	50	80
Final	New York	91	61	St. Louis	82	71
	Pittsburgh	87	67	Brooklyn	65	88
	Chicago	86	68	Phil.	60	92
	Boston	83	71	Cincinnati	58	94

Ring Lardner and the "Br'er Rabbit Ball"

Terence Malley

As biographers of Ring Lardner have pointed out,[1] he began as a devoted baseball fan, achieved great success as a baseball writer covering the Cubs and White Sox, and then even greater success with his baseball stories (most notably the *You Know Me Al* letters, collected in book form in 1916). However, by the 1920s Lardner's interest in baseball had diminished. Although he continued to cover the World Series through 1927, he increasingly saw these assignments as burdensome.

Anyone who has seen John Sayles' film *Eight Men Out* (1988) will probably remember the Ring Lardner character (played by Sayles himself, who, by the way, looks astonishingly like Lardner in the role) expressing utter contempt for the Black Sox. "I'm forever blowing ballgames," he sings, parodying a popular song.[2] There's no doubt that Lardner was embittered by the White Sox swoon in 1919; for one thing, he lost money on the Series! But, as Jonathan Yardley points out, the Black Sox incident was only part of the story. Lardner was also offended by the livelier ball of the post-World War I era; in a 1930 *New Yorker* article he called it the "Br'er Rabbit Ball."[3]

It's possible, however, to push Lardner's disenchantment with baseball back almost another decade—to the lively ball of 1911. In a letter to his fiancee, Ellis Abbot, in May of that year, Lardner complained, "They are using a new ball this year. It's livelier and more hitting means longer games.... It appears to be impossible to finish a game in less than two hours."[4]

Terence Malley , a retired college English professor, is on the editorial board of Nine. *He recently completed a long essay on Ring Lardner's eldest son, John, a distinguished sports columnist.*

(Pause for a moment to let that sink in. In late June, 1994, the Yankees and Indians played consecutive nine-inning games that each lasted over four hours.)

As we hear every day in this "Br'er Rabbit Ball" season of 1994, a livelier ball is only one possible reason for a sudden upsurge in offense. But, for whatever reasons, there is no doubt that the baseball was jumping (comparatively speaking) in 1911. The offenses generated in the two leagues were somewhat different, though. In 1910, the National League as a whole scored 5,007 runs, with 214 home runs (that's the whole league, not the 1994 Tigers); the league batting average was .256, the slugging average .338. The American League had lower numbers in all four categories: 4,573, 145, .243, .314, respectively. Low as these AL offensive totals were, they represented an *increase* in run production and home runs over 1909 (4,264 and 109). Batting and slugging averages in the AL stayed about the same (.244 and .309 in 1909).[5]

In 1911, the National was a real power league. Runs were up only 10 percent (to 5,506), but home runs rose almost 50 percent (to 316). Lardner's friend, Frank (Wildfire) Shulte hit 21, the most since 1899,[6] and five other players had between 12 and 16. No NL batter had hit more than 10 the previous year. The league batting average, however, increased only slightly, from .256 to .260. (Strikeouts were up slightly in 1911, too, from 4,511 to 4,792.)

In the American League in 1911, the home run increase was perhaps less dramatic than the rise in collective batting average and in runs scored. Homers were up a hefty 37 percent (to 199), but the league batting average soared to .273, an increase of thirty points over 1910. Ty Cobb and Joe Jackson were both over .400 (.420 and .408, respectively); Sam Crawford (.378) and Eddie Collins (.365) also had big years. Although the home run leader (Frank Baker) only had 11, the AL as a whole scored over 1,000 more runs than in 1910 (5,658), an increase of almost 24 percent.

If the ball was indeed juiced in 1911, as Ring Lardner insisted, it must have been unjuiced again by 1914, when the American League offensive numbers fell back to their 1910 levels (4,611 runs scored, 148 home runs, .248 batting average) and the National League was *down* in runs scored and batting average (4,798, .251) compared to 1910. Home runs (267) were up over 1910 but way down compared to 1911.

In each of the five years 1910-1914, the National League outhomered the American by a large margin; in 1913, in fact, the disparity was almost two-to-one (310 to 160). Overall, the NL hit 73 percent more home runs than the AL during this period (1394 to 806). Not surprisingly, the American League led the National in stolen bases in each of these years, though the overall margin was a relatively slim eight percent (8,524 to 7,873). The stand-and-slug NL and the run-run-run AL—it almost seems as if the National League should have had the designated hitter!

In June, 1932, Ring Lardner wrote to John McGraw, who'd just retired as manager of the Giants. Br'er Rabbit, of course, had become more explosive than ever. "Baseball hasn't meant much to me since the introduction of the TNT ball that robbed the game of the features I used to like best," like "intelligent managers" managing and "smart ballplayers [getting] a chance to do things."[7]

Lardner could probably have gotten over the Black Sox mess (he forgave Jack Dempsey, who, he was convinced, had thrown the first Tunney fight), but he couldn't forgive the desecration of the game as he knew it.

What would he think of baseball in the '90s? The mind reels!

Notes:

1. The two full-length biographies of Lardner are Donald Elder, *Ring Lardner* (Garden City, L.I.: Doubleday, 1956) and Jonathan Yardley, *Ring* (N.Y.: Random House, 1977). The first section of Yardley's book, "Frank Chance's Diamond" (pp. 3-41), is a detailed account of Ring Lardner's relationship to baseball.
2. Mathew J. Bruccoli's edition of Lardner's complete baseball fiction, *Ring Around the Bases* (N.Y.: Scribner's, 1992), reprints this parody in an appendix.
3. Yardley suggests that behind Lardner's dislike of the lively ball may have been a nostalgic yearning for baseball to remain "what it had been—or what he remembered it as being—when he was young" (p. 41).
4. Quoted in Yardley, p. 13.
5. My data for the 1909-1914 seasons are from the *Baseball Encyclopedia*, 9th edition (N.Y.: Macmillan, 1993); so is my information on home runs totals in other years.
6. In 1899 Buck Freeman of Washington (NL) hit 25 home runs. Shulte's 21 remained the most homers in the twentieth century until Gavvy Cravath hit 24 in the 1915 season. It might be argued that Cravath's achievement was tainted by the dilution of pitching talent caused by the emergence of the Federal League.
7. In *Letters from Ring*, Clifford M. Caruthers, ed. (Flint, Mich.: Walden Press, 1979), p. 270.

And don't forget: the *Times* is the paper of record

YOU KNOW ME, AL. By Ring W. Lardner. George H. Doran Company. $1.25 net.

Mr. Lardner's book is sub-titled "A Busher's Letters" and consists of a series of communications sent by Jack Keefe, a professional baseball player, to his friend Al. In these letters he tells how he was sold to the White Sox, then shifted to various other organizations, winding up with the Giants, describes his games and his grievances, his wife, his baby; and his constant and consistent endeavors to live at some other person's expense. The author was for some time sporting writer on a Chicago newspaper, and so may be supposed to know his subject thoroughly, but, for the honor of the national game we trust that his "busher" is not typical of the majority of its players. A glutton and a braggart, mean, inordinately vain, an ignoramus, and without even a glimmer of ordinary human intelligence, he is not precisely what may be truthfully described as a charming individual. Callahan, the manager, tells him: "You have got no brains," and the reader heartily indorses the statement. However, he is entirely satisfied with himself, and writes: "Matthewson [sic] *could not learn me nothing...he has not got my stuff but they can't everybody expect to have the stuff that I got or 1/2 as much stuff." The publishers describe the book as being written in "Pure United States...bad grammar and baseball slang." As it contains many accounts of baseball games strung on the thinnest possible thread of a plot, it may please the "fans."*

—New York Times Book Review, *July 30, 1916, submitted by A.D. Suehsdorf*

Cobb Never Supported Cochrane

Norman L. Macht

One of SABR's missions is to study the stats of the past and, where justified, to correct the record. It is something we are good at. We take pride in following whatever path the research trail leads us down, without fear or favor, whether it leads to the discovery of a hitherto uncounted Walter Johnson strikeout or to question the validity of Honus Wagner's 1911 batting title.

But we seldom have the opportunity to set a personal record straight, like correcting the spelling of Elden (not Eldon) Auker's name, or misrepresentations about a player's life or character.

The more a myth is repeated, the more credibility it acquires. One writer states something as fact that is not. A second writer, using the first as a source, repeats it. When a third writer sees it in print in *two* sources, the misinformation gains four times the weight, in the quantum physics of journalism. And so it goes.

For several years Mickey Cochrane's wife, Mary, and daughters Joan and Sara have been bristling, fretting, fuming, and unsuccessfully fighting the fable that their husband and father (who died in 1962) had been so down and out in the 1950s that a charitable Ty Cobb had to keep the family afloat with a steady flow of welfare checks.

Sara first came across the story a few years ago in a column in the Los Angeles *Times* by Al Stump, who did not check it out with the family.

"It so angered me," she told me, "I faxed a letter asking where the reporter got his 'facts' and refuting the story. Not only was no retraction printed, I never even heard from them."

Over the years I have seen this story several times myself. In Charles C. Alexander's biography of Cobb, he wrote that Cochrane was thoroughly down on his luck in the 1950s, when Cobb began sending him regular checks. Although Alexander footnotes practically every other paragraph in the book, he gives no source for this statement.

About five years ago, while slogging through my eternal research for a biography of Connie Mack, I asked Mary Cochrane if there was any truth to the story. She told me there was none. I tucked that away with my notes for future follow-up.

The story surfaced again recently in connection with the movie, *Cobb*, and its companion book by Al Stump. I saw it repeated in a story about the making of the movie. It prompted me to write once again to Mrs. Cochrane for confirmation or denial of its accuracy.

The Hollywood version—Meanwhile, out in Scottsdale, Arizona, Cochrane's younger daughter, Sara, went to see the movie. As she watched it, her disposition went from dyspeptic to choleric, "not only at the one-sided portrayal of Cobb," she wrote to me, "but by the false characterization of my father."

Unaware of what was in the movie, I called her and she described the scene that upset her the most.

"There is an episode at what appears to be the induction weekend at the Hall of Fame in 1961. My father generally avoided those events. His vision had started to go, but he had come east for a speaking engagement and the Cooperstown event. Mother came with him to

Norman Macht has written 20 books, the latest of which is Rex Barney's Orioles Memories.

Sara Cochrane Bollman

Sitting in his Grosse Pointe, Michigan study, a financially independent Mickey Cochrane gets the news in 1950 that he has been appointed general manager of the Philadelphia Athletics. With him are his wife, Mary, his older daughter, Joan, and his younger daughter, Sara.

help with the driving. Their itinerary included stopping to play golf with Connie Mack, Jr. and his wife, and Fred Waring (of the Pennsylvanians' music fame), and afterward to visit me in Pottsville, PA, and my cousin in Washington, DC.

"In Cooperstown they had lunch with Mr. and Mrs. Tris Speaker. They never intended to stay in Cooperstown long enough to attend the formal dinner that evening, and my father had not brought a tuxedo with him because he did not expect to do anything where he would need one.

"But the inference in the movie was that he wanted to go to the dinner but he did not have a tux, and the reason he did not have one was that he could not afford it. There's a scene where Cobb picks up the phone and orders one for Mickey Cochrane and has it put on his own bill. The character representing the writer, Al Stump, says something to the effect: 'You've been supporting Cochrane and Rogers Hornsby for a long time, haven't you.'

"Cobb says, 'You know how these old ballplayers are. And after Cochrane was hit in the head he was never the same,' or words to that effect.

"This was the last year of Cobb's life. Stump admitted that Cobb was on heavy medication at the time and that a lot of the things he said were not true. But he never made any effort to check out the statements about Cochrane with his family."

Writing in The New York *Times* November 27, 1994, Michael Sragow said, "[*Cobb* director] Ron Shelton took liberties with the facts admittedly...."

Taking liberties with the facts of time and place is one thing, albeit inexcusable in itself. But taking liberties with the facts about people's lives and circumstances is another, more reprehensible matter.

The truth—Cobb did offer financial advice to many players in the form of investment tips. He was an early investor in what became General Motors; that and Coca-Cola made him a multimillionaire. Most of the players did nothing with the information; either they lacked the money to invest or the confidence that Cobb had in his own judgment. Cochrane was one of those who failed to heed Cobb's advice until one night in 1960. The phone rang in Cochrane's home. Sara's fiance answered it.

"Get me Mike!" a voice demanded.

"He's gone to bed."

"Get him up."

"Who's calling?"

"Ty Cobb."

The young man hesitated. Was somebody playing a joke? Should he risk his future father-in-law's anger by getting him out of bed for a prank? Or risk not telling him and find out it really was Ty Cobb on the phone? He decided to wake Cochrane.

"Cobb wanted to tell Dad that Coca-Cola was about to come out in cans and he should buy the stock," Sara recalled. "This time he took the advice. The stock has since grown and split several times and has been a big help to my mother's financial security. But that's the only financial 'help' Ty Cobb ever gave him.

"The point is," she concluded, "Dad had the money to buy the stock and to pay for my wedding all in the same summer. Does that sound like an indigent old ballplayer getting by on Ty Cobb's handouts?"

Although Cochrane made more money in business than he did as a player, he did have some reverses, but no more so than most people. In 1939 he and Frank Book bought the 4K ranch in Dean, MT. The 4K stood for "Keen's Kozy Kountry Klub," but either the offbeat spelling or the 62-mile gravel road from Billings to the ranch had spelled its failure as a golf club, and made it available for purchase. They operated it as a dude ranch, and their families and friends enjoyed it for about ten years.Cochrane sold his interest in the late 1950s.

During this time he helped his brother, Archie, buy a Ford agency in Billings, across town from his own Lincoln-Mercury agency. (Archie Cochrane Motors is still in Billings; it is owned today by former Orioles pitcher Dave McNally.) He also made the down payment on a small pony farm near Denver for his daughter, Joan.

"At that same time, he provided me with a college education, paying the University of Colorado's high out-of-state tuition," Sara said. "He paid cash for his cars, homes, everything. I would hardly call that being indigent."

Cochrane's daughter Joan summed up the family's feelings in a letter to me dated January 17, 1995:

"As to the ridiculous story of Ty Cobb helping Gordon S. Cochrane financially, I want you to know that it is pure fiction. Anyone that ever knew Mickey Cochrane would know that he never needed any financial help and that he was certainly never indigent. It has been my experience that most writers and/or media people never let the facts get in the way of a good story. Anything you can do to set the record straight would be appreciated."

Setting the record straight is what SABR is all about.

Another oft-repeated canard about Mickey Cochrane has it that he was so depressed over his stock market losses, it affected his catching in the 1931 World Series, when Pepper Martin stole everything but the water bucket. Mary Cochrane confirms that, like many of the Philadelphia A's, Mike invested his 1929 World Series check in the stock market just before its collapse, and lost it all. But the following year he paid cash for a new Packard convertible "which was something Mike had wanted for a long time." A few years after the '31 Series Lefty Grove admitted that the Cardinals had stolen on him, not the catcher.

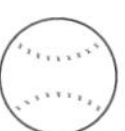

A personal history

Baker Bowl

Edward F. "Dutch" Doyle

Philadelphia's Baker Bowl is remembered today as a comical bandbox of a park, inhabited by bad Phillies teams with worse pitching. In fact, it was the first modern ballpark, it was the home grounds for pretty decent teams during its early years, and it didn't gain the name by which we all know it until a quarter century after it was built.

Philadelphia was an early hotbed of baseball, and it had a team in the new National League in 1876. The Athletics, however, failed to complete the season's schedule, and were expelled from the league. The league returned to town in 1883, and the history of the Phillies began that year, with the team playing in Recreation Park.

As soon as owner A. J. Reach obtained the services of Harry Wright as manager in 1884, the Phillies developed into a force in the National League. But Reach was unhappy with Recreation Park. He and his son looked at many locations, but they fell in love with the area at Broad Street and Lehigh Avenue, which had the railroad across the street and another railroad a block away. The park they built there opened on April 30, 1887.

The main entrance to the new Philadelphia National League Park was at 15th and Huntingdon Streets; and despite its official name, it was often called the Huntingdon Street Grounds. Even less formally, the ballpark became "the Hump" in the sport columns. There was good reason for this: to this day, when you reach this site, Broad Street rises to a gentle peak before falling off again.

Dutch Doyle is the author of Al Simmons, the Best, *and* Babe Ruth, the Only One.

The first year the Phillies were in their new location they finished second, 3-1/2 games behind Detroit, but even though he put exciting teams on the field, Wright couldn't bring Philadelphia a championship before poor health forced him to resign in 1894. During the nineteenth century, the Phillies never led the league.

On August 6, 1894, the ball park was burned completely to the ground in a fire that was started by a plumber's stove or torch. The records claim that the team's temporary field was the University of Pennsylvania's athletic grounds, but by working around the clock, carpenters had the Phillies' field ready to play in twelve days. After the season, Reach commissioned a complete rebuilding of the facility.

On May 2, 1895, the Phillies opened the most advanced park in the United States. Its cantilevered grandstand—the first of its kind—offered an unobstructed view for everybody. The pavilion between first and third bases was double-decked, with bleachers down the left and right field lines. The outfield was clear of seats, but a 15-foot-wide bicycle track encircled the outfield.

The four exceptional Phillies players of this period were Bill Hamilton, Ed Delahanty, Sam Thompson, and Nap Lajoie. All are enshrined in Cooperstown. Elmer Flick had four solid seasons with the Phillies, hitting .338 before jumping to the new American League. He's in the Hall, too. Pitchers are another story. Only three of them won more than 90 games: Charlie Ferguson, 99; Jack Taylor, 96, and Kid Carsey, 94. Some of the other pitchers who were considered decent were Kid Gleason, Charlie Buffinton, Dan Casey, Gus Weyhing, Al Orth, Wiley Piatt, and Ed Daily.

The first ten years of the twentieth century, the Phillies operated in the first division six times. Bill Shettsline, who would work every position in the organization from office boy to president, managed the first three years, with finishes of third, second, and seventh. The seventh-place finish must have been a bit much for Bill, as he passed the job over to Chief Zimmer, who did no better with another seventh-place effort.

Hugh Duffy took over in 1904, and the team promptly dropped to last with a record of 52-100, but Hughie rebounded to fourth place finishes in 1905 and 1906. To play out the decade, Billy Murray did an admirable job, finishing third, fourth, and fifth.

New favorites were "Gravel-Voiced" Sherry Magee, "Tight Pants" John Titus, "Fancy Dan" Mike Doolan, and William "Kid" Gleason came back to the Phillies in 1903 as a second baseman. Two other favorites were Bill "Kitty" Bransfield and Charlie "Red" Dooin. Everyone just seemed to have a nickname.

One of the old sports writers, Jack Kofoed, grew up at Germantown Avenue and Lehigh Avenue, which was four city blocks from Baker Bowl. Jack's father sold shoes, and Jack related that the first major league player that he saw eyeball to eyeball was Sherry Magee, who came in his father's store to purchase a pair of patent-leather shoes. Sherry did not impress Jack's mother, and she did not want him to go near the ball park.

Toward the end of his career, Jack Kofoed wrote a story for *Sports Illustrated* in April of 1958, "The Bandbox at Huntingdon and Broad."

In this article, Jack relates an incident at Baker Bowl in 1906 between the Giants and the Phillies, and he gives some excellent information about the park and the area. In those days, visiting teams did not dress at the park. "Splendid in uniform," writes Jack, "they rode from hotel to park in a horse-drawn bus. It labored in the heat up Broad Street, the horses shaking white spittle from their whiskers with annoyed head tossings."

The Giants were different. As World Champs, they traveled in barouches drawn by animals made handsome with black-and-yellow blankets. Jack said, "It was a braggart gesture which roused our fury. We gathered on the curbstone to jeer. Peering from those carriages were the faces of America's most exalted athletes. John McGraw seemed chronically red and angry… Christy Mathewson's eyes were thoughtful and tired…Iron Man Joe McGinnity's chin thrust like the prow of a tug…and Roger Bresnahan swept us with a look which made us lower our lids and shuffle uneasily. I stood in awe of these men of Manhattan, not only because they were champions, but because some were said to be paid as much as $5,000 a year."

Kofoed's description of John Titus is a gem. "My favorite on the team was outfielder John Titus, a stocky, heavy shouldered man who, because robust buttocks crowded his nether garments like watermelons in a small sack, was known as Tight Pants. Though mustaches for players had gone out of fashion, for many years Titus stubbornly refused to shave off the straw colored hair shadowing his upper lip."

On this particular day there were some bad feelings with the Giant and Phillies players. Titus, sensing trouble after the game, told his young friend Jack Kofoed to get away from the park when the game ended. Jack's description:

> The Giants came out of the park, shoulder to shoulder, tough looking, ready for anything. A spate of booing rose from the crowd. A few more venturesome fished into nearly empty lemonade cans of vendors and hurled slices of fruit at the carriages.
>
> I stood in the front of the grocery store. My heart was beating fast. It was all right for the Phillies and Giants to fight, but a thousand against 20!
>
> The players piled into their carriages, and the jehus clucked to their horses. Somebody yelled, "Get 'em," and the crowd surged forward. The barouches at the head of the line went off at a gallop. I was watching the last one in which Roger Bresnahan rode.
>
> Bresnahan was alone, except for the frowsy at the reins, but there was no fear in his harsh face. The coachman whistled his whip more at the crowd than the horses. The people in front fell away, and the barouche began to move.
>
> Roger stood up, holding on with one hand and kicking with spiked shoes at men trying to climb up to him. He lost his balance and fell to the street. The fall was broken by the bodies of his attackers. You never saw anybody come up so fast, slugging with both fists at every face that dared to come into sight.

Along Came Tight Pants

Through the mass of humanity came Tight Pants Titus, still in uniform, wriggling and fighting his way. Bresnahan fell in beside him, and they forced a lane of bloody noses and bruised shins until they reached the grocery store, I opened the door. They bolted in and locked it.

"Thanks," said Bresnahan, grinning through split lips. Tight Pants looked at me. "I thought I told you to stay out of this," he said. "Such things ain't for a kid of your age."

"The hell with that," grinned the Giant catcher. "Boys gotta learn some time. Come on John, I'll buy you a beer before I go back to the

Baker Bowl's grandstand and the Field Seats up the left fie

hotel. You hit pretty good against us today."

On Saturday, August 8, 1903, a large crowd was on hand. At the top of the bleachers along the first and third base lines was a walkway or balcony which was attached to the outside walls on Huntingdon and 15th Streets. People would get up and stretch their legs on this structure, and congregate there between games of a doubleheader.

On this particular day, there was a disturbance on 15th Street, on the third base side of the ballpark. The people in the bleachers rushed up to the balcony to see

National Baseball Library, Cooperstown, NY

what was going on, and the balcony and the outside wall collapsed onto 15th Street, killing 12 people and injuring 232. The youngest person injured in this misfortune was four-year-old Harry Ickler, who was celebrating his birthday with his father and brother, and who later became a close family friend. In the confusion, the three Icklers were taken to three different hospitals.

For the Phillies this disaster meant another reconstruction job at these historic grounds. During the work, they played at the Athletics' Columbia Ball Park.

In 1910, the Phillies extended the grandstand beyond third base and first base. On the first base side, they exended them all the way to the right-field wall. They built bleachers in the outfield, and the original bleachers along the left-field foul line were curved to meet the new bleachers in the outfield. These curved bleachers were called the Field Seats.

Baker Bowl hosted its only World Series in 1915, when the Phillies lost to Boston four games to one. Babe Ruth made his first appearance in World Series play when he pinch-hit in the first game.

Another disaster struck on May 16th, 1927. The Phillies were playing the World Champion Cardinals before 18,000 fans on a beautiful Saturday afternoon. The field seats beyond third base and the bleachers in left field were crammed to capacity.

The game was moving normally when an abrupt severe rain shower struck the area. The people in both stands were getting drenched, so they jumped the short fences and headed for the lower right-field grandstands. Under the added weight, the grandstands collapsed, injuring 50. One man had a heart attack and died.

In later years, this incident gave birth to a great trivia question: What player hit two home runs in one game in two different ball parks? The answer: Chuck Klein. The explanation was that on May 16, 1927, he hit a home run in Baker Bowl before the disaster, and that when the game was continued at Shibe Park he hit another. The only thing wrong with that great answer is that Chuck did not make it to the big leagues until July of 1928.

Though it was built for baseball, every possible means was used to utilize the facility to obtain revenue; consequently, the right-field wall, many years prior to the famous Lifebuoy sign, had many different advertisements. Money was the key!

Harry Ickler, for example, told me that after the ball season a circus always came to the park. In the early days a huge hole was dug in the third base area. It was filled with water and a platform was set up and they had a diving horse.

As early as 1904 boxing matches came to the Bowl. On July 23, 1904, the great Bob Fitzsimmons fought Philadelphia Jack O'Brien at the park. It was a $5,000 gate with top ticket price at $3.00. It was a six-round no decision fight.

On September 15, 1928, the Baker Bowl scene became my neighborhood. Another fight was my introduction to the park, and the next 10 years were probably the most enjoyable days of my life.

Heavyweight champion Gene Tunney had retired, and a series of elimination fights had been promoted to determine the new champion of the world. October 1, 1928, was a Monday night; consequently, there was school the next day. I was only seven years old, and new to the neighborhood, but I was at the ballpark, absorbing everything. I was mesmerized. Stadiums in those days did not have lights, so temporary lights had to be set up. Baker Bowl, bulging, could squeeze in 18,000. But for a big fight, 7,000 to 10,000 extra seats could be set up on the playing field.

The fight was between local fighters, Jack Gross and Tommy Loughran. Loughran was the light heavyweight champ who was moving up to the heavyweight division. Jack Gross, a Jewish fighter, was undefeated and this was his big chance. Loughran had fought Tunney, Greb, Impellitiere, Sharkey, and others at this location. He was the favorite, even though he was moving up in weight. He won easily and became my favorite fighter.

I learned this night that everyone who ever worked in the park, no matter when or what his current age, came back on fight night. They all started at the park as cushion boys, and Leon Gumpert, a very excitable individual, seemed to have been in charge of this department forever. Leon never forgot a cushion boy, so they were back on fight nights. From about 4 P.M., Leon could be found periodically at the gate on Huntingdon Street, just east of 15th Street. If you were spotted by Leon in the crowd, he motioned you forward, and as you reached him, he literally threw you inside the park.

At Baker Bowl, there was a gate at 15th and Oakdale Streets. This gate's proper use was to permit supplies to enter the park, but it was extremely important to men who didn't have the price of admission. The gate was in direct line with the center-field scoreboard. During the Depression years, grown men drilled holes into the fence that would let them see the entire scoreboard and the center fielder. The men who had their own peepholes kept score. They did not know if a player hit a single, double or triple, but they knew if he got on base because an out wasn't put up on the board. At the end of the inning, they knew how many runs scored. Kids rarely got a hole. Our only edge was that we could lie flat on the pavement and look under the wooden gate. But we didn't have the patience to stay at this long. There were many ways for a boy to get into the park.

I had five ways to get into Baker Bowl. Our family lived two doors from a Jewish tailor, Mr. Twer, who took a liking to me when I was a very young boy, and became a lasting friend. Mr. Twer pressed the dress suits of the visiting players if they so desired. He would go to the park a couple of hours before game time (3:15 P.M.) and return around the third inning. If he had three or four suits, he let me carry one back to the park. We would enter at 15th and Huntingdon Streets, which was the home plate area, and walk through the park to the center-field clubhouse. Even though we went to the clubhouse nearly every day, I almost never saw a player, because they were all on the field.

Mr. Twer didn't get to see the players when he picked up the suits, either. He dealt with the clubhouse man, Teddy Kessler. Mr. Twer was unable to please one visiting player. Bill Terry's suit was never pressed to his satisfaction, and Mr. Twer invariably had to press it again for nothing.

There were other ways to get into the park to see a game. My main means was a gentleman by the name of Eddie Martin. Eddie was a World War I veteran who had lost a leg, although you'd never have known it. He had a cork leg and he walked with a very slight limp. He did an enormous amount of bicycle riding. Eddie, very meticulous in manner, was a gambler who also studied the stock market.

Eddie did his betting at Baker Bowl in the field seats beyond third base. As kids we named the men who bet in this area small-time gamblers, because they bet as low as a quarter on the batter. But they were betting on every batter. Some of these men, like Eddie Martin, made a good living out of their baseball betting. How did they win? They knew the players and the game thoroughly, and they were quick to pick up on situations that changed the odds.

Most of the kids had a gambler. They would double us in the stile so that two got in on the one admission. My gambler, Eddie Martin, got me in all the time even if the field seats were packed. He would say to those in charge, "Some day this kid will be paying your wages." They would back off and let me in. Fifteen minutes after the game, I had to meet him at Chadwick and Huntingdon Streets to have a 15-minute catch with a pimple ball. This was his activity. My pay was a nickel on weekdays, and 10 cents on Saturday. There were no Sunday games in Philadelphia until 1934.

There was another group of gamblers in Baker Bowl, beyond first base in the lower grandstand. We called these the big-time gamblers. Jack Lynch was always present with three chorus girls from Jack Lynch's Walton Roof, which was a nightspot in center city Philadelphia. Jack was a large, good-looking Irishman, who always rented the thickest, hardest cushion he could find, and one of the girls carried it to his location. The older guys would always joke that Jack had a very gentle anus brought about by hemorrhoids, and we young kids didn't know what they were talking about.

Eddie Gottlieb was often in those seats, too. He was as well known in Philadelphia as Connie Mack. Eddie was a booking agent of another kind. He arranged for semipro teams from all over the area to come together to play baseball, football, and basketball. Eddie normally collected 50 cents from each team for arranging the game. When the teams were good enough to give guarantees of money, Eddie's stipend was much greater. Eddie bet baseball and was always coach of a basketball team, mainly the SPHAS (South Philadelphia Hebrew Association). Eddie is definitely the founder of pro basketball after World War II. It has been said that Eddie made up the basketball schedule in his head.

The ballplayers always knew about these big-time gamblers. When Heinie Manush was traded to Brooklyn from the American League he always had fun with them. If he was having a good day at the bat, he would holler to them, "I bet you bums are betting on me today."

The third way to get into the ball park easily came about in 1933, when the Phillies started the "Knothole Gang." A knothole card qualified young boys to get into five games during the summer. Tickets were distributed at different boys' clubs and recreation centers in the Philadelphia area. The influx of boys caused the small-time gamblers to move out of the field seats and into the left center-field bleachers. The Phillies lost 25 cents a ticket on this deal.

At a very young age, Jackie Flood became a ticket collector for the knothole gang. Those of us who knew him would go in and pretend we gave Jack a ticket. We didn't like to sit with the knotholers in the field seats, though, so we always tried to get into the grandstand or the bleachers.

If things were getting desperate, Tom Dunn would be my fourth opportunity to enter Baker Bowl. His job was to let people leave the park early from the field seats and bleachers. After the fourth inning, he'd stand at the bleacher entrance at 15th and Lehigh Avenue. Tom always kept this door closed, but some of the men who had knotholes at the gate on 15th Street would always come around and try to get Tom to let them in to see a few innings. Sometimes they gave him a trolley pass so that he could jump the number two trolley which took him home. A cigar was sure entrance fee.

Tom liked me, but on his bad days, he simply wouldn't let anyone in. When this happened, I just ran past him when he opened the door to let someone out. Looking back, I wonder why the men never squealed on me. Tom always said, "someday I am going to catch that kid," but he never did. At the time I thought that I was too quick for him, but now I'm not so sure.

My last means to enter the park was Firpo. All the kids were afraid of Firpo. He was a huge crippled man, whose speech was slightly slurred. Firpo policed the walkway at the top of the bleachers. The Phillies had advertisements on billboards outside the bleacher wall facing Lehigh Avenue. Kids would scale this wall and drop down into the bleachers. Sometimes, though, they dropped into Firpo's arms, which was an extremely frightening experience. Besides patrolling the walkway, Firpo's other duty was to open the center-field gate at the top of the bleachers to let fans out. With one or two outs in the ninth inning, Firpo would fling the gate open and all the kids outside would pour into the bleachers. With the Phillies, you often got to see four or five extra innings.

In the immediate area of the park, parking was in the hands of the "Unholy Seven," who invented valet parking. The "Unholy Seven" were grown men, and during the summer months this was one of the main sources of their income. The group had the Kennedy brothers (Norman, Moon, and Francis), Jim McDonough, Patty Rowbottom, Johnny Nixon, and a gentleman named Hoffman. They took care of the judges, city officials, lawyers, and other big shots. They stored cars wherever they wanted, even in the safety lane in the middle of Broad Street. Francis Kennedy doubled as the announcer inside the ball park with his megaphone. Francis was known to take a drink, and people often played tricks on him. In 1934, Benny Bass was scheduled to fight Cleo Locatelli. When some of the gang saw that Francis was ready for a trick, they changed the pitcher's name in the batteries from, say, Mungo, to Locatelli. The fans would really get on him, but all in fun.

The "Unholy Seven" were not the only adults who mooched (that was what it was called) cars. A man we called Andy Gump was a fixture on 16th Street. We thought Andy was ancient because he had a bald head. Jim Barry, who had a lame leg, patrolled Tucker Street while a guy named Tommy Carr had Huntingdon Street between 16th and Bancroft. The younger kids were deep in the outfield, as my partner, Bill Alpuche and I had 17th Street, where we guided drivers to empty spaces. Lynn C. Doyle, a writer for the *Bulletin,* was a regular customer, and he gave us a nickel every day.

In the '20s and '30s in Philadelphia, sandlot baseball was at its peak, as men played into and beyond their thirties before they threw in the sponge. Legions of players at the top rung supplemented their income and also sent children to college with the proceeds from sandlot baseball. The great Art Sharkey told me that he sent three of his children through college on the money he made playing sandlot ball.

The most significant item in a baseball game is the ball, which has always been costly. One gentleman, Ball Hawk George, realized it very early, and he knew that this was a source of income. George was a large, weatherbeaten, rawboned man, who walked everywhere. George lived in South Philadelphia, six or seven miles from the ballpark. If you lived in the area of Baker Bowl, it wasn't too long before you met and were knocked down by Ball Hawk George. His station was the southwest corner of 15th and Huntingdon Streets, behind home plate. George shagged foul balls to sell them to the best sandlot teams in Philadelphia for 50 or 75 cents. The cleaner the ball, the more money he got. He had capturing foul balls down to a science. His ears were fine-tuned to the crack of the bat, and he knew immediately whether to head for Huntingdon Street or 15th Street. Everything in his path was simply bowled over.

George became a celebrity of some note. When you went to the movies in the '30s, before the main feature there were photos of world happenings. Ball Hawk George was caught hawking balls outside of Baker Bowl by Fox Movietone News.

George was not the only one who had a strategy for making money out of marketing baseballs. There was one person inside the park who had a better racket, and he never got caught. Southstreet was a carpenter by trade, but during the Depression he worked on the grounds crew, which probably paid him a dollar or dollar and a half a day. He was an excellent pool shark, too, capable of playing with the big boys. And he'd learned a great drop-ball pitch from Cy Blanton and Mace Brown of the Pirates, which he used to great effect as a pitcher for Bancroft A. C. But his real money came from none of that.

Southstreet's job, once the game started, was to handle all foul balls off the screen behind home plate. He always wore baggy pants, and he had two bank money bags sewed in the inside of the front of his pants. When he caught three balls off the screen, he slipped one ball inside his pants into one of the bags and took the other two balls up to the umpire. It was a bad day when Southstreet didn't get at least six balls.

There was another gentleman who collected baseballs at Baker Bowl. George Brand worked the press gates at Shibe Park and Baker Bowl and had his own ball club, the Lancaster Roses. If you brought a ball to George, he would let you into the game. His team probably got more balls this way than they bought.

Prior to World War II, the concessions rented cushions for ten cents. There were 1,800 of these thick, hard leather pads. Some oldtimers would say that they were bought for the World Series of 1915. If that is true, they lasted until the place closed for baseball in 1938. You started as a cushion boy, and made a penny for each cushion you rented, so the only way to really make money was on tips. You carried a rag to wipe off the seat or seats. You always wiped off seats for ladies. If you got a nickel tip that was the same as selling five cushions. On good days at Baker Bowl, 1,500 or more cushions might be rented, and the cushion and scorecard sellers could not go home until we collected all the cushions. If we were missing one, we searched for it.

Leon Gumpert handled the cushions and the selling of the score cards. Always dressed in a suit with a felt hat, Leon was a good guy, very excitable, never forgot a face. Leon never counted money. He did not want to be short. He always had an assistant. I eventually got to be one.

The main boss of the concessions was John Mallon, brother of the owner, Mrs. Gerry Nugent. He was not a likable man.

The Phillies at Baker Bowl always vended lemonade (at Shibe Park it was orange). Baker Bowlers consumed Burk's hot dogs, a big name in this area, (at Shibe Park it was Voigt's skinless). The Phillies' lemonade was made fresh. There were a couple of large vats, and Moon Kennedy, one of the "Unholy Seven," would come in from his parking chores and stir the lemonade. If the sales of the lemonade were good, lemons would run short and water would simply be poured over the used ones. Because of this, we were always taught to holler, "Get your cold drinks," not "Get your lemonade."

In the ten-year period that I was at Baker Bowl, the two biggest crowds for baseball happened on consecutive Saturdays, first with the Gashouse Gang, the Cardinals, followed by the Giants. These were two torrid days. Naturally, the concessions ran out of lemons, and the vendors, of whom I was one, were really selling water. I was 14 when a guy grabbed me in the bleachers and said, "Is this lemonade?" and I said, "I don't know because I am selling cold drinks." Whenever a fan complained and got that answer, all the other fans around him would laugh and we would be on our way.

There were a number of tricks to make extra money, some not very sanitary. When there was a good crowd, cushion boys would sell the so-called lemonade after the cushion sales. This is where the unsanitary part took place. When we collected cushions after the game, we also collected cups that weren't smashed. On a good day we might get five or 10 good cups and hide them. The day of a big game when we got our tray of 12 lemonades we were on our way. After we sold three or four, we went under the stands and put four empty used cups in the tray, poured a little lemonade into them from the full cups and went back to the concession stand to say we needed some ice. A guy with a shovel threw ice on the top of the trays, which made all 12 cups full again. This would net us 40 cents profit.

Another way was with scorecards. Phillies scorecards were a nickel. Every time a new series started, the concessions had enough cards printed for the entire series. Once again when collecting cushions, we looked for clean scorecards and hid them away (other vendors would steal your cards if they saw where you hid them). This was a nickel profit for every one that we sold. One time we were selling Braves scorecards and the Giants were playing. Someone had switched scorecards on us.

None of the kids that I grew up with sold hot dogs at Baker Bowl. That was a tough job. You had that metal box with hot water. Lugging that case up the steps was no easy task, so we stayed away from that chore. We never made a ton of money, but every day in Baker Bowl was a fun day.

Kid Beebe vended in the bleachers and field seats with his large wicker basket, selling peanuts, peanut chews, and everything else that he was permitted to sell. Kid was a former pug, and all the gamblers knew him. He stood no more than 5'4" in his stocking feet. When we knew him as kids, his hair was already white, but he was still around and I was still his friend thirty years later. Kid Beebe had a strong little body which got him through 637 fights without getting knocked out. He fought three fights in New York in one night. It was my pleasure to work the front steps with him at Shibe Park selling scorecards for a number of years. One day when the Kid had to be well past sixty some young punk tried to give him some static, and like a cat the Kid hit him with a left hook and put him right on the seat of his pants. He said to the guy, "Go home and tell your father you were knocked out by grandpa."

Sam Payne had been the groundskeeper dating back to the turn of the century. At one time he and his wife had lived in the clubhouse. Sam was well known in the neighborhood and he always hired boys to do jobs around the park. In the wintertime the kids shoveled lots of snow. Mrs. Payne at one time offered meals right after the game in the clubhouse. Sam was a character. He always had a couple of sheep or goats under the bleachers. After the game Sam turned them loose, and Baker Bowl was expertly sheared.

What made Baker Bowl a so-called bandbox? When the first park was built in 1887, the distance to right field was about 300 feet. When the fire burned it down in 1894, the new grandstands were wider which cut down on the distance. This still wasn't a problem until 1910, when the cork center ball was invented. This is when the park became a bandbox, and when the right-field wall became a famous target. The rest of the ballpark always held its own with other parks. No ball was ever hit over the clubhouse in center field, although Hornsby hit one through the window, 408 feet from home plate. Down the left field line was 341 after the bleachers were built in 1910. Prior to that it was about 400 feet.

When the park was rebuilt after the fire of 1894, it had a brick wall around the entire field. From the flagpole in right center field to the right-field foul line was the famous wall, to which a wooden framework was attached to hold advertising signs. Practically from its inception, the wall was used to produce revenue. In the twenties, there was the Bull Durham sign. During my ten years at Baker Bowl, the only sign was the Lifebuoy sign. It said, "The Phillies Use Lifebuoy." The kids would write, "and they still stink."

For years, the scoreboard was divided into three sections. In right field on the foul line side of the wall was listed the Phillies lineup. In right field was a board that gave the score of the game. In right center field was another board that gave the batteries. In my time, there was one score board in right center field on the center field side of the flag pole. This was a good-sized board that carried all the National League scores as well as the score of the Athletics game. It gave the batter, the count, and the number of outs.

In 1922 , balls started to fly out of the right field section of the grounds so the Phillies moved home plate back six feet. The new dimensions were right field: 279'6" (some publications put it at 280'6"); center field: 408, and left field 341. On Memorial Day, 1922, Cliff Lee hit the first ball ever hit out of the park to left field. It would happen only four more times: by Wally Berger, Jimmie Foxx, Hal Lee, and Joe Medwick.

In July of 1929, owner Baker decided the Phillies were being sued too often because Chuck Klein was hitting too many cars on Broad Street. So he set up a screen over the wall that extended it to about 60 feet high. The screen cut down on homers (especially Klein's, which didn't help the Phillies any), and gave the fielders more chances at assists.

For me, the real treat of the right-field wall was watching the fielders play it. Some, like Johnny Moore, Paul Waner, and Mel Ott, were exceptional, but the king was Chuck Klein. He established an assist record of 44, which has never been broken. Klein's throws were quick and accurate no matter where he was throwing. He had better control to the plate than the Phillies pitching staff.

May 29, 1935, was Babe Ruth day, but the Babe went hitless. The next day, Memorial Day, turned out to be the Babe's last as a player. Baker Bowl was the only major league park he never got a hit in. He was 0 for 4 there.

On June 30, 1938, the Phillies played their last game at Baker Bowl. We were all on hand. It was like a funeral. The Giants, who had helped open the park so many years before, now helped close it with a vengeance. They battered the Phillies, 14-1.

My friend Bob Butler cried. Bill Alpuche of our gang saw his favorite, Bill Atwood, make the last out. Phil Weintraub of the Phillies had the last single, and Pinky Whitney the last double. Lonnie Frey, of the Reds, had clubbed the last triple. Hank Leiber, the Giant center fielder, blasted the last home run, while Mel Ott got the last base on balls (off Bill Hallahan) and scored the last run. Ray Stoviak, fresh out of Villanova, was the last strike-out, a victim of the Giants' Slick Castleman. Jimmy Wilson, practically a neighborhood boy from Kensington, was the last to leave the park, as the Phillies shifted five blocks west to Shibe Park. The change of venue didn't help our Phillies. They finished in last place, at 45-105.

Elmer Flick

Scott Longert

On a warm summer's morning in 1891, fifteen-year-old Elmer Flick stood barefoot on the railroad platform, helping the large crowd in a rousing cheer for the departing Bedford baseball club. Two games were to be played against nearby rival Garrettsville. As the train slowly pulled in, the enthusiasm gave way to panic, when a head count revealed only eight players lined up to board. The team captain, unwilling to risk a forfeit, scanned the group of well wishers for a replacement player. He spied the muscular Flick, motioning the teenager to come forward. Without hesitation, Elmer dashed toward the passenger car, elbowing his way through the throng of fans. After he convinced the captain he could play ball, the train left the platform with a full complement of ballplayers ready to do battle. Despite the lack of shoes and a uniform, Flick held his own against the big boys, hitting several drives deep into the outfield.

Elmer Harrison Flick was born in Bedford, Ohio, January 11, 1876, one of four children of Zachary Taylor and Mary Flick. A mechanic by trade, Zack owned and operated the Eagle Chair Company in the downtown business district. It was there that Elmer used a wood lathe to fashion the bats that he used throughout his career.

In the fall of 1895, Flick traveled to Youngstown to collect a bill for his father. On the way he made a stop in Akron, where he knew the manager of the Youngstown club settled for the winter. He located the man relaxing in one of the local pool halls. After a lengthy plea from Flick, the manager agreed to a tryout in the following spring. Elmer received a contract for the grand sum of forty dollars monthly, provided he stuck with the club. After blasting balls to the outfield fences, Flick became a star in short order, prompting admiring fans to nickname him, "The Demon of the Stick." At five feet nine inches and 165 pounds, Flick possessed tremendous power to go along with above-average foot speed. Soon National League clubs bid for his services, with the Philadelphia Phillies winning out. In April of 1898 he made his debut, batting .302 in his initial season.

Two years later, Flick showed he was a man to be reckoned with by holding his own in a clubhouse fight with Napoleon Lajoie. The brawl occurred over the possession of a bat. Despite giving away thirty pounds to the bigger Lajoie, Flick battled his nemesis to a bloody draw. The fray ended when Lajoie missed with a haymaker and broke his thumb on the clubhouse wall. Flick walked away with a black eye and new-found respect from his Phillies teammates.

Jumping leagues—The creation of a new league to compete with the established National, brought forth lucrative opportunities for the game's best players. In 1902, Flick and others left the Phillies to join the American League's cross-town Athletics. Weeks after his departure, the Phillies owner went to court to get his stars back. Faced with an injunction to keep him from playing in Philadelphia, Flick worried about his status as a player. He watched as the court system handed down injunctions against Lajoie and pitcher Bill Bernhard. Both players had jumped the previous sea-

Scott Longert is a free-lance writer and business consultant. He is working on a biography of Addie Joss.

son, and had been stars for the fledging League. Flick presumably faced the same fate as his renegade teammates. Several weeks passed while he remained in limbo, waiting for the court to issue a ruling. Some type of action, legal or otherwise, needed to be taken to get Flick on the baseball diamond where he belonged.

Cleveland Blues owner Charles Somers watched the proceedings with keen interest. He very much wanted to bring Flick back to his home town, where he anticipated a boost in attendance would surely take place. Using his influence as vice-president of the American League, Somers worked out a deal with Ban Johnson for the rights to Elmer Flick. Several weeks later the Blues had a new right fielder, who quickly became a fixture in the outfield for the remainder of his career.

National Baseball Library, Cooperstown, NY

Elmer Flick with his stick.

Appearing in front of family and friends, Flick established himself as one of baseball's premier players. He led the American League in stolen bases twice, while banging out the most triples three years in a row. In 1905 he captured the batting title with an average of .306. (Until Carl Yastrzemski hit .301 to take the AL title in 1968, Flick was known to moderns mainly as the man with the lowest league-leading batting average ever.) As an outfielder he was fearless, chasing balls with reckless abandon. While playing against Philadelphia, Flick dove headlong into an overflow crowd along the right-field line. He didn't come up with the ball, but he did manage to upend one of the sandwich vendors, causing a spray of mustard to shower the helpless spectators.

Generally a good-natured fellow, Flick sometimes exhibited a feisty side to his character. Several times he refused to report to spring training, going as far as announcing his retirement. He grew to dislike going south for spring training, advising reporters he planned to ship down his own food supply rather than eat the awful food there.

In 1907 Flick became part of a controversy that is still talked about today. During training camp, Charles Somers received a phone call from the Detroit management. It offered to trade Ty Cobb to Cleveland, straight up for Elmer Flick. The Tigers had grown tired of the unruly antics of their young star, and wanted him out of Detroit. Somers considered the trade, eager to have a player of Cobb's caliber. However he feared the disruptive force Cobb could be on his ballclub, ultimately turning down the offer. At the time it made sense, as Flick was a star in his own right. One year later it became apparent that Somers had made a grave error. Cobb enjoyed the distinction of being recognized as the American League's best player while Flick came down with a stomach ailment that ended his career. Doctors were unable to find the cause of Flick's problem, which saw him drop 25 pounds and left him sidelined for the entire 1908 season. After 66 games in 1909 and 24 in 1910, Flick reluctantly gave up the game. In a sense, Somers could have acquired Cobb for practically nothing.

With his baseball career finished, Flick returned to his Bedford farm, where he began a new vocation as a builder of residential homes and office buildings. He had a fondness for raising horses, often exercising them through Bedford's downtown streets. In later years he scouted on a part-time basis for the Cleveland Indians.

Shortly after his 87th birthday, Flick received a most unexpected gift. The Veteran's Committee elected him to membership in the Baseball Hall of Fame. Despite a weakened physical condition, Flick made the long journey to New York to take his place among the game's immortals. Leaning heavily on his cane, he slowly walked to the microphone to accept his plaque. Smiling to the crowd, Flick said, "You see my cane and how I walk. But I feel good today. I feel good. This is the biggest day I ever had." His sincerity warmed over the audience, which gave him a spirited reception. The "Demon of Swat" had spoken.

Elmer Flick died January 9, 1971, just two days shy of his 95th birthday. He played baseball when the ball was dead and the outfields were large enough to graze cattle. The pitchers threw spitballs and tobacco balls, while the hitters stood their ground without helmets. He rode to the ballpark in a horse-drawn carriage, waving to fans who lined the streets to shout their encouragement. Elmer Flick lived in a long-forgotten era when baseball really was a game and giving your best was all that mattered.

Lady Baldwin forced his hand

Captain Anson's Platoon

Tom Nawrocki

Abner Dalrymple must have been surprised to see that he was not in the starting lineup for the Chicago White Stockings on May 6, 1886, against the Detroit Wolverines. Dalrymple was coming off a season in which he had played left field every day for the pennant-winning White Stockings, leading the league not only in at bats but in homers as well. Yet for the home opener of the following season Dalrymple was on the bench.

Chicago's manager was trying out a new idea. "The team presented by Captain Anson had particular reference to the effectiveness of [Lady] Baldwin, Detroit's lefthanded pitcher, and Dalrymple and Gore, both left-hand batters, were accordingly laid off, Flynn and Ryan taking care of left and center field," the Chicago *Inter Ocean* reported. The writer didn't have the full story; center fielder George Gore was merely out with a sprained ankle and would play regularly for Chicago that season. But Anson fully intended to platoon Dalrymple, playing one of his rookies, Jocko Flynn or Jimmy Ryan, in left field against lefties. Through two-thirds of the season, Dalrymple would lead off and play left field against righthanded pitchers, who would make up the bulk of the opposing moundsmen, but see almost no action versus the handful of lefties Chicago faced.

In addition to his left–right platooning, Anson alternated catchers depending on who was pitching. This was a common practice of the day, naming a battery where a modern manager would name a starting pitcher, but Anson carried it further. His best hitter, Mike "King" Kelly, was a top catcher in an era when it was physically impossible to catch every day. The greatest catcher of the nineteenth century, the New York Giants' Buck Ewing, only once caught more than 81 games in a season. Kelly's bat was too valuable to leave on the bench that long, so Anson shuttled him back and forth between right field and behind the plate, with stops nearly everywhere else. At the outset of the 1886 season, Anson set into place a system whereby Kelly would catch Chicago's second starter, Jim McCormick, and usually play right field when the team's ace, John Clarkson, or third starter, Jocko Flynn, pitched. Clarkson was caught by veteran Silver Flint (the papers called them the Jersey battery). Flynn and a fellow rookie, George "Prunes" Moolic, made up the so-called pony battery. So Chicago's lineup was determined not only by the opposition's pitcher but by its own pitcher as well.

Southpaws and platooning—Bill James has written that platooning would have been nearly impossible in the nineteenth century because of a lack of lefthanded pitching and the small size of the rosters. While lefties made up a tiny fraction of the National League's pitchers—only three southpaws started more than ten games in 1886—each pitcher started so often in those days of two- and three-man rotations that a manager could effectively platoon. Detroit's Lady Baldwin started 56 games, Philadelphia's Dan Casey 45 games, and Washington's Dupee Shaw 44 games. Not counting games started by the White Stockings' pitchers (all righties), lefties started about one-seventh of all league

Tom Nawrocki is an editor at Worth *magazine. He lives in Hoboken, New Jersey.*

games.

And while the rosters were relatively small—13 was the normal size—the largest difference from today's roster was the size of the pitching staff. The White Stockings carried only three regular pitchers, and one of those saw almost as much duty in the outfield as on the mound. That leaves 11 position players available each day (10 when Flynn pitched), enough to maintain a regular platoon.

Coming into the 1886 season Anson was facing a manager's favorite problem: a talent glut. His team had won its fourth pennant in six years in 1885 and boasted some of the game's biggest stars. Kelly, Clarkson and Anson himself are now Hall of Famers. Center fielder George Gore was a consistent .300 hitter who often led the league in walks; he regularly scored 100 runs a season in a 120-game schedule. Third baseman Ned Williamson set the NL home run record in 1884 with 27. Left fielder Dalrymple, shortstop Tommy Burns and Fred Pfeffer, the greatest defensive second baseman of his day, were established stars.

To this team Anson added a rookie sensation in outfielder Jimmy Ryan, headed for an 18-year major league career and a lifetime average over .300. Rookie pitcher and outfielder Jocko Flynn would go 24-6 that summer. And Anson already had Billy Sunday, one of the most valuable reserve outfielders in baseball, on his bench.

Where would they all play? To begin with, Anson made heavy use of his fourth outfielder by switching Kelly between catcher and right field. Against lefties, the righthanded hitting Ryan generally went to right field when Kelly caught. Facing a righthander, the left-swinging Sunday often took right.

Against righthanders, Abner Dalrymple was the everyday left fielder and leadoff man. But apparently Anson didn't feel he could hit lefties at all. Although Dalrymple played a total of 82 games that year, in Chicago's 16 starts against lefties, he played twice, batting ninth and seventh. Sunday got only one start in left field against a southpaw; otherwise it was Ryan or Flynn, depending on whether Flynn pitched that day (he started 29 times; there is no pattern of his pitching more frequently against righties or lefties).

Against lefties, Flynn often led off, playing left or right or pitching. Ryan played left or right against lefties, depending on whether Kelly was catching or not and Flynn was pitching or not. Or depending on what Anson had for breakfast that day, for all I know.

Dalrymple and Sunday saw almost no action against lefties. Gore, also a lefthanded hitter, played center field every day except for injury time-outs, so Anson recognized that some lefthanded hitters could hit southpaws better than others. With the overwhelming proportion of righthanded pitchers in the league, Anson couldn't afford to completely bench a righthanded hitter against them, but Flynn's batting-order position showed a definite platoon effect. Against lefties he led off or batted third through the first two-thirds of the season; against righties he generally batted ninth. Although the Macmillan *Encyclopedia* doesn't list a batting style for Flynn, I am convinced based on the *Inter Ocean* information quoted above and Anson's treatment of him that he was a righthanded batter.

Complications—The whole thing was incredibly complicated. The only regular strategy was that Dalrymple played against righties but not lefties, and that Flynn led off against lefties but not righties. In 16 games against southpaws, Anson never started the same lineup twice. Against righties, there was a much more regular pattern. Despite the fact that he swapped positions between third baseman Williamson and shortstop Burns before the season opened, Anson had his infield set in stone, with the same players playing every day and hitting in the same slots every day. (Williamson did not play an inning at third base all year and Burns never again played short. The New York Mets should take note.) The most regular lineup against righties:

Abner Dalrymple

Dalrymple, LF
Gore, CF
Kelly, RF
Anson, 1B
Pfeffer, 2B
Williamson, SS
Burns, 3B
Clarkson, P
Flint, C

And it worked. Chicago had gone 87-25 in winning the pennant the year before and started out almost as hot in 1886. But the Detroit Wolverines were even hotter, winning 18 games in a row at one point. The White Stockings went to Detroit on June 19 to open the biggest series of the year: the defending champs, in second place with a 26-7 record, against the first-place upstarts at 30-6. On the morning of the 19th, the *Chicago Tribune* reported: "In answer to queries as to the probable team that will represent the Chicagos in the game tomorrow, Capt. Anson said that he had not fully made up his mind. McCormick will probably pitch, but the rest of the makeup will depend largely on whom the Detroits put in the box." The Detroits put their left-handed ace, Lady Baldwin, in the box, and the White Stockings beat him, 5-4; it was Detroit's first home loss all year.

"Anson showed fine judgment in substituting Flynn for Dalrymple and putting Gore at the bottom of the batting list," the *Tribune* said the next day. "Of course the reason for the change was that the lefthanded batters can't do anything with Baldwin." It was the sixth time that year that Dalrymple had been bumped from the lineup against a lefty, but apparently the *Tribune* hadn't noticed before. Now the reporter was aware of Anson's platooning. A week later, after a game against the Washington Nationals, the *Tribune* said: "Dalrymple got a two-base hit off [Dupee] Shaw yesterday [a lefty on in relief of right-hander Bob Barr], the first time on record that he has hit a left-handed pitcher." On June 28, Dalrymple made his first start of the year against a lefty, Philadelphia's Dan Casey, batting ninth. "Dalrymple managed to pound two singles off the lefthanded twirler for the Quakers," the *Tribune* said. "If he keeps on it will not be necessary to put him at the foot of the list when facing a pitcher of that kind."

The system falters—By July 4 the White Stockings were 34-13. Unfortunately, the Wolverines were still on fire at 39-9. Anson's system, which had been quite consistent the first part of the season, began to fall apart. In July he broke up his regular batteries and started catching Kelly more. Kelly hit a league-leading .388 that year, scoring an astonishing 155 runs in 118 games, while Flint hit .202. If Kelly caught more, Anson could get Ryan's or Flynn's bat in the lineup rather than Flint's, so by August Kelly began catching almost every day. (Anson found other ways to keep from burning out his catchers; he sent himself behind the plate in the late innings of blowouts 12 times during the season, usually moving Kelly or whomever to first base.)

Dalrymple continued to sit against lefties, but in mid-August he began sitting against some righties, too. Why Anson chose Dalrymple for this treatment after he had been one of the leading hitters in the league for the first half of the 1880s is a mystery, but he knew what he was doing, for Dalrymple, it became clear, was virtually through as a player by this time. In his autobiography, Anson conceded that Dalrymple "excelled as a batsman," but added: "I have said that he was a fair fielder, and in that respect perhaps I am rating him too high, as his poor fielding cost us several games that in my estimation we should have won." Although he led the league in homers with 11 in 1885, his batting average had dropped from .309 to .274. In 1886, when he became a platoon player, Dalrymple hit just .233. He then spent two years as a part-timer for Pittsburgh, never clearing .220, before dropping out of the league.

The Wolverines refused to give in through August, despite the charge of Anson's Colts, and the league had a heated pennant race on its hands. In the middle of August Anson benched Dalrymple, whose hitting had dropped to next to nothing, for good, so the platoon experiment was over. Through September the lineups against lefties and righties were identical for the first time all season. With Dalrymple cut loose from the leadoff spot, everyone else moved up a notch, so that by September Gore was leading off, followed by Kelly, Anson, Pfeffer, Williamson and Burns. The two other outfielders—or an outfielder and a catcher when Kelly played right field—and the pitcher rounded out the lineup. Ryan usually took left, and Flynn, Dalrymple and Sunday saw occasional action. Although Sunday is one of the best-remembered players of the era because of his later fame as an evangelist, he was in reality no more than a Henry Cotto type; one of the fastest men in the game, he was an excellent outfielder and base runner but a weak hitter and therefore never more than a bench player for Chicago. If anyone had thought to invent pinch running, he probably would have done a lot of that, too.

On August 27 the White Stockings (64-24) finally caught Detroit (64-25). Through September Anson stuck with a set lineup, disrupted only by a late-season injury to Tommy Burns. Kelly and Ryan primarily filled in at third—despite Ryan's being a lefthanded thrower—but with the deep bench Anson had developed, his outfield was covered easily. On September 23 the lead stood at 6-1/2 games for Chicago. The powerhouse Chicago offense had proved too relentless for Detroit. The White Stockings would score 900 runs on the year, more than seven a game. Kelly and Gore were one-two in the league in runs scored; Anson hit .371 (second to Kelly) and led the league with 147 RBIs.

Chicago relaxed down the stretch after a torrid 21-2 stretch drive, losing eight of its last 14, but the team still won 90 games while losing 34. Detroit finished 2-1/2 back at 87-36. Staking their claim as the greatest team of all time, the White Stockings won their fifth pennant in seven years.

It all comes tumbling down—Captain Anson was not to win another pennant. A fanatic about conditioning, Anson grew impatient with the lax fitness standards of some of his stars and began to peddle them off. King Kelly, who probably would have been the NL MVP of 1886 had such a thing existed, was sold to Boston before the beginning of the next season. John Clarkson followed a year later. Hugh Fullerton would later write, "The cause of that sale was never made public, but the real reason was a woman, and the club was compelled to sell the men, although the act brought down the wrath of the city upon them." Dalrymple was sold to Pittsburgh. George Gore was released to the Giants, apparently as a result of Anson's irritation over his preoccupation with "women and wine." Anson had six outfielders seeing playing time in 1886; in 1887 he had to import yet another rookie, Marty Sullivan. Two more rookies joined the pitching staff following the departures of Jim McCormick, a holdout early in the 1887 season who was shipped to Pittsburgh, and Jocko Flynn.

National Baseball Library, Cooperstown, NY

Cap Anson, platooner and "fascinating manager."

Flynn was just 22 years old and adept at both pitching and hitting in 1886. His "arm gave out while he was with us," Anson wrote in his autobiography. "Besides, he got into fast company and, attempting to keep up the clip with his so-called friends, found the pace much too rapid for him and fell by the wayside." The pace began to get too rapid for Flynn in the middle of the 1886 season. In August Anson dropped him in the batting order against lefties to eighth or ninth, when he played him at all. Flynn never batted again in the majors after 1886.

A great, innovative manager—Anson is remembered today as a symbol of an era, as a great player who collected 3,000 hits, as a blowhard and a racist, as the bulwark of the early National League and the primeval Cubs. He managed the White Stockings for 19 years and led them to seven pennants, yet most fans seem to think managing began with John McGraw. During the latter stages of his career, Anson became seen as a parody of himself, a figure of ego and self-conscious rectitude.

Anson was a fascinating manager, innovative in his training system, a keen judge of talent, a strategist who made the best of what the game had to offer. He was known to work the rules in his favor: Before it became obligatory to announce the full lineup before the game started, Anson would wait to see how the first inning was going and then decide whether he was hitting third or fourth. In 1910 Johnny Evers and Hugh Fullerton, neither of whom was a fan of Anson's, wrote, "The Chicago team of 1880...was the pioneer of 'inside baseball,' and from that team came more original plays, now in common use, than from any other source." That was Anson's second year running the White Stockings. He is often credited with inventing spring training. Decades before Babe Ruth, Anson's Colts discovered the use of the home run as a weapon, leading the NL in homers seven times. The press of the day paid little attention to managerial moves, so much of Anson's work is lost to history. His reputation as a field leader deserves some measure of rehabilitation. In the early summer of 1886, he was the proto-Earl Weaver. Until someone can show otherwise, Adrian Anson has earned the credit for inventing platooning.

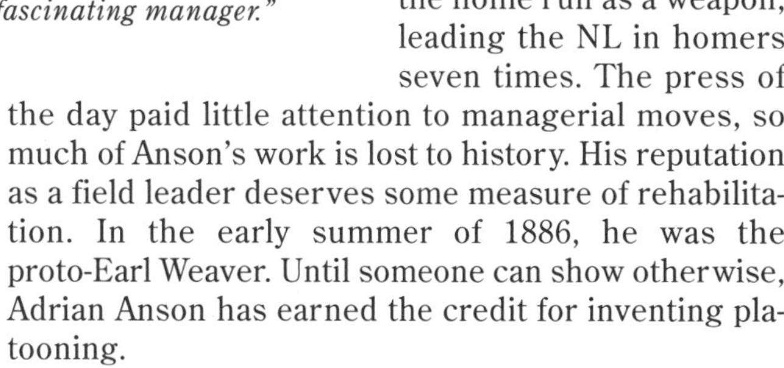

Some teams change a lot. Some don't.

Notes on the Uniform Distribution

David C. King

On opening day at Fenway, 1994, I caught a glimpse of the Tigers' new warm-up jackets—traditional navy throughout but for one shock-orange arm from shoulder to sleeve. The fearsome likes of Fielder and Fryman devolved into pathetic one-clawed lobsters. Ugly. Ridiculous. Welcome to high fashion.

The fellow next to me, a Boston sportswriter of some note, explained that lots of teams are redesigning hats, jackets, and jerseys these days. Why? Licensing fees, he said. See that kid in a White Sox jersey over there? It's a 1991 design. Made Major League Baseball a mint. Think about it, he said. Even kids in Kansas City are buying Marlins and Rockies hats. Why did the Indians change uniforms this year, and the Reds last year? Money, he said. Nothing's sacred anymore.

True? There certainly are plenty of redesigned jerseys in stores. The Brewers are looking better lately, at least before they hit the field. And the Astros finally stopped dressing like night-shift managers at Taco Bell. But is there really a wave of innovation going on across baseball? And what causes design changes when they happen? Is it money, as my writer friend says, or something more insidious, like a new cadre of fashion consultants pigeonholing team owners at their occasional national meetings?

Thanks to Marc Okkonen's wonderful picture book, *Baseball Uniforms of the 20th Century* (New York: Sterling, 1993), we can see if the wags and cynics are right. Are uniform changes more common today than back in the good old days, whenever they were? The answer is clear, and the answer is no. Major league ball teams are no more likely to be sporting redesigned uniforms in the 1990s than they were in the 1940s, or any decade since World War II. That is true for home and road uniforms, and home and road hats, too.

To understand how turbulent the uniform distribution can be, I randomly selected 17 of the current 28 baseball teams, nine from the American League and eight from the National League.[1] With the help of a research assistant, I studied every jersey and hat design for each year in a team's history, as shown in Okkonen's book. We used conservative coding rules, ignoring times when design changes were slight, like different colored socks, varying sleeve lengths, and the occasional appearance of commemorative patches. Instead, we only recorded major modifications, such as new color combinations, pinstripes, and the appearance of those pullover pajamas in the 1970s.

For an example of how often uniform styles change, recall what the Kansas City Athletics looked like. In 1960 they sported an off-white[2] button-up jersey with black piping and a red script "Athletics" on the chest. The 1961 Athletics showed up in pinstripes with a large navy "A" over their hearts, and their look was topped off with a new hat. They were in new hats the next year too, as the 1962 Athletics dressed in black and red "tank top" jerseys, with block letters spelling out the team name. Not to be out-done, the 1963 A's came to camp introducing their now-familiar green and gold combination.

The way the Athletics tinkered with uniforms is not some historical fluke. Most teams have gone through similar spurts of innovation. The table below shows the

David C. King is assistant professor of public policy at the John F. Kennedy School of Government, Harvard University. Many thanks to Michael Terra and Kirsten Syverson for their help.

percentage of major league clubs in our sample that redesigned uniforms in a given year. The percentage varies widely, from 75 percent in 1909 to zero in 1984, but the trend is unmistakable. Despite the general impression that there are more uniform changes happening in the 1990s, the greatest flux came before World War II.

Take the Yankees. Originally the Highlanders after moving from Baltimore in 1903, the young New York team went through six home and road jerseys by 1909. Since Babe Ruth joined the Yankees in 1920, however, the Bronx Bombers have changed their look just once, and it was minor. Likewise the Boston Red Sox and Chicago Cubs tried out various uniforms in the 1920s and 1930s, but they have made relatively few changes since the 1940s. This has been the pattern across baseball, as anyone collecting old uniforms will note.

The table shows what has happened to home uniforms over the years, but there are important marketing niches for hats as well. Just think about the Rangers' new logo, or the return a few years ago of Baltimore's stylish bird. Maybe teams are increasingly likely to play head games for the sake of clever marketing in the 1990s. Again, the answer from our data is clear, and the answer is no. Hat designs are as stable now as they have ever been.

There have been two general types of caps in baseball history. The "Chicago style" pillbox looked like a layer cake. (Recall those old pictures of "Home Run" Baker, or, if you dare, imagine Kent Tekulve with the Pirates in the early 1980s.). The "Boston style" from the turn of the century was, as Okkonen notes, "the forerunner of future cap styles with a rounded close-fitting crown." This Boston style presumably includes the shockingly red cap that Bernie Carbo wore for the Red Sox in the mid-1970s.

In the 1930s, clubs were much more likely to have separate home and road hats, doubling the number of hats diehard fans could buy. Even if it seems as though every kid on the block is wearing a fancy new cap, your parents probably thought so too.

Average Annual Percentage of Major League Teams with Redesigns, by Decade (1901-1993)

	Home Uniform	Away Uniform	Home Hat	Away Hat
1901-1909	47	46	50	43
1910-1919	43	39	38	35
1920-1929	33	36	23	36
1930-1939	36	38	21	25
1940-1949	15	14	12	13
1950-1959	15	18	13	12
1960-1969	14	18	7	11
1970-1979	13	16	4	7
1980-1989	16	22	5	6
1990-1993	18	18	6	6

The aggregate statistics paint a different picture than one expects, based on what we have been hearing about the new marketing push for licensed baseball products. Still, the table can be misleading, because some teams have indeed been going through spurts of redesign. The San Diego Padres have modified their uniforms, on average, every 2.33 years. Since 1940, Cleveland has had a new look every 3.38 years, on average. And thanks largely to Bill Veeck's years as the White Sox's owner, Chicago has averaged a new home jersey every other year since 1976. Contrast this with the stability in uniform designs found in Detroit and St. Louis.

Why is there such team-by-team variation? Why do some teams go through spurts of innovation, followed by long periods of stability? A team-level analysis of the uniform distribution highlights a few things that make teams more likely to scrap their old jerseys and start anew.

- This is obvious, but when franchises change cities, as when the Washington Senators became the Minnesota Twins in 1961, teams almost always redesign their jerseys. (The Braves are a notable exception. Both times they moved, only the letter on the hat changed.)

- Related to this, we should mention that when there are new franchises, like those in Florida and Colorado, there are naturally more new licensed products on the market. But that does not mean that established teams are changing their looks.

- New hats and jerseys usually come with new stadiums, such as those in Cleveland and Arlington in 1994.

- When ownership changes, a team is more likely to go for an image overhaul.

- Pennant-winning teams are much less likely to tinker with their wardrobe.

- Teams in smaller than average media markets (Milwaukee, Seattle, Pittsburgh, and San Diego), are slightly more likely to change designs. Teams with below-.500 records, and teams with below-average attendance records are much more likely to redesign hats and jerseys.

These last two findings make sense if marketing decisions drive uniform changes. What teams need the most help with marketing? Those in small markets and those with losing records and poor gates.

Maybe my writer friend had the story half right. No, we baseball fans are not drowning under a new wave of hats and jerseys. Our grandparents survived much more turbulence in the uniform distribution than we are seeing now.

Still, the almighty dollar probably does play a role in the design changes we are seeing. In baseball, teams market jerseys but they also market dreams. When our favorite team fails in September, we hope against hope, whispering, "Wait until next year." It is easier, I suppose, to dream that dream when your favorite nine no longer looks like the scraggly bunch of losers that disappointed everyone the year before. Anyone remember what the Brewers looked like when Dave Bristol was their skipper and they lost 97 games? Me neither. Thank goodness.

Notes

1. American League: Baltimore, Boston, California, Chicago, Cleveland, Detroit, Milwaukee, New York, Oakland. National League: Chicago, Cincinnati, Houston, New York, Philadelphia, Pittsburgh, St. Louis, San Diego.

2. The 1960 jersey was off-white. The 1959 jersey was pure white. I do not code such minor changes to be "redesigns."

A marriage made in heaven

No. Audre and I weren't married at home plate. You never met my mother-in-law.

Instead, I sent my pals, Billy and Don, on a reconnaissance patrol to Wrigley Field for the Chicago Cubs doubleheader against the Brooklyn Dodgers.

After Audre and I tied the knot on Sunday, June 30, 1957, my informants called from the ballpark and said the Cubs and Dodgers were knotted 1-1 going into extra innings and they would keep me posted for later developments.

Everyone at the reception thought I was just another nervous bridegroom. IO was. But it was because I didn't know the score, And then the phone finally rang.

"The Cubs won 3-2 in 11 innings," shouted my spy ring. "Bob Speake walked and circled the bases after Ernie Banks doubled over Duke Snider's head against the center-field ivy."

I then proposed a toast—to Ernie Banks.

Maybe getting married wasn't so bad, after all.

And now for the honeymoon. Our first stop was Detroit. We checked into the Detroit Leland Hotel, where Audre registered and i raced to the newsstand. I scanned the sports pages and learned that rookie Dick Drott had tossed a four-hitter and the Cubs had drubbed the Cincinnati Reds, 6-0.

I also learned the Chicago White Sox were playing the Detroit Tigers that evening, and Briggs Stadium was only a few blocks from the hotel. Audre went to bed—and I went to the ballgame.

Briggs Stadium is rich in baseball lore. It's the site where Ducky Medwick of the St. Louis Cardinals was showered with fruit in the seventh game of the 1934 World Series; where Ted Williams hit his game-winning three-run homer in the ninth inning of the 1941 All-Star Game, and were Ty Cobb filed his spikes before tearing around the bases.

The Tigers' current stars were Harvey Kuenn and Al Kaline. But when the lineups were announced, their names only drew a smattering of applause. The Detroit fans saved most of their cheers for Charlie Maxwell, chanting "Paw Paw." That's the nearby town where the renowned Sunday slugger resided.

The question was: Should I root for the Tigers or be a loyal Chicagoan and go-go with the White Sox? I went with the crowd and cheered as the Tigers won 5-2, highlighted by Al Kaline's two-run homer.

Our next stop was Niagara Falls, where Audre marveled at the scenery and i went exploring—for a newspaper. I finally latched onto a St. Catherines (Ontario) paper and discovered the Cubs dropped a doubleheader. The headline should have read, CUBS FALL AT THE FALLS.

No honeymoon is complete without a visit to Cooperstown, New York, a picturesque hamlet that by coincidence is where Baseball's Hall of Fame is located. Audre was just ecstatic.

And finally, we hit Broadway. The bright lights, the big shows, the Statue of Liberty, the Empire State Building, and —you guessed it— Yankee Stadium, the Polo Grounds, and Ebbets Field.

On the tollway back to Chicago, we stopped overnight in Cleveland. Audre stayed in the motel and i went to see the Indians play, but they were rained out. No. It didn't put a damper on our marriage.

When we got home to our tiny three-room apartment, I could tell the honeymoon was over. Audre was going to make a new man out of me. She mentioned something about culture and said we were going to see "Swan Lake." I thought it was a resort.

And now, after 38 years of wedded bliss. Audre owns a baseball bubblegum card store. Our sons, Steve and Bruce, are among here employees. She has approximately four-and-a-half million cards.

So much for culture!

—Eddie Gold

A great leadoff man of the old days

Roy Thomas

Ralph C. Moses

The Dickson *Baseball Dictionary* defines the term "leadoff batter" as follows: "The first player in the batting order. Because this batter comes to bat more than any other player on the team, the position is normally reserved for a top player, ideally one with a high on-base average and with the ability to steal bases."

This definition brings to mind such contemporary stars as Rickey Henderson, Tim Raines, Brett Butler, and Kenny Lofton. Older fans may recall the exploits of Richie Ashburn, the great Philadelphia Phillies' center fielder of the 1950s, who was the consummate leadoff batter of his era. However, it was another Phillies center fielder, the little-known Roy Thomas, who personified the term "leadoff batter" when it was introduced into baseball lexicon at the turn of the century.

Despite having the lowest total of extra-base hits by any player with 1,500 or more total hits in baseball history (160 of 1,537, or a percentage of only .104) and a slugging average of just .333 compared to his career batting average of .290, Roy Thomas found his way to first base with greater consistency than any other leadoff man of his time, as evidenced by his on-base percentage of .413.

Hitting over .300 five seasons in his 13-year career (1899 to 1911), Thomas also drew 100 or more bases on balls seven times. Once he reached base, Thomas knew how to move around the diamond, stealing 244 bases and scoring 100 or more runs in four separate seasons, the marks of a truly unique and valuable ballplayer.

Ralph C. Moses lives in Chicago, where he is a social worker, a teacher, and a long-suffering Cubs fan.

Roy Allen Thomas was born on March 24, 1874 in Norristown, Pennsylvania, a suburb of Philadelphia. The member of a very religious family that strictly observed the Christian Sabbath, Thomas later refused to appear in Sunday ballgames. He was also an intelligent young man who attended and eventually graduated from the University of Pennsylvania. College graduates who aspired to be major league baseball players were rarities at the turn of the century.

The 5-foot-11, 150-pound Thomas signed with the Phillies for the 1899 season. Despite the presence of three future Hall of Famers (Ed Delahanty, Elmer Flick, and Napoleon Lajoie), the Phillies had finished in sixth place the previous season. Manager Bill Shettsline installed Thomas in center field and the leadoff spot in the batting order, instructing the 25-year-old rookie to "get on base by any means." Thomas made his major league debut on April 14.

If the Rookie of the Year Award had existed in 1899, Thomas certainly would have been a leading candidate for the honor. In what may have been the best season of his career, Thomas immediately established himself as a superb leadoff man, batting .325 with 178 hits, 115 walks, 42 stolen bases, and 137 runs scored. His on-base percentage that first year was .457, his lifetime best.

Thomas' positive effect on his team was immediate and significant. Joining him to form an all-.300 batting outfield were Delahanty (with a league-leading .410) and Flick (.342). In addition, Lajoie batted .378, and the Phillies as a whole batted .301, highest in the NL. The Phillies finished in third place with 94 victories, 16 more than in the previous season.

In 1900, Thomas had another fine season, batting .316, drawing a league-leading 115 walks (the first of five consecutive years that he would lead the NL in walks), scoring 131 runs and achieving an on-base percentage of .451, while leading the Phillies to another respectable third-place finish.

It was also in 1900, when fouls were still just counted as wasted pitches, that Thomas established his reputation as an expert in deliberately fouling off pitches. Thomas drew many of his bases on balls after spoiling a dozen or more good deliveries until the exasperated pitcher threw a wide one. Thomas claimed to have once fouled off 27 pitches in one at bat against Bill Phillips of Cincinnati.

After Thomas had hit foul after foul against a Brooklyn hurler, Manager Ned Hanlon, a member of the rules committee, shouted from the dugout, "Have your fun now, kid, because we're going to take care of you for next year."

That winter, the rules committee enacted the rule that the first two fouls should be counted as strikes.

The new rule had little impact on Thomas' effectiveness the following season. Thomas batted .309, walked 100 times, scored 102 runs, and had an on-base percentage of .437. Thomas also hit the first of only seven home runs that he collected in his entire career. The Phillies finished in second place, their top ranking during Thomas' years.

National Baseball Library, Cooperstown, NY

Roy Thomas

1901 also marked the establishment of the American League, and the following season saw many of the National League's star ballplayers jump to the junior circuit. The Phillies were particularly hard hit, losing Lajoie in 1901, and Delahanty and Flick in 1902. They fell to seventh place. Thomas also fell off, batting just .286, although he led the NL in walks (107) and on-base percentage (.415). Thomas' younger brother, Bill, appeared in six games for the Phillies that same season.

The Phillies again finished seventh in 1903, but Thomas batted a career-best .327, with league-leading totals in walks (107) and on-base percentage (.453). Thomas again fell off to .290 as the Phillies finished in the cellar in 1904, but in 1905 both Thomas and his teammates rebounded, finishing fourth with Thomas batting .317, his final .300 season.

Thomas' career began to decline in 1906, and after playing in just six games in 1908 he was sold to Pittsburgh. Joining future Hall of Famers Honus Wagner and player-manager Fred Clarke, Thomas was involved in what was later termed by author G. H. Fleming as "the unforgettable season" as the Pirates battled the Cubs and Giants until the final week, finishing in a second-place tie with the Giants, one game behind the pennant-winning Cubs. Thomas played in 102 games for Pittsburgh that season and batted .256.

That winter, Thomas was again sold, to Boston of the NL where he hit .263 in just 83 games in 1909. Thomas returned to the Phillies as a part-time player in his two final seasons.

In addition to his prowess as a hitter and baserunner, Thomas was an outstanding defensive center fielder. He led NL center fielders in fielding percentage five times and was the league leader for all outfielders in 1906 with a .986 percentage. Thomas's lifetime fielding percentage of .972 was a league-record when he retired in 1911. He led all NL outfielders in putouts three times, assists once, and total chances per game twice. Thomas had an excellent range factor of 2.43.

At various times in his life, Thomas had been associated with an automobile firm, a coal company and a morticians' supply concern. Back in 1903, he had coached baseball at his alma mater, and following the end of his major league career, he returned to Penn in 1912. Thomas remained as coach of the Ivy League school through 1919, compiling a record of 88-81-3. From 1928 through 1933 he was head coach at Haverford College. In between, Thomas briefly served as a minor league manager at Bradenton (Florida State League) in 1923 and Oneonta (N.Y.-Penn League) in 1924. Later, he became a successful coal salesman in Philadelphia.

Thomas retired to his birthplace in Norristown, Pennsylvania, where he died on November 20, 1959, at age 85. A handsome, articulate, and talented ballplayer, Roy Thomas was one of the most distinguished, but least-remembered stars of baseball's Dead Ball Era.

The Greatest Fielding Outfielder of All

Jerry Mathers

Was Richie Ashburn the greatest fielding outfielder of all time? Statistics compiled in the many baseball encyclopedias of today say he was. Definitely.

Better than Mays, Mantle, Snider, DiMaggio? Yes. Better even than the best, Tris Speaker? Yes.

The stats say absolutely, positively. So why did Ashburn have to wait until this year to be admitted to the Hall of Fame?

Bad timing. Ashburn played about the same time as three of the greatest center fielders of all time—and they played in New York City, Navel of the Universe, epicenter of sports hype. And Richie's competitors hit home runs. Ashburn hit singles, doubles, and triples.

Willie Mays of the New York Giants hit tons of homers, drove in runs and patrolled the gigantic Polo Grounds center field. He made flashy catches while running out from under his artfully arranged cap.

Mickey Mantle of the New York Yankees also hit hundreds of homers, some of record distance. Very fast, he roamed the huge center field in Yankee Stadium.

Duke Snider was one of the key sluggers in the great, power-packed Brooklyn Dodger lineups that dominated the National League for ten years from 1947 through 1956. He was a noted fielder in a smaller park.

These great hitters almost always batted third in their lineups. Their teams almost always contended for top honors.

But the 5-10, 170-pound Ashburn outhit them all in percentage: His lifetime batting average was .308; Mays was .302, Mantle .298 and Snider .295.

The blond flash from Tilden, Nebraska, didn't bat third, he led off, and he was one of the best in history. In 1948, he was the Philadelphia Phillies' Rookie of the Year. He led the league in hitting twice (1955 and 1958). He led in hits three times, walks four times, triples twice. He stole 234 bases in an era during which stealing was virtually obsolete. In his career he had 2,574 hits, 1,322 runs, and nearly 1,200 walks. He ranged from 84 to 111 runs 12 straight years. He played in 150 or more games 11 times when the season was 154 games long.

Ashburn was not a good field-no hit player.

But it is in fielding that he really shines in comparison with other center fielders. He ranked first in putouts nine times, assists three times, chances per game 10 times, and double plays three times. Only six times in 154-game seasons did an outfielder make 500 or more putouts; Ashburn accounted for four of these. (Taylor Douthit of the 1928 St. Louis Cardinals holds the record with 547 putouts and 3.7 chances per game.)

In comparison we find that Snider never led in any fielding category. Mantle led once each in assists, errors, double plays and percentage—never in putouts or chances per game.

Now the real surprises. DiMaggio rarely led in any category. Mays ranked first only once in putouts, and once in assists. He led twice in chances per game (the best single measure of a fielder), and four times in double plays.

Ashburn even outshines the greatest of them all, Tris Speaker. Ashburn led in putouts nine times,

Jerry Mathers is unofficial high-school sports historian for Nebraska. He has written two books, and is a board member of the Nebraska High School Sports Hall of Fame and of Nebraska High School History.

Speaker seven. Both led in assists three times. Speaker led in errors once, Ashburn never. Ashburn led in chances per game 10 times, Speaker seven. Speaker led in double plays six times to Ashburn's three. Speaker led twice in percentage, Ashburn never.

The numbers prove it. Ashburn was the greatest fielding outfielder of all time. Ashburn's fielding record:

		PO	A	E	C/G	FA	
1948	Phillies	344	14	7	3.1*	.981	
1949	Phillies	514*	13	11	3.5*	.980	
1950	Phillies	405*	8	5	2.8*	.988	
1951	Phillies	538*	15	7	3.6*	.988	6 DP*
1952	Phillies	428*	23*	9	3.0*	.980	5 DP*
1953	Phillies	496*	18*	5	3.3*	.990	
1954	Phillies	483*	12	8	3.3*	.984	
1955	Phillies	387	10	7	2.9	.983	
1956	Phillies	503*	11	9	3.4*	.983	
1957	Phillies	502*	18*	7	3.4*	.987	7 DP*
1958	Phillies	495*	8	8	3.4*	.984	
1959	Phillies	359	4	11	2.5	.971	
1960	Cubs	317	11	8	2.3	.976	
1961	Cubs	131	4	3	1.8	.978	
1962	Mets	187	9	5	2.1	.975	

*led league

National Baseball Library, Cooperstown, NY

Richie Ashburn climbs the ladder

The story of Harry Heilmann's four batting titles

Harry Who?

Jamie Selko

Whenever I looked at Harry Heilmann's four American League batting championships in the past, I wondered whether he had slumped away from .400 or driven toward it. After all, not only did he have a .400 season to his credit, but in each of the other three years he had batted over .390. In the end, curiosity overcame lethargy and, determined to uncover the burning secrets of "Heilmann: The Story That Had To Be Told", I went to work on this piece.

I decided to pick up all four of the batting races on July 1, after most of the non-serious contenders had fallen by the wayside. Ideally, I would have liked to pick up the race when both Harry and his main challengers had 200 at bats under their belts, but the July 1 start date approximated that closely enough. It should also be emphasized that this is not a Harry Heilmann biography. It is just a search to determine whether Harry swallowed the apple whole, or bit the bullet in 1921, 1923, 1925, and 1927.

1921: Harry hits the bigtime—On July second, 1921, Harry Heilmann was hitting .413, just a tad above Tris Speaker's .407. Ty Cobb, at .394 and sidelined with injuries (a self-inflicted spike wound incurred on June 30 that would sideline him for two weeks), and George Sisler, .367, trailed the leaders. Most wagering money would have gone on any of the other three to cop the title, with Cobb the favorite off of his record, and Sisler next as the "coming thing" in AL batting circles. After all, Speaker had hit over .380 three times before, and Cobb had done it seven times. Even Sisler, who trailed badly at this point, already had surpassed the .400 mark in his career. But who was this Heilmann character? With only two .300 seasons under his belt and a lifetime high of a mere .320, he was definitely the outsider of this group. His lifetime BA of .291 was paltry, compared to Speaker's .342, Sisler's .347, and Cobb's lofty .370. And yet, here he was, battling it out with the big boys.

After July 2 Heilmann went on a tear, as if to prove he belonged in the race with his more noted companions. From then until the 15th, he went 34 for 58 (.534), and raised his average to .430. On the 8th, by the way, the New York *Tribune* reported that Heilmann hit a 610-foot homer. This would be quite a blow if there were other corroboration. Cobb, who returned to action on the 15th, peaked at .405 on the 31st. Speaker's challenge fell by the wayside as he hit just .322 from the 15th until the end of the season to wind up hitting "only" .362. Sisler, who bottomed out at .356 on August 10, would peak at .379 about a month later, but he was never a factor in the race, finishing at .371.

The race narrowed to Heilmann-Cobb, coach versus pupil, legend versus veritable nobody. Ty never had a slump after returning to earth following his 8-12 rampage after leaving the DL for good on July 28—in fact, his average never dipped below its final .389. The same cannot be said of Heilmann. From his peak of .430, he had fallen to .401 by August 20, and below .400 by September 2. Since the 15th of July, Harry had hit a weak .212, no doubt prompting many observers to comment, "there goes what's-his-name".

Harry responded, however, with a mini-tear the first

Jamie Selko lives in Eugene, Oregon.

week of September. He went 9 for 16 (.563) to climb back over the .400 mark. On September 11, he was at an even .400, with Cobb right behind at .396. On the 14th he fell below .400 for the last time, and by the 17th he was a mere two points ahead of the steady Cobb, .397 to .395. Unfortunately for Cobb, he picked this moment to falter, and by the 27th was "down" to .390. He would bat but twice more that season, serving a three-game suspension for a temper tantrum earlier in the season. In this instance his temper certainly cost him a 200-hit season, and possibly a final batting title. A three-game surge such as he had when he returned from the DL would have sufficed to give him the title, and Cobb certainly was capable of such a surge. The likelihood of him catching his fellow Bengal flyhawk is even more imaginable when you note that Heilmann hit (and I use the term in its Mendoza sense) .176 the last week, going 3 for 17 to drop to .394, the lowest point of the season. Who knows what would have happened with Tyrus the Fierce snapping at his heels?

In the event, "Harry Who?" won the title, but given his end run, who could tell at the time whether or not his title was a fluke or a foreshadowing?

1923: Harry plays Duck-and-Cover—In 1922 Harry was never in the hunt for the title, finishing 64 points behind George Sisler's .420 (note to all you career-constructors out there: what does Sisler's career look like if he never gets sinusitis?) 1923, however, saw another hot race, with Harry in the thick of it.

On July 1, Heilmann was batting a lofty .429. He was 61 points better than his closest competitor, Charlie Jamieson, who was back at .368. Trailing were Eddie Collins at .367, Fred Haney at .364, and Babe Ruth at .354. One would have presumed that a lead of such magnitude, even this early in the season, would have been safe. One would have presumed falsely. Haney soon disappeared, hitting only .226 the rest of the season to finish at .282. Jamieson, too, dropped by the wayside, fading to a .303 clip the rest of the year to wind up at .345. Collins remained steady at .353, but never mounted a charge. But the Babe...ahh, now that is a steed of a different hue.

By July 8 Heilmann, by virtue of a 9 for 33 stretch, had dropped to .407. Ruth, who went 14 for 32 over the same span, had climbed to .365, gaining 33 points on Harry in one week. And Harry kept dropping: to .400 on the 11th, .390 on the 15th. Then he went on another of those tears which were beginning to become a trademark, going 11 for 20 over the next week which brought him back to .401 on the 22nd. On the 24th both he and Rogers Hornsby in the NL were batting .399. As July wound down and August began, the race for the AL title became positively torrid. During the month of July, Heilmann had gone just 33 for 105 and lost 39 points from his BA. The Babe, meanwhile, had belted the ball at a .454 (55 for 117) clip to close to within one point of the now struggling Bengal, .390-.389.

The batting race in August was a real scorcher. From the 7th until the 9th, Heilmann and Ruth were in a virtual dead-heat: .3927-.3924, .3905-.3896, and .3906-.3903. On the 11th AL President Ban Johnson decreed that the Babe must give up his "Sam Crawford" bat. The bat, handmade by Sam for Ruth, was "four pieces of seasoned wood, carefully glued together." The Babe was at a loss to understand why he was singled out for such harsh treatment. On the 11th, before the ruling, the Babe had gone only 3 for 8 in a doubleheader versus the Tigers, while Harry had gone 5 for 10 against the Yankee staff to open a four-point gap over Ruth. The next day, while Heilmann sat, the Babe went 3 for 4 and overtook him, .3939-.3932.

For the next couple of days the Babe's playing was confined to exhibitions. The first, in Cincinnati, saw Ruth held homerless in the game. In BP, however, he had hit one completely out of the park which bounced into the second story of a factory across the street. The next day, in Indianapolis, the Babe hit three homers—one to the opposite field and two out of the park. In this game, he pitched the last five innings of the game, giving up five runs.

On the 17th Babe passed Harry again, and the next day climbed to over .400 (.401 on 150 for 374), and possessed an eight-point lead over the streaky Heilmann. On the 21st Ban Johnson ruled that thenceforth, only one-piece bats would be used in league play. (Ken Williams had also been a culprit, using a plugged bat.) The following day, the Babe opened what would prove to be his biggest lead over Harry, 16 points, as he moved to .404 while the Tiger dropped to .388. On the 30th the Babe reached his high-water mark, entering the last month of the season at .405.

At the beginning of September, Ruth hit a 2-for-17 dead spot which dropped him behind Heilmann by the 4th, .3916-.3923. His slump was so bad he even went hitless in an exhibition against Allentown on the 6th. The Babe's slump was to continue until the 13th, when a 3-for-4 day brought him back over .390. On the 25th, only two points separated the combatants, with Ruth on the short end of a .387-.385 stick.

The 28th was a red-letter day for both gladiators. The Babe went 5 for 6 in a 24-4 obliteration of the Red Sox, with two doubles and a home run. Harry went 4 for 4 in a 17-3 massacre of the Indians to bring his average to .398. On October 2 Heilmann went 2-2, getting back over the .400 mark for the first time since July22. Since bottoming out at .387 on September 25, Harry had hit .545 in 22 at bats. At this point, whether by Cobb for Heilmann, or at Heilmann's request, the decision was made to sit Heilmann for the rest of the season.

Meanwhile, the Babe, fresh from a series of exhibi-

National Baseball Library, Cooperstown, NY

Harry Heilmann, in an uncharacteristic non-hitting pose.

tions (including one on September 30 where he hit the "longest home run ever seen in Baltimore" and one on October 2 when, playing for McGraw in the Polo Grounds, he hit the first ball ever over the right field roof of that storied ballyard) made a valiant run at the title, ending the season with a 6-for-10 rush to end with a career-high .393, but with Harry riding the pine it was all for naught. Heilmann, with the title (and his .400 season) secure, did pinch-hit the final day of the season and got a hit to close at .403.

From the beginning of July to the end of the season, Harry hit a more than respectable .385. The Babe, however, hit a tremendous .419. Both of these batting titans were streak hitters, and Ruth just happened to have a bad one at the wrong time. Some examples for the Babe: from June 30 until July 11, he hit an even .500 (21 for 42). From June 30 until August 17, he hit .472, including a 15 for 27 (.556) binge from August 7 until the 17th. During July and August, he hit .461 on 93 for 193. Then he hit that killing stretch from the end of August until September 11, batting only .219 (9 for 41), which effectively took him out of the chase.

Heilmann, who hit only .258 from June 30 until mid-July, had a 20-47 surge from August 22 until September 7, just as Ruth was slumping, which enabled him to catch up. Ruth led the race from August 17 until September 4. Incidentally, leaving out that disastrous 2 for 17 slump, The Babe would have hit an even .400 (.4004, to be exact).

For the second time, Harry had won a championship. But, for the second time, there is a sense that more than just his own efforts, Herculean as they were (and make no mistake, hitting .394 and .403 is an enormous feat), were responsible for his titles.

1925: Harry plays "role reversal"—The strangest thing about the American League stats on July 1, 1925, was not the fact that three Tigers were batting over .400. It was the fact that Babe Ruth was not in the top 36 in home runs. He had but six to Cobb's eleven. As

June turned to July, Ty was batting a cool .415, Absalom Holbrook "Red" Wingo was batting .409, and Heilmann was batting .403. The man who stood fourth, Bill Lamar of the A's, was hitting .384. He would hit a respectable .338 the rest of the way to finish at .356, but in the hard-hitting '20s, that would hardly qualify as a run for the title. Tris Speaker made his first appearance among the leaders at .369, 49 points behind the seemingly ageless Cobb.

Harry seemed to start his annual summer decline early, losing eight points in just three days, but he regained his touch the next week, going 8 for 11 at one stretch to climb to .412. Other bats were starting to rumble, as pitchers throughout the American League were having a hard time getting anyone out. On the 4th, Speaker went 6 for 9 to climb to .385. Speaker and Sam Rice both reached .391 on the 12th, and Rice would peak at .405 on the 14th. Two days later Speaker reached .4044, just ahead of Cobb's .4042.

Geo. Brace

Tris Speaker

On the 17th Cobb was suspended indefinitely for arguing with an umpire (as Gomer Pyle would so succinctly put it, "Soo-prize soo-prize!"). On the 19th, Harry went 4 for 5 to raise his average back to .391 in a game that saw the Bengals trounce the Yanks 18-12 and featured 31 non-Heilmann hits. The next day Harry went 3 for 3 and climbed to .398. Terrible Tyrus returned to the lineup the 22nd and went 0 for 4, dropping him to .399. He also went 0 for 4 the next day (.393) and 1 for 4 the day following, dropping all the way to .388. While Cobb was in a tailspin, Speaker climbed back up to .403. As July wound down, so did Cobb and Heilmann, both of whom sank under .380.

Speaker entered August hitting .402, but neither he nor any other American Leaguer would see that plateau by season's end—except, of course, for Walter Johnson. On the second, Spoke was at .399, Cobb at .382, and Harry at .379. By the 19th, a new face had entered the race, one which for the next decade would figure prominently in many AL batting races: Al Simmons. He stood at .380, ahead of Harry's .377 but trailing Speaker's .391. By the 24th, Heilmann's now familiar August slump was in full swing as he dropped all the way to .370, still 20 points behind Speaker.

In the batting race Harry seemed to be treading water. On September 3 he went 1 for 5 in a 17-hit Bengal barrage, and on the 5th he was fourth, his .371 trailing Speaker (.388), Simmons (.380), and Cobb (.379). On the 7th and 8th, he gave evidence he might have been about to start one of his streaks when he went 7 for 14, but he followed this by going 0 for 8 in his next two games and falling 20 points back of Speaker once again. On the 10th, Harry went 0 for 8 in a doubleheader, dropping 20 points behind Speaker yet again, with time running out.

From the 17th on, the attention of the baseball world began to focus on the AL batting race. From this point, over his last 16 games encompassing 69 at bats, Harry would do a complete reversal of his fadeouts of '21 and '23. He would garner 38 hits in those 69 times up, a torrid .551 clip. From the 22nd until the end, he even improved on that to the tune of .581 (25 for 43). On the 27th Harry trailed the idle Speaker .3875-.3893. On that day Harry went 0 for 6, which should have put paid to his efforts to annex another crown—but, as fate would have it, he wore the collar in an exhibition against the Reds. He was obviously saving himself for his final burst. Over the season's final three games, he went 8 for 13 (.615), including a Ted Williams-like final day doubleheader in which he went 6 for 9 to overtake Speaker in the season's last game. Going into that game he still trailed .3883-.3893, but he won going away, .393-.389.

All the calumnies which had been heaped upon him for winning the title from the bench the previous two times were forgotten in this great run for the crown. What a race!

1927: Harry gets charged up—Harry had to figure the odds were in his favor to cop another title going into the '27 season. After all, baseball players are a superstitious lot (or at least they were in Harry's time), and he had to be aware of his odd-numbered-year streak. Once again, however, it did not look particularly good for the big guy going into August. He was 38 points out of the lead—and 19 out of fifth, which was held by none other than the ancient Ty Cobb at a cool .369.

In the lead was the young slugger, Lou Gehrig, at .388, followed by his teammate Bob Meusel at .381, Jimmy Dykes at .381, and Al Simmons at .379. Meusel would hit .310 the rest of the way and Dykes .297 to drop by the wayside, but Gehrig would be in the race almost to the end, and Simmons until...well, let's see how the race developed.

On the 5th Gehrig had climbed to .399 and Wally Schang, deemed too old by the Yanks two years earlier, climbed to .374 for the Browns.

On the 8th the Yankees and the Tigers faced each other in a doubleheader. While Harry went 2 for 8 and plunged to .335, Lou would climb to .404 after the first game, which would prove to be his peak for the season. In the first week of July, Harry had hit .257 and Lou, .577. Harry would reach his nadir on the 11th when he dipped all the way to .331. On that same day Simmons would overtake Gehrig, rising to .403 on the 12th, having hit .532 so far in July. On the 13th Harry began to hit again, going 7 for 9 in a doubleheader against New York, including a 5 for 5 in the second game.

Geo. Brace

Babe Ruth

As July passed its midpoint, Harry was back up to .347. Cobb had slipped a bit to .358, Gehrig held steady at .390, Simmons was still over .400 at .402, and the Babe had climbed to .375 on the strength of 23 for 58 in two weeks. On the 18th and 19th Harry went 7 for 7 to climb to .363. On the 26th the Babe went 7 for 8 in yet another doubleheader that saw the Yankees score 27 runs, including six by Ruth.

As the month drew to a close Harry was hitting .361 and was 14 games into a hitting streak that would reach 22 games. In the July portion of the streak he would hit .500, including an incredible stretch from the 13th to the 19th when he went 15 for 20! With the help of the streak he would hit .380 for the month on 41 for 108. The Babe, who hit .416 in July (42 for 101,) was up to .377. Simmons, who was injured, still led the pack, and Gehrig, who was not, was still second.

In the batting race news for August, the 3rd saw Gehrig hit two homers against the Tigers to go three up on the Babe. Harry went 3 for 7 that day. The next day he was described as "flirting the flail" after going 4 for 4. The next day his streak ended, and he was still 24 points behind Simmons. On the 12th, 40-year-old Ty Cobb and 39-year-old Zack Wheat combined to go 8 for 9 for the Athletics in what surely must have been a record performance for most hits in one game, oldest teammates.

On the 14th Harry decided to fool around at first fielding practice and wound up getting hit in the eye, getting two stitches, and missing the game. He came back to go 4 for 6 in his next two games, and on the 20th went 7 for 10 in a doubleheader to bring his average up to .381, 11 back of the idle Simmons. On the 21st he went 3 for 4 to climb to .385, and the next day reached .390 on the strength of a 4-for-6 doubleheader against Washington, as the Tigers won their 13th in a row (with one tie) to overtake the Senators in the battle for second. After an off day on the 23rd, Harry beat up the Yanks to the tune of 4 for 4, finally passing Simmons as he reached .397, his high-water mark for the year. He had gone 18 for 24, .750, over his last five games, all against the league's top two teams. He would close out August going 9 for 27, "sinking" to .388 on the 29th before going 4 for 6 in a month-ending doubleheader to enter September at .392. (Incidentally, he had gone 20 for 37, .541, in those five doubleheaders during the second part of the month.)

On the 2nd, Harry's 15-game hitting streak ended. During the streak he hit a cool .500 on 28 for 56, climbing back to .393 to once again overtake the still idle Simmons. Al finally came off the DL on the 6th and went 0 for 3, a day in which Ruth hit three homers in a doubleheader, including one which was described as having "soared like an eagle, spiraling into the sky."

The race was still tight on the 7th, with Harry's .395 just a couple of 0-fers ahead of Gehrig and Simmons, both at .390. One of those came the very next day as he was fitted for the collar by Grove, who went 2 for 3 with a homer, three RBIs, and a stolen base himself. This was the start of 0 for 12 spin which put the race back up for grabs. Unfortunately for Gehrig, he too picked this time to plunge, going 1 for 13, and Simmons once again took the lead in the three-man hunt, .390-.384-.382. On the 15th Simmons went 1 for 4, getting his first hit since going on the DL. On the 17th the race was just about as close as it could get: Heilmann, .3899, Simmons, .3896. Ty Cobb, who had gone 48 for 103 (.466) since August 20th, including 17 for his last 25 (.680), reached .362, not a bad spot for a washed-up old forty-year-old.

On the 20th and 21st Harry went 5-12 to reach .391, but was outpaced by Al's 7 for 12 as he reached .396. On the 26th Harry dropped to .387, four points behind Simmons after going 0 for 3. The next day Al went 0 for 4 to drop to .389. Neither played on the 28th, but on the 29th, Simmons went hitless once again to drop a point behind Harry. On the 30th Al didn't play while Harry was going 4 for 7 in yet another doubleheader to reach .389. The next day, it was Harry who was idle while Al went 5 for 7 in his doubleheader to retake the lead at .3915.

Geo. Brace

Al Simmons

On the season's last day Simmons went 2 for 5 to close at .392. Although hurt by his stay on the DL, he never had a slump until his 2 for 15 from the 22nd until the 28th, but he recovered to go 7 for 12 his last three games to make a real race out of it. (In fact, what Simmons's stay on the DL probably cost him was 3,000 hits. He averaged 1.5 hits a game that year. Had he played in 40 more games and hit at the same pace—and there is no reason to believe he would not have—Al would have reached the 3,000 mark for his career.)

Al's try, though gallant, was just not good enough, for (shades of 1925), Harry went 7 for 9 in his final day doubleheader to vault over the helpless Simmons and finish at .398. Hitting .688 over his last four games, Harry added nine points to his average when it really counted. The whispers of '21 and '23 were stilled forever. Harry was legit.

Conclusions—So, was Harry a warrior or a rabbit? Did he slide backward into his titles or claw them from the unwilling grasp of lesser batsmen? The results would seem to show a clear 50-50 split. The young Harry swooned and sat his way to his first two titles. A .430 hitter heading into summer, he was hard-pressed to stave off his challengers, winning the first of his titles while Ty Cobb was on the bench, and sitting out the final dance to protect his second one.

His second two titles were cut from a different cloth. For these, it was Harry who was the charging challenger, breathing fire and racing fate to the finish on the very last day of the season, hitting a gargantuan .655 his last seven games those two years to wrest the title away from the would-be winners. It hardly seems like the same fellow.

Why the two different Harrys? Was it some wellspring of confidence which came after the first two titles which was not there for the first two? Was he simply a more relaxed fellow later on, impervious to the pressures which had almost submerged him previously?

The reading I get is that Harry tended to "sit on his laurels," as it were, when he had a huge lead at midseason, and then was simply unable to gear back up at crunch time. When it was he who was trailing, however, as long as he was still in the hunt, he was focused and dangerous. The real answer, of course, will never be known, but there must have been some internal adjustment that transformed him from the man who backed into his titles in '21 and '23 to the aggressive '41 Williams he was in '25 and '27.

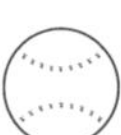

One Team, Two Fields

Bob Boynton
(data provided by Bob Tiemann)

"When construction started on Municipal Stadium in 1930, it presaged the demise of League Park. After 15 years (1932 through 1946) of dividing their schedule between the two parks, the Indians, in their first season under the presidency of Bill Veeck, switched all their games permanently to Municipal Stadium in 1947."

This statement appears on page 98 of Lowell Reidenbaugh's *Take Me Out to the Ballpark.* It is ambiguous because it could be interpreted to mean that the Indians divided their schedule during every season of the period cited, which, as we will see, was not the case. Furthermore, although 1947 was Veeck's first *full* season as Cleveland president and owner, he had purchased the team in June of the previous year, after which the Indians played 22 of their remaining 49 home contests in the old ballpark.

These ambiguities are trivial compared to errors that can be found in other books that discuss how the Cleveland Indians divided their home games between the two ballparks (see references). It is my aim to correct the record in the hope that these errors will not be perpetuated.

Nearly a decade ago, reacting to similar concerns, Bob Tiemann collected relevant data and sent this information to SABR headquarters and a few members of the Ballparks Committee, with the following comment:

"This data was culled from two different sources. The Cleveland park was determined by whipping through the Plain Dealer to see if the game was at the Stadium or at League Park. In almost all cases I found confirmation in at least two of three places: (1) the 'Today's Games' list below the daily standings usually stated where the game would take place; (2) the club always had a two-inch advertisement which told the park, time, and opponent. (3) The story in the next day's paper usually made some casual mention of the park.

Being aware of my special interest in the Cleveland ballparks, Bob Bluthardt, chairman of the SABR Ballparks Committee, called my attention to Tiemann's work and sent me a copy of it. I am grateful to Bluthardt, and especially to Tiemann for his subsequent cooperation in reading drafts and for correcting mistakes I had made in reworking his data to create the accompanying figure, which shows the percentage of home games that were played in the Stadium from 1930 through 1948. It reveals that there was a gradual return of the Indians from League Park to the Stadium during the decade before Veeck finally took over and completed the transition.

Without attempting to describe in detail the various changes of team and park names that occurred from time to time over the years, a few basic facts about League Park are in order. The grounds at Lexington Avenue and East 66th Street were occupied by the National League Cleveland Spiders from 1891 to 1899. From opening day in 1901 through July 30, 1932, the American League Cleveland team played all but eight of its home games there in a facility owned by the ball club. (Six games were played in the Ohio cities of Canton, Columbus, and Dayton, and two in Fort Wayne, Indiana—all during the 1902 or the 1903 seasons.)

Bob Boynton has been secretary of the San Diego Ted Williams Chapter of SABR since 1991.

Originally a classic wooden structure, League Park was extensively remodeled for the 1910 season using steel and concrete, although these materials did not replace all of the wood. Most conspicuously, "the old wooden bleachers" (as announcer Jack Graney used to call them) remained in left-center field. Although photographs reveal that temporary stands were added in center field for the quartet of World Series games in 1920, there appear to have been no important changes for regular-season play after 1910, other than the chicken wire used to turn home runs into doubles when batted balls landed between the girders above the concrete portion of the right field wall.

By the late 1920s, Cleveland officials reached a decision to finance a huge multipurpose facility on the lakefront, to be known as the Cleveland Municipal Stadium. Construction began during the summer of 1930 and the structure was completed in only a year in the vain hope of attracting the 1932 Olympic Games. To this end, an oddly shaped quarter-mile track rimmed the field area, producing an enormous outfield expanse for baseball within a structure that has often been described, with good reason, as "cavernous." It had been assumed that the stadium's tenants would include the Cleveland Indians, who would abandon League Park and become the first major league club to play its home games as a tenant in a facility owned by a government agency.

The Stadium opened with a boxing match during the summer of 1931, but contract negotiations with the Indians proved difficult and the baseball team continued to play in League Park throughout that year. In 1932, contractual arrangements were completed, but too late for the opening of the season. What was supposed to have been the last game ever played in League Park took place on July 30, and the first major league baseball game in the Cleveland Municipal Stadium was staged before a record crowd the very next afternoon, as the A's Lefty Grove bested Cleveland's Mel Harder, 1-0. Billed as a grand new facility, which it truly was, the Stadium was greeted with enthusiasm by players and writers alike.

For the remainder of the 1932 season, and throughout 1933, all home games were played in the new facility. (This can be seen in the figure where the plotted lines rise steeply from zero in 1931 in two steps to 100 percent in 1933.) But it would be fourteen years before another full season would be played in the Cleveland Stadium. In 1934, the Indians moved back to League Park, and remained there full-time for three seasons with the exception of a single Stadium game played on a summer Sunday in 1936.

This was part of a special event staged to help celebrate the Great Lakes Exposition, which was being held nearby during the first of the two years that it would run. The ballgame, which was called on account of darkness as a 4-4 tie after four hours and fifteen minutes, was played against the Yankees before almost three times as many fans as could have been accommodated in League Park. Before the game, there were many special events. The Yankees won a heel-and-toe walking relay race. There were contests for fungo hitting (won by Joe Glenn of the Yankees at 400 feet), and for bunting and running to first (won by Cleveland catcher Billy Sullivan in 3.4 sec). Bobby Feller, age 17, showed promise as he easily won the pitching accuracy

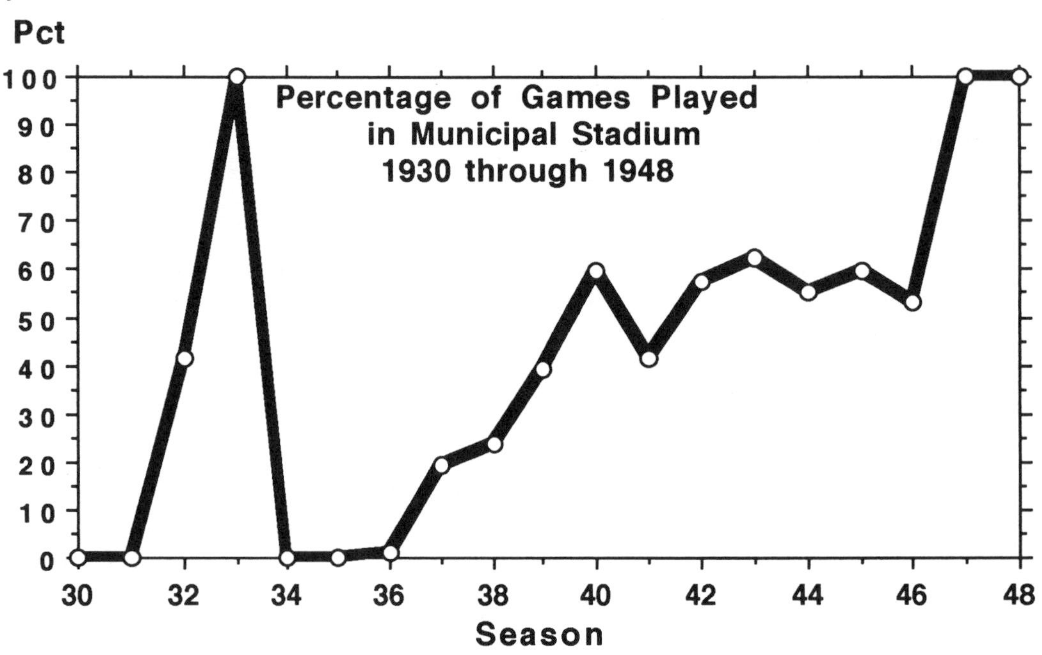

contest, while Joe Becker was the only catcher able to throw a ball through a hoop at second base. A Cleveland *Plain Dealer* account of the day's festivities added that "The three Marx Brothers, who are appearing at the Palace Theater, stormed the field just before the game and took charge of matters, aided by a dozen chorus beauties." League President Will Harridge was on hand, but Commissioner Landis "was detained by a hearing in Chicago."

Back to League Park—It was not long before the long-ball hitters, especially those who had peppered the right-field wall at League Park, started to complain about the vastness of the Stadium with its 435-foot power alleys and literally unreachable center-field bleachers. The Indians had won 59.3 percent of their games during their brief stay in the new facility, so it is unlikely that the owners' decision to return to League Park in 1934 had anything much to do with the gripes of sluggers about outfield dimensions. Instead this was simply a matter of a financially-strapped ballclub saving on rent by returning to a wholly owned facility during difficult Depression years. The move took into account the chronically poor attendance in the 78,000-seat lakefront facility. Evidently it was expected that the 22,500-seat capacity at League Park would be adequate for most games with only a few tolerable exceptions.

One such instance occurred on the occasion of the first major league game that I attended, at age 10, when my father took me to League Park on opening day in 1935. There was an overflow crowd, and I can still recall that fans were standing behind ropes in the outfield. I became hooked on baseball for life that afternoon, and no wonder: I saw a three-run Cleveland homer (Odell Hale) in my very first inning, and the Indians won with a two-run ninth-inning rally. Then in July of that same year, Dad took me to see my first game in the Stadium, which was the third All-Star Game (the only one ever staged in a facility not being used concurrently by a major league baseball team). Even today, I can visualize Jimmie Foxx's home run disappear into the stands well beyond the 435-foot sign in left as the American League won for the third straight year.

A gradual return—In 1937, in anticipation of larger crowds and in conjunction with the second year of the Great Lakes Exposition, a decision was made to play fifteen Sunday and holiday games in the Stadium (for which the baseball ticket also entitled the holder to be admitted to the Exposition). In 1938, a couple of weekday doubleheaders, the Friday and Saturday games of a three-game series with the Yankees, and the opening game were added (see the accompanying table). Dad had taken me again to League Park for the 1936 and 1937 openers. Unlike League Park, the Stadium was accessible to public transportation from the suburban area where we lived. On April 18, 1938, at age 13, I noted the following in my diary:

"Tomorrow, Cleveland meets the Browns in the opening battle. I have selected my ticket from the bunch and shall endeavor to battle my way through the crowds all by myself directly from school. This means that I can get there as early as I please."

I don't recall how I managed my joyful escape from junior high school at a time of my choosing! It is evident that I had learned my way to the Stadium during the 1937 season. Over the years, I enjoyed a very substantial number of games in both ballparks, and bore witness to the Indians' gradual return to Municipal Stadium.

Night ball—In 1939 light towers were erected atop the commodious Stadium roof, and major-league night baseball came to Cleveland. (The Stadium already had some very inadequate field lighting and I had earlier seen an amateur night game played there in the gloomy glow.) I was on hand for the first Indians night game, which turned out to be one of Feller's numerous one-hitters. Limited by agreement among the owners to seven night games per season, I recall that these were promoted as very special events that started at eight-thirty. (Because of the huge roof, relatively little light reached the back of the stands, and when the crowds were large one could observe a continuous flickering of tiny lights caused by cigarettes being lit.)

The entire three-game opening series of the 1939 season, together with a scattering of other games and the addition of night games, raised the percentage of Stadium play that year to nearly 40. By 1940, for the first time since 1933, more than half of the Indians' home games would be played in the Stadium. This proved to be a temporary phenomenon. With the Indians in contention for a pennant until the final weekend of the 1940 season, all remaining home games were shifted to the lakefront starting with a Labor Day doubleheader. In 1941, with the team out of contention, games were divided much as they had been in 1939, causing the percentage of Stadium contests to dip once again below 50 percent. The increase for the first wartime season of 1942 resulted mainly from increasing of the number of night games from seven to 16. (Night game totals in the table include the first games of some twi-night doubleheaders.) From 1942 through 1946, almost all of the Stadium games were played on Sundays, holidays, or at night. Besides the home openers, there were only nine other exceptions.

As already noted, Veeck bought the team during the summer of 1946. Anticipating the vastly increased attendance that his promotional efforts would soon help to create, it was his decision to abandon League Park (which had *not* suddenly deteriorated during the winter) and to move all games to the Stadium beginning with the opening game of the 1947 season. Fewer than 3,000 fans had attended the last game at old League Park on September 21, 1946. Unless Veeck overlooked a promotional opportunity, which seems impossible to believe, he had not yet made his decision (or at least the necessary arrangements) to use the Stadium exclusively during the following season. In any event, beginning with the opening game in 1947, the Indians would play all of their home games in the lakefront facility for 48 consecutive seasons through 1993. In addition, five World Series games were played there (three in 1948 and two in 1954) and the All Star Game returned in 1954, 1963, and 1981.

For the lakefront finale on October 3, 1993, with Jacobs Field under construction, the Indians enjoyed a promotional success that Bill Veeck surely would have appreciated. For the third straight day, the Stadium was packed in celebration of abandoning a place which by then had become known, cruelly and unfairly I think, as the "Mistake by the Lake." Although it is very unlikely that the statistical record of the Cleveland Indians will ever again be complicated by the use of two home ballparks, one never knows. The Cleveland Municipal Stadium remains, and could, if needed, be used for major league baseball yet again.

References [Pages listed contain incorrect statements about the League Park–Stadium split use.]

Benson, Michael, Ballparks of North America. *Jefferson NC, MacFarland & Company, 1989 [p. 111].*

Gershman, Michael, Diamonds: The Evolution of the Ballpark. *New York, Houghton Mifflin Co., 1993 [p. 99].*

Jedick, Peter, League Park. *Cleveland, Society for American Baseball Research, 1990 [p. 18].*

Lewis, Franklin, The Cleveland Indians. *New York, G.P. Putnam's Sons,1949.*

Lowry, Philip J., Green Cathedrals: The Ultimate Celebration of All 271 Major League and Negro League Ballparks Past and Present. *Reading MA, Addison-Wesley Publishing Co., Inc., 1992 [p. 37].*

Ridenbaugh, Lowell, Take Me Out to the Ballpark *(Revised edition). St. Louis, The Sporting News, 1989 [p. 92].*

Ritter, Lawrence, Lost Ballparks: A Celebration of Baseball's Legendary Fields. *New York: Viking Penguin, 1992 [pp. 101 and 108].*

Shannon, Bill and Kalinsky, George, The Ballparks. *New York: Hawthorn Books, Inc., 1975 [p. 92].*

Tackach, James and Stein, Joshua B., The Fields of Summer: America's Great Ballparks and the Players Who Triumphed in Them. *New York: Moore & Moore Publishing, 1992 [p. 92].*

Toman, James A., Cleveland Stadium: Sixty Years of Memories. *Cleveland: Cleveland Landmarks Press, 1991 [p. 70].*

Veeck, Bill, Veeck as in Wreck. *New York, G. P. Putnam's Sons, 1962.* (box)

Breakdown showing the number of playing dates of various kinds on which baseball games were played in the Cleveland Municipal Stadium, for seasons (excluding 1932) during which the remainder of the Indians' home games were played in League Park. The right-hand column verifies that some Sunday and holiday games were played in League Park as late as 1942.

Yr	Sunday	Opener	Holiday	Night	Other	Total	Total Home Games	Pct. at Stadium	Sunday & Holiday Games at League park
1936	1	0	0	0	0	1	81	1.2	18
1937	11	0	4	0	0	15	78	19.2	6
1938	9	1	2	0	6	18	76	23.7	4
1939	14	1	2	7	6	30	77	39.0	6
1940	16	1	4	7	21	49	82	59.8	0
1941	18	1	4	7	2	32	77	41.6	2
1942	20	1	4	16	5	46	80	57.5	1
1943	22	1	4	19	2	48	77	62.3	0
1944	23	1	2	17	0	43	78	55.1	0
1945	23	1	4	18	0	46	77	59.7	0

Dusting off the American Association for a second look

Not Bad for A Beer League

Robert E. Shipley

The American Association (1882-1891) was a major league, but it was also in many ways a stepchild of the older National League. Formed largely through the aggressive planning and capital of four large brewers, the Association survived (and sometimes prospered) by marketing itself with 25 cent seats, Sunday baseball, and the sale of beer. At times antagonistic, at times cooperative, it coexisted with the more established league until a weak economy, internecine conflicts, and poor planning eventually weakened it to the point that it was absorbed by the National League in the early 1890s.

In no instance is this subordinate status more apparent than in the widespread perception that the Association was a much weaker league and that its players, events and records were somehow less legitimate, less professional, and less worthy than those of the National League.

Past voting patterns for the Baseball Hall of Fame are one excellent indication of this perception. Twenty-nine players who took the field during these years have been inducted into the Hall. Of these, only 12 played even one game in the AA. Only three of the 12 played over three years in the Association (Wilbert Robinson, Charles Comiskey, and Tommy McCarthy), and two of these—Robinson and Comiskey—were elected as much for later managerial and ownership accomplishments as for their playing skills. No player who toiled entirely in the AA has ever been elected.

There are two primary reasons why this perception has continued to flourish. First, the AA did not survive as an independent entity after 1891, although several players and entire teams switched to the NL before and during the consolidation. History is normally written by victors and survivors; losers rarely have a wide audience for their own interpretation of reality.

Second, the AA fared poorly in the World Championship series held during several of these years. Between 1882-1891 the two leagues engaged in seven sanctioned series, with the NL winning four, the AA one, and two ties:

Robert E. Shipley has a Ph.D. from Rutgers University and is employed by the Department of Defense.

Table I

World Championship Series 1884-1890

Year	Teams	Wins
1884	Providence Grays (NL)	3
	NY Mets (AA)	0
1885	Chicago White Stockings (NL)	3
	St. Louis Browns (AA)	3
	Tie	1
1886	St. Louis Browns (AA)	4
	Chicago White Stockings (NL)	2
1887	Detroit Wolverines (NL)	10
	St. Louis Browns (AA)	5
1888	NY Giants (NL)	6
	St. Louis Browns (AA)	4
1889	NY Giants (NL)	6
	Brooklyn Bridegrooms (AA)	3
1890	Brooklyn Bridegrooms (NL)	3
	Louisville Cyclones (AA)	3
	Tie	1

SOURCE: *Total Baseball*, Edited by John Thorn and Pete Palmer, Third Edition, pp. 329-335.

The problem with this indicator is that championship series between two teams may not be representative of the overall level of competence and ability in one league compared to the other. Indeed, they may not even be an accurate portrayal of the true strength of two teams participating. Fortunately, there are other methods of measuring the relative strength of the two leagues. As we will see, these indicators suggest that, at least during the four-year period 1886-1889, the AA was comparable to, if not stronger than, the NL. In fact, a case could be made that the overall period of relative parity actually lasted from 1885-1890.

Exhibition games—One weak but interesting initial indicator is the record of AA against NL teams in exhibition games. There are two major problems with this information. First, much like present-day spring training contests, winning may not always have been the foremost goal of the teams, nor did all teams and players take these contests as seriously as regular season contests. Second, the *Spalding Base Ball Guide* and *Reach's Base Ball Guide*, the semiofficial house organs of the National League and American Association respectively, did not publish aggregate statistics for the period 1888-1891, choosing instead to mention only various city and state "championships" that occurred during these later years.

The evidence that is available suggests that the AA was capable of holding its own against the NL by 1885 and 1886 (although it suffers a setback in 1887).

Table II

NL - AA Exhibition victories, 1882-1887

Year	NL	AA	Ties
1882	25	2	0
1883	66	23	0
1884	58	26	2
1885	28	29	5
1886	27	37	3
1887	47	33	1

SOURCES: *Spalding Base Ball Guide* and *Reach's Base Ball Guide*, 1883-1892 editions.

Bushers—A better indicator concerns the incidence of players who reached the majors for only one year. Normally, the reason these "bushers" played only one year was that they simply weren't good enough. Logically, the higher the percentage of bushers in a league the lower the overall skill level of the league during that particular year.

For example, let's look at the case of another designated major league of the same period, the Union Association of 1884—a veritable busher's paradise. Consolidating statistics from *Total Baseball*, we find that the 118 bushers in the UA batted only .220, while the combined average of everyone else in the league was 31 points higher (.251). Busher pitchers were equally weak, with a winning percentage of .239 versus a percentage of .539 for the other pitchers in the league, and an ERA of 4.33 while all other pitchers combined for an ERA of 2.74.

Graph I demonstrates the percent of bushers to total players making appearances for each league and year during the period. This distribution suggests several points about relative league strength. Although the NL normally had a lower percentage of bushers, the American Association had slightly lower percentages for 1883, 1885, and 1887. More important, the two leagues were within six percentage points of one another between 1883-1888 and within 10 percentage points in all years except 1882 and 1890. This suggests at least a rough parity between the two leagues for several of the years under question.

A few sidebars from the data: One, during the years 1884 and 1890, when a third major league was present, the overall skill level in the major leagues was diminished (i.e., the percent of bushers sharply increased). Two, the data suggests that the Union Association was not really worthy of major league status—a whopping 44.5 percent of all players were bushers! Three, the Players' League was probably the most skilled and professional league in 1890, with only 10.2 percent bushers compared to 18.2 percent for the NL and 32.5 percent for the AA.

[graph I]

Transferred players—The final indirect indicator available involves players who performed for both leagues during the period. By looking at how well they performed in each circuit, we can get a rough idea of each league's relative strength.

According to the data in *Total Baseball*, 384 of the 652 hitters who made a plate appearance (59.1 percent) and 165 of the 567 players who made a mound appearance in the American Association during the period 1882-1891 (29.1 percent) also played in the National League. This in and of itself establishes a sort of parity based on a common talent pool. It also confirms that there is sufficient data to draw the comparison. Nonetheless, there are a few controls that must be placed on the data to ensure its reliability:

1. Because the strength and overall level of play changed over time, it is not very useful to make a list of all players who played in both leagues and compare their career statistics in each league. Therefore we will only compare statistics in the year prior to the transfer and the year directly after the transfer.

2. We will compare only those players who transferred in back-to-back years in order to minimize changing conditions. For example, a player who performed in the National League in 1885 and the

GRAPH I
BUSHERS
PERCENT TO TOTAL PLAYERS

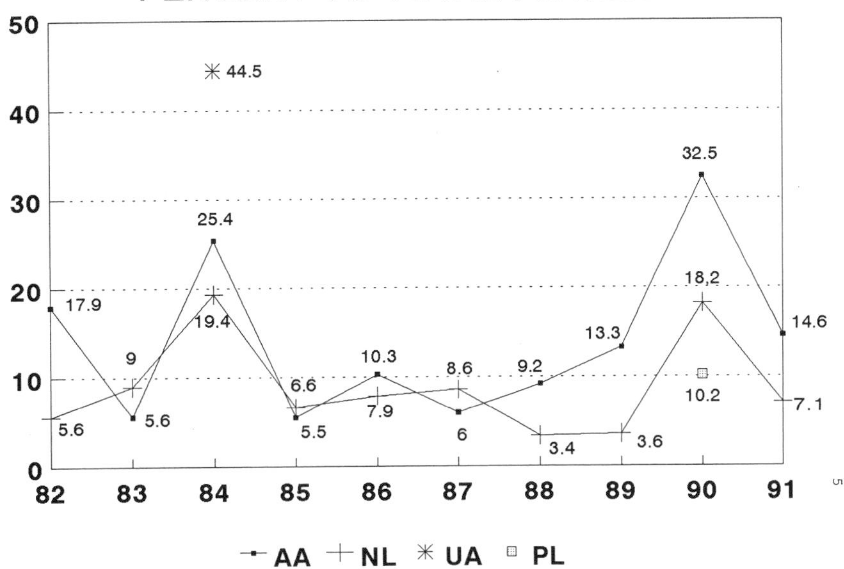

American Association for 1886 would be included in the statistics for "NL to AA" players for 1886. A player who performed in the National League in 1884, did not play anywhere in 1885 and then switched to the American Association in 1886, would not. The same would hold true for a player whose career was broken by a complete year in the Union Association or the Players' League.

3. In order to better compare league strength rather than the strength of individual players, we will compare transfers to themselves (i.e., the percent who improved in their new leagues) and not how they compared to the rest of the league. The latter method would better measure the caliber of players who transferred during that year, rather than the strength of the league. Likewise, we need to measure the percentage of those who improved and not how much they improved (e.g., five points higher in batting average) to reduce the risk of skewing the data with one or two players who played in several innings or at bats with significantly superior or inferior statistics.

What we need to look at is the collective percent of all transferred players in both leagues who improved statistically during their transfer year compared to the previous year in the other league. By comparing the percent of transfers who improved in one league to the percent who improved in the other during a given year, we can get a better sense of the relative strength of the two leagues at that point. For example, if 75 percent of all transfers from the American Association improved their statistics over the previous year and only 30 percent of the transfers from the National League during the same year improved their statistics, it is likely that the American Association was a somewhat stronger league during that year.

Granted, this is not an infallible method of statistically determining the issue. A player's performance can change from year to year based on factors other than the overall strength of the league. Age may be depleting his skill or a younger player may be coming into his own as he gains more experience. Some players' statistical performances tend to rise and fall in cycles throughout their careers based on injuries or other factors less open to determination. But by giving all players equal weight in the data, these phenomena should be minimized.

Another potential objection might be that different rules, field dimensions, or conditions in one league might reflect more on statistical improvement or decline than the overall skill level in the league. Fortunately, during this period most major rule changes (e.g., shoulder high pitching in 1883, four strikes in 1887) were made in both leagues at the about the same time, so conditions in both leagues were comparable.

Table III and Graph II demonstrate the combined results of comparing percentages of improved performance for two of the most critical statistics: batting averages and earned run averages. These data for all first-year transferred players in both leagues suggest

GRAPH II
FIRST YEAR TRANSFERS -
PERCENT WHO IMPROVED

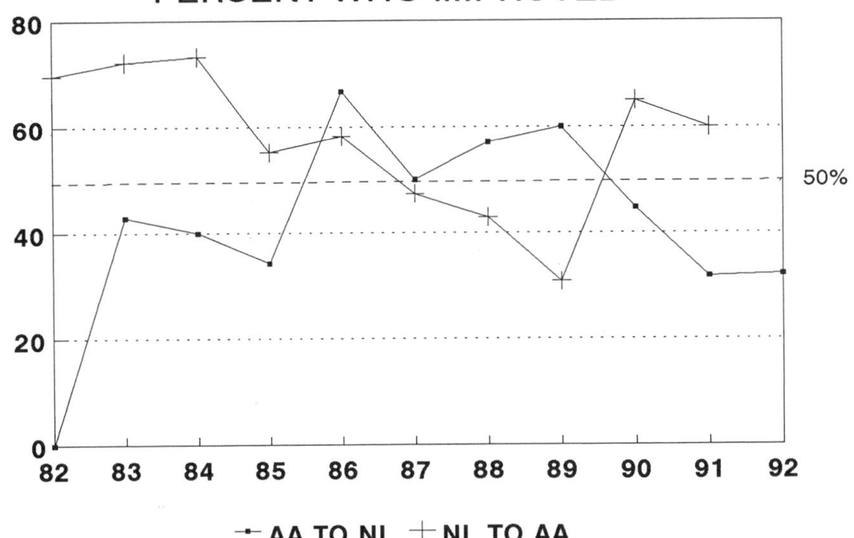

BA & ERA

definite trends in overall league strength. Between 1882-1885, National League players transferring to the American Association fared much better than those going in the opposite direction, although the gap had narrowed from almost a 70 percent differential in 1882 to about 21 percent by 1885. On the other hand, between 1886-1889 those transferring from the AA to the NL fared better than those going from the NL to the AA. In 1890 the trend switched back to a 20 percent gap in favor of the transferred players from the NL, a gap which increased for 1891.

These trends suggest that the AA was at least as tough to play in from 1886-1889, a status achieved largely through aggressive recruitment of top minor leaguers like Bob Caruthers, Toad Ramsey, and Curt Welch, along with serviceable NL players not held under the reserve clause. The NL showed superior strength during the early years, when the AA was still struggling to find quality players and suffered from owner skullduggery such as the dual ownership of the AA NY Mets and the NL NY Giants. The NL likewise demonstrated stronger abilities in the later years as many of the best AA teams and players were switching to the senior circuit.

Table III

First year transfers—Percent who improved

	AA to NL			NL to AA		
Year	**BA**	**ERA**	**Total**	**BA**	**ERA**	**Total**
1882	0	0	0	70.6	66.7	69.6
1882	42.9	0	42.9	70.3	77.8	72.2
1884	50.0	0	40.0	68.0	100.0	73.3
1885	33.3	40.0	34.3	66.7	25.0	55.2
1886	71.4	60.0	66.7	66.7	33.3	58.3
1887	58.3	37.5	50.0	50.0	42.9	47.4
1888	60.0	50.0	57.1	45.5	33.3	42.9
1889	62.5	50.0	60.0	44.4	0	30.8
1890	36.3	64.3	44.7	72.7	55.6	65.0
1891	33.3	28.6	31.8	52.4	77.8	60.0
1892	26.2	46.2	32.2	-	-	-

SOURCE: Computed from data in *Total Baseball.*

All of the available evidence—championship series, exhibition games, incidence of bushers and the experience of transferred players—suggests that relative parity was achieved between the two leagues between 1886-1889. Partial evidence (exhibition wins, percent of bushers, a tied championship series) supports the theory that this state of parity was achieved as early as 1885. (Indeed, even the *Spalding Guide* of 1886 admitted that the American Association clubs had shown "marked improvement in the strength of their teams" in 1885.) One could even argue, although with much less evidence and conviction, that the AA remained close to the NL in 1890, when both were weakened by the Brotherhood War and the Players' League and the championship ended in a tie.

The best league ever? No!

The best league of the nineteenth century? Nah.

The best league of the 1880s? Maybe.

All in all, not bad for a beer league.

A salute to baseball in the Army's black infantry, 1894-1919

The 25th Infantry Regiment Takes the Field

Jerry Malloy

The 25th Regiment of United States Infantry was one of four African-American Regular Army units created after the Civil War, the others being the 24th Infantry, and the 9th and 10th Cavalry. Its baseball program began in Missoula, Montana, in 1894, and 25 years later six players from the 25th, including Bullet Rogan and Dobie Moore, formed the backbone of the Kansas City Monarchs, the Negro League's powerhouse of the plains. So strongly were the Monarchs identified with the ballplaying soldiers of the 25th Infantry that in the early 1920s they commonly were called "the Army team."[1]

Reveille—Colonel Andrew S. Burt decided to form a regimental baseball team upon observing the hoopla of an informal game at Fort Buford, North Dakota, in 1893. The post was garrisoned by three companies of the 25th as well as one company of the (white) 20th Infantry and Troops D and H of the (black) 10th Cavalry. A game was played between an interracial infantry team and an all-black cavalry team, with the Doughboys whipping the Cavalrymen, 7-0. "This certainly was a holiday," recalled the 25th's pitcher, Master Sergeant Dalbert P. Green, "the whole garrison was out in force, such noise and fireworks...."[2]

Burt's choice of Green to organize a regimental team was fortunate for historians of African-American military baseball. Twenty years of close association with the team enabled him to recount its genesis for a regimental history compiled in 1927.[3] "As Captain of the team," Green wrote, "I spent the happiest days of my life, and was proud of the honor of being a member of one of the scrappiest teams in the U.S. Army."[4]

Initially, players wore makeshift uniforms, improvised by company tailors. Games were played on Sundays and holidays, and players practiced and maintained the grounds on their own time. Baseball was not permitted to interfere with any drills or training. Indeed, ballplayers "had to show soldierly qualities of the very highest type," wrote Green, and withholding permission to play for or watch the regimental team proved a useful disciplinary tool.[5]

The culmination of the Indian Wars gave African-American soldiers the most recreational time they had ever known, and competition on the baseball diamond became fierce. Although the second commander of the 24th Infantry was none other than Abner Doubleday, it was the 25th Infantry that attained supremacy in baseball among the Army's four African-American units, followed by the 10th Cavalry.[6] The 25th Infantry "played gilt-edged ball" from 1894 until 1898, when war with Spain carried the 25th overseas, and the 25th carried their emergent baseball tradition with them.

Cuba and the Philippines, 1898-1902—The Spanish-American War brought changes in the use of the Army's four black regiments. Participation in larger military operations and assignments near population centers east of the Mississippi River brought them into unprecedented proximity with white soldiers and civilians, and not always harmoniously.

The 25th Infantry, the first United States Army unit

Jerry Malloy compiled and introduced Sol White's History of Colored Base Ball *(University of Nebraska Press, 1995). This paper was presented at the Cooperstown Symposium of June, 1994. He wishes to thank Sonja Tanaka for her help on this article.*

ordered into wartime duty, was assigned to Chickamauga Park, Lyle, Georgia, where an intercontinental baseball rivalry arose, pitting the 25th Infantry against the (white) 12th Infantry. "The 12th Infantry," wrote Green, "with its well known practically semi-professional team...won handily and the 25th with the Colonel leading, swore to get even if it took twenty years."[7] Nonetheless, he added, "all other teams fell before our prowess."[8]

Colonel Burt and his men would not have to wait 20 years to extract revenge. In the summer of 1899, the 25th Infantry arrived in the Philippine Islands, and immediately defeated the 12th Infantry in a game that "was played with that fighting spirit that both regiments are noted for," according to Green. The black soldiers agreed to play on Christmas Day, 1899, at 12th Infantry Headquarters, and "delivered the goods," with another dose of vengeance. Green described the 12th Infantry as "our old rival and best friend," but battlefield events in Cuba must have made the 25th's baseball field triumph in the Philippine Islands all the sweeter. At issue was not a pennant, but the Spanish flag that both regiments claimed to have taken in the surrender at the battle of El Caney on July 1, 1898.[9]

Initial response to the performance of the Regular Army's four black regiments in Cuba was quite favorable in both the military and the press. But martial exhilaration soon gave way to the accrued momentum of the nation's racial mores, and Jim Crow would follow the flag overseas.

The regiment was sent to Fort Logan, Colorado, for a few months before being assigned to the Philippine Islands from 1899 until 1902. Green wrote cavalierly that, while in the Philippines, "the regiment was busy engaged in policing the territory that was assigned to them of the many insurgent bands that were roaming through the country at that time, but a small matter like that never caused a moment of laxity in playing ball." Nonetheless, Green, like his teammates on the diamond, was a soldier first and foremost. In November, 1899, he single-handedly rescued four unarmed civilians from a band of 30 armed insurgents, prompting his commander to recommend him for a Medal of Honor.[10]

Green called the 25th Infantry's baseball team the champions of the Philippines from 1899 through 1902. They usually played twice a week and attracted the attention of the local population.[11] The army encouraged the regimental baseball team for its contributions to camaraderie and morale. Chaplains, however, were of a mixed mind. On one hand, baseball was an attractive alternative to more unsavory diversions. On the other hand, it also presented a diversion from chapel attendance on Sundays. And while the national pastime helped alleviate many of the vices that accompany barracks life, it positively fostered one of them: gambling.[12]

In 1901, when the 25th was sent to Manila for a month, the team issued a challenge in the *Manila Times* to play anyone—"For money, marbles or chalk, money being preferred."[13] This braggadocio nearly came to a ruinous conclusion. The team entered a five-game competition with $500 at stake to win at least three—and lost their first two games. But, as Green informs us, they came back and won the last three.

> The last and final game was played against the famous Battery H, 6th Artillery, a great team, and at that time considered the champions of Manila, and since this game was for the championship of the Islands, we won, as usual. Their scalps, added to our already well-filled belts, was a trophy worth fighting for.[14]

In 1902 Major Arlie Pond, who had compiled a 35-19 record as a pitcher for the Baltimore Orioles from 1895 to 1898, became the manager of the 25th Infantry team. When the regiment was ordered back to the United States, it defeated several teams en route, most notably the champions of the Manila League, "Major Archie Butt's Quartermaster Team."[15]

Department of the Missouri, 1903-1905—Rotation back to the United States in 1902 resulted in the fragmentation of the regimental baseball team. Four companies were sent to Fort Reno, Oklahoma Territory, while the remainder of the unit (including Sergeant Green) was ordered to Fort Niobrara, Nebraska. Events on the field one year later reveal how strong and deep the 25th had become in baseball, even when broken into separate components.

In 1903, both elements of the 25th were ordered to Fort Riley, Kansas, for fall maneuvers. The 25th Fort Niobrara contingent won every game it played against local competition along its 254-mile march to Fort Riley, where a Department of the Missouri baseball tournament was arranged. Though teams from several white units participated, the co-favorites, as identified by the gambling community, were two African American teams: the 25th Infantry's Fort Reno team, and the 10th Cavalry, then stationed at Fort Robinson, Nebraska. The 25th's Fort Niobrara squad was given little chance, due to the arduous march it had recently endured.

But Fort Niobrara fared well, and even knocked their Fort Reno brethren out of contention. Eventually all the white teams were eliminated, and the championship game featured two African American units: the 25th Infantry of Fort Niobrara, and the 10th Cavalry of Fort Robinson. "These two teams battled desperately for 12 innings," wrote Green, "play after play of the sensational order were made, until finally the 25th Infantry won the game by a score of 3-2...." As for the vanquished players of the 10th Cav, "their excellent playing and gameness will be long remembered by the fortunate ones who witnessed that hard-fought contest."[16]

The *Army and Navy Journal* reported a final score of 4-3, not 3-2, and in 10 innings, not 12 (*Army and Navy Journal*, November 3, 1903). But in any case, the 25th Infantry's Fort Niobrara contingent was crowned champions of the Department of the Missouri and took proud possession of the handsome banner that accompanied the distinction. During the regiment's tour at Fort Niobrara, from 1902 through 1905, the team lost only three games, one to a squad from Deadwood, South Dakota, and two to what must have been a pretty good team in Gordon, Nebraska.[17]

Brownsville, Texas, 1906—The 25th Infantry had survived desperate battles against Native American warriors in the west, Spanish soldiers in Cuba, and guerilla insurgents in the Philippines, but nothing prepared them for the wounds inflicted on the racial battlefield of Brownsville, Texas, in 1906.

In June, the 25th Infantry was dispersed once again, this time to three posts in Texas. One battalion was sent to Fort McIntosh. Sergeant Green was ordered to Fort Bliss, along with the regiment's main body, where "games played were minor affairs."[18] Affairs would prove far from minor for the three companies sent to Fort Brown, on the Rio Grande near its mouth at the Gulf of Mexico. Gunfire in the adjoining town of Brownsville, during which a bartender was killed and a police officer wounded, resulted in President Theodore Roosevelt discharging without honor 167 African-American soldiers, six of them Medal of Honor recipients, without any sort of judicial proceeding. The Brownsville affray remains the only documented case of mass punishment in the history of the United States Army.[19] In 1970, John D. Weaver vindicated the honor of the soldiers of the 25th in *The Brownsville Raid*, illustrating how Jim Crow attitudes of that tragic year turned racial predators into prey, and vice versa.

Weaver cited a typical incident in which a government investigator distorted a soldier's identification of players in a team portrait of Company B's baseball team into a bogus "confession." A witness to the proceeding called the report "the most absolutely false, the most willful misrepresentation of the truth, and the most shameful perversion of what really did take place ...that I have ever seen over the signature of any person."[20]

The Brownsville affair, which was not mentioned at all in Nankivell's history of the 25th Infantry, was a clear illustration of the severe deterioration of the status of black soldiers in the United States Army. African-American soldiers responded in part by strengthening their grip on one of the few remaining realms governed by rules that were blind to race: baseball. The first step was to recapture baseball supremacy in the Pacific.

To the Philippines and back, 1907-1912—In August, 1907, the regiment arrived in Mindanao Province, Philippine Islands, and immediately won a baseball tournament that included teams from the 6th Cavalry, and 18th and 23rd Infantry. As departmental champions, the team toured the islands playing ball. During this tour they were defeated by two teams, the 26th Infantry and the 5th Artillery. "These two defeats," wrote Green, "were the only ones that the team suffered during this tour of 1907-08 and '09."[21]

Reassignment to the United States once again divided the 25th Infantry, this time within the state of Washington, Fort Lawton, and Fort George H. Wright. Green's Fort Lawton team twice defeated their Fort Wright rivals during maneuvers in 1912, with both games "hotly contested, and...won by close scores."[22]

Hawaii, 1913-1918—The regimental baseball team was reunited in 1913, when the 25th Infantry was shipped to Schofield Barracks in the Hawaiian Territory. Under the leadership of Lieutenant O. H. Saunders, "one of West Point's brightest stars," according to Green, the 25th formed a "Plan and Strategy Board," which closely analyzed the team's performance after every game. Perhaps this brain trust contributed to the great success the team enjoyed in Hawaii. They won the championship of a post league that included teams from the 1st Infantry, 4th Cavalry, and 1st Field Artillery. Then they won the championship of a city league in Honolulu, and conquered the Oahu Island League, defeating the Coast Artillery, All Chinese, and Portuguese teams.[23]

The 25th Infantry played many games during the winter months against touring college teams, as well as barnstorming teams of professional players. In 1913, a barnstorming team consisting of players from both major leagues and the Pacific Coast League arrived in Hawaii to play the 25th. "A holiday was declared for this great event," Green recalled, "and a parade with both of the teams in line, led by the 25th Infantry Band, preceded the game; the whole garrison turned out to do honors to both teams." The 25th lost a brief series, "eagerness and nervousness, and a big case of stage fright being the main reasons for the loss of these games," according to Green.[24]

Yet the team quickly recovered. In 1914, the 25th won nine of 10 games in winning the Army championship of Oahu. Two years later they compiled a record of 42-2 against military, civilian and college teams. They even attracted the attention of promoters. A representative of the Spalding Company asked the Army for permission to sponsor the 25th Infantry baseball team for a tour of the west coast of the United States, but the request was denied because there was "no special end of military athletic training served thereby" (Marvin E. Fletcher, "The Black Soldier Athlete in the United States Army, 1890-1916, *Canadian Journal of History of Sport and Physical Education*, 3:2 December 1972, p. 19).

In 1914, Sergeant Green retired from the Army. Green had given birth to the 25th Infantry Regiment's baseball program in Fort Missoula, Montana, in 1894, and had seen it blossom into one of the Army's most powerful teams by the time he retired 20 years later. Yet the best was yet to come. A transition in personnel took place during the unit's tour at Schofield Barracks that would propel the 25th to even more exalted heights.

The Rogan Years, 1914-1919—With the retirement of Dalbert Green in 1914, the 25th Regiment lost its baseball historian, so accounts of the last five years of its heyday are sketchy. John Nankivell, editor of the regimental history, wrote that after Green's retirement the team "continued its winning streak, and defeated practically every team that it played in the Hawaiian Islands." Unfortunately, he felt that "[i]t would be wearisome to recount here the many and hard-fought games that were played," but he did list a number of players who distinguished themselves on the diamond. "First of all," he wrote, "there comes to mind Rogan, whose masterful pitching carried the regimental team to victory in many a tight game...."[25]

A wire service later reported that, while in the Army, Wilber "Bullet" Rogan had once won 52 games in a single year, striking out 25 batters in one of those victories. A sergeant of the 25th recalled that John McGraw, upon watching Rogan in Hawaii during his world tour of 1913-1914, concluded that "if Rogan was a white man he would burn the league up." John Holway writes that Rogan shut out the Portland, Oregon, team of the Pacific Coast League in Hawaii in 1917, allowing just three hits, striking out 13, and hitting a double for good measure.[26]

Sergeant Rogan, a fire-balling righthanded pitcher and power-hitting center fielder, went directly from the 25th Infantry into the Negro National League and forged what is arguably the greatest career of any player not in baseball's Hall of Fame. Rogan's prodigious Negro League accomplishments are all the more impressive when it is noted that he already was 30 years old by the time he began playing for the Monarchs in 1920.

Rogan spent most of his twenties playing ball for United States Army teams. He caught for the 24th Infantry in the Philippines from 1911 through 1913. After leaving the Army to play in the California Winter League in 1914, he joined the 25th Infantry as a pitcher in Hawaii in 1915, having been spirited away from 9th Cavalry's zealous recruiters, according to one account. Ironically, Rogan's nickname in the Army was not "Bullet." Rather, it was "Cap," because, in the words of one veteran of the 25th, "in the army at that time a Captain was some body and on the ball field Cap Rogan was some body." By his account, khaki-clad soldiers of the 25th would chant "Touch 'em all, Cap, touch 'em all," when the mighty Rogan strode to the plate.[27]

In 1918 the 25th Infantry was transferred to Camp Stephen D. Little in the Mexican border town of Nogales, Arizona, some 60 miles south of Tucson. There, the team was known as the Wreckers, and was far from a one-man team. Among Rogan's teammates were no fewer than five future Kansas City Monarchs: Dobie Moore, Hurly McNair, Oscar (Heavy) Johnson, Lem Hawkins, and Bob Fagan.

The ballplayers of the 25th Infantry were brought to J. L. Wilkinson's attention when he was creating the Monarchs by a tip from fellow Kansas Citian Casey Stengel, who played the 25th in Arizona during a barnstorming trip in the fall of 1919. "We were down near the Mexican border," as he told John Holway, "and the army brought these buglers and made all the soldiers line up and march across the ball field...and pick up pebbles and rocks so we could play." According to Robert Creamer, Stengel recalled the star pitcher as being named "Grogan," and praised the infantry team's shortstop, Dobie Moore, as well. "They were as good as any major-leaguers," he said.[28] The astute Stengel benefitted from watching Rogan's no-windup delivery, an unusual motion that he adapted for several pitchers while managing the New York Yankees in the 1950s.

On June 29, 1920, Sergeant Rogan, Service Number AT 3 349 211, was honorably discharged from the 25th Infantry Regiment's machine-gun company. Just three days later he shut out Rube Foster's Chicago American Giants on one hit in Kansas City in his Negro League debut. Bullet Rogan was on his way to glory. By midseason Moore, McNair, Johnson, Hawkins, and Fagan, Rogan's teammates with the Wreckers, had joined the Monarchs.[29]

Bob Fagan's luster would soon fade, but Lem Hawkins found a niche as a slick-fielding first baseman. "Heavy" Johnson was sometimes called the Babe Ruth of the Negro Leagues in the 1920s. Hurley McNair, who had played for Rube Foster's Chicago American Giants in 1915, *before* he joined the 25th, had a long, distinguished career with the Monarchs, including service as an umpire when his playing days were over. Dobie Moore, the roly-poly shortstop, was as unorthodox as he was brilliant, both at bat and in the field. The *Chicago Defender* once proclaimed Moore "the greatest Negro shortstop of all time," and there's no telling where he might have ended up in the pantheon of African-American ballplayers if his knee (and career) had not been shattered by a gunshot wound in 1926.[30]

Retreat—The instant success of the Monarchs reveals how far the 25th's baseball program had progressed in the 25 years of its existence. The *Army and Navy Journal* reported that the recreation hall proclaimed the unit's many victories in sports: "Every bit of wall space was covered with banners won by the companies, battalions, and the regiment in athletic contests during many years past."[31]

Black soldiers took pride in their baseball teams, as black citizens took pride in their soldiers. All four regiments boasted of its athletes, not only in baseball, but also in boxing, track and field, football, and basketball. Their sporting triumphs were prominently reported in the leading African-American newspapers of the era.

Ascendancy in sports occurred during a time when African-American status within the Army was in rapid decline. Gone were the days of frontier duty, when isolation not only sheltered them from Jim Crow's early successes, but also enabled them to display their ability in comparison with white units performing similar assignments. The lesson of Brownsville was that military service, even of the highest order, did not shield African Americans from discrimination and injustice. Against this backdrop of accelerating racial animosity, black ballplayers in the Army seized upon a mission to excel in baseball, where they still held the trump cards.

Legislation creating the four black regular Army regiments was one of the few Reconstruction programs to survive the nation's later abandonment of its black citizens. With Jim Crow triumphant in the 1890s, military life offered African Americans an uncommon measure of economic well-being and even, occasionally, the thanks of a grateful nation. Once professional baseball drew the color line, the 9th and 10th Cavalry

Jerry Malloy

The 25th Infantry Regiment baseball team, c. 1918.

and 24th and 25th Infantry became keepers of a flickering flame of interracial play.

The Kansas City Monarchs' signing of the team's best players put an end to the 25th Infantry's baseball supremacy just as, a generation later, the major leagues would kill the Negro Leagues. After "Cap" Rogan joined the Monarchs, the 25th Infantry's regimental newspaper (ironically called "The Bullet") reported that he had written "a long and very interesting letter."

> He had many things to say concerning himself and the other players who are making good in the Negro National League....The former 25th Infantry star said that there is a bright future for colored players in civil life and especially army players....[M]anagers are anxious to employ ex-soldiers.[32]

Military veterans such as Oscar Charleston, Spottswood Poles, Dick Redding, Rube Currie, and Dave Malarcher prospered in the Negro Leagues. The next generation of African-American servicemen helped pry open the door to the major leagues, among them Larry Doby, Monte Irvin, Willard Brown, and, of course, Jackie Robinson. The narrow stream of black baseball history initiated by Sergeant Dalbert Green eventually flowed into a meaningful tributary of desegregation in the military, baseball and the nation.

Notes

1. Janet Bruce, *The Kansas City Monarchs: Champions of Black Baseball*, University of Kansas Press: Lawrence, Kansas, 1895, p. 21.
2. Dalbert P. Green, "History of the 25th Infantry Baseball Teams, 1894-1914," in John H. Nankivell, ed. and comp., *History of the Twenty-Fifth Regiment of United States Infantry, 1869-1926*, Smith-Brooks Printing Co.: Denver, Colorado, 1927; repr. Negro Universities Press: New York, 1969, p. 164.
3. Green/Nankivell, pp. 163-172.
4.Green/Nankivell, p. 163.
5. Green/Nankivell, pp. 163, 164.
6. Bernard C. Nalty, *Strength For the Fight: A History of Black Americans in the Military*, New York: The Free Press, 1986, p. 55.
7. Nankivell, p. 67.
8. Green/Nankivell, p. 166.
9. Green/Nankivell, p. 166.
10. Nankivell, pp. 166, 109-110.
11. Green/Nankivell, pp. 163, 167.
12. Fletcher, *Black Soldier and Officer*, p. 105 107.
13. *Army and Navy Journal*, June 22, 1901, cited in Fletcher, p. 18.
14. Green/Nankivell, p. 167.
15. Green/Nankivell, p. 167.
16. Green/Nankivell, p. 168.
17. Green/Nankivell, p. 168.
18. Green/Nankivell, p. 169.
19. Jack D. Foner, *Blacks and the Military in American History*, Praeger: New York, 1974, p. 102.
20. John D. Weaver, *The Brownsville Raid*, W. W. Norton: New York, 1970, pp. 221, 222.
21. Green/Nankivell, p. 169.
22. Green/Nankivell, p. 171.
23. Green/Nankivell, p. 170, 171-172.
24. Green/Nankivell, p. 172.
25. Nankivell, p. 172.
26. Nankivell, p. 172; unidentified newspaper clipping dated November 30, 1923, from Rogan Scrapbook; Beagle letter, Rogan File, National Baseball Hall of Fame Library; Holway, p. 172).
27. Master Sergeant Bertran T. Beagle, retired, to "the Colored Base Ball Hall of Fame," undated letter, Rogan File, National Baseball Hall of Fame Library.
28. John Holway, *Blackball Stars: Negro League Pioneers*, Meckler Books: Westport, Connecticut, 1988, p. 169; Robert W. Creamer, *Stengel: His Life and Times*, Simon and Schuster: New York, New York, 1984, p. 130.
29. Questionnaire completed by Rogan's son, Wilbur S. Rogan, in Rogan File, National Baseball Hall of Fame Library; National Archives and Records Administration Statement of Service; "Rogan Stops the American Giants," unidentified newspaper article, Bullet Rogan Scrapbook.
30. Holway, p. 196.
31. *Army and Navy Journal*, September 12, 1914, cited in Arthur R. Ashe, Jr., *A Hard Road to Glory: A History of the African-American Athlete, 1619-1918*, Warner Books: New York, New York, 1988, p. 87.
32. Bullet Rogan Scrapbook.

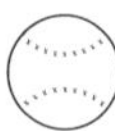

An interview with Sidney Howell

"I Did The Best I Could"

Gordon Olson and Frank Schubert

Occasionally, a quiet, white-haired man with an erect bearing and a spritely walk takes a seat in Lakeland, Florida's Joker Marchant Stadium to watch the Detroit Tigers in spring training. As he watches the game, Sidney Howell's thoughts drift back to an earlier time when the Tigers were new to Lakeland, and the Great Depression-wracked city was doing its utmost to make them feel welcome.

It is 1934 and the Tigers have just announced their decision to move their spring training camp from San Antonio, Texas, to Lakeland, Florida. Eighteen-year-old Sid Howell is helping his attorney father support his family of six children by caddying at Cleveland Heights Country Club. Detroit manager, Mickey Cochrane, is in town to check on promised improvements to the local baseball field before his team arrives and to get in a few rounds of golf. Young Howell, a standout on Lakeland High School's state championship team, becomes a favorite of Cochrane's and his regular caddie. When the team arrives he is offered a job as the Tigers, bat boy and quickly accepts.

I met Mickey Cochrane at the Cleveland Heights Golf Course in Lakeland. He came down in December of 1933 and I got pretty well acquainted with him. He played golf pretty near every day, and he gave me $3 a day to [be his caddie].

Sidney Howell was interviewed by Gordon Olson and Frank Schubert as part of their research for a forthcoming book, Tigers in the Sun, *about the 60-year history of the Detroit Tigers and Lakeland, Florida, the longest-running spring training association between a Florida City and a major league baseball team.*

I caddied all through high school. I just about supported our family. I graduated in '32, and that was the very depths of the Depression. My father was an attorney. He stayed an attorney throughout the Depression, held things together. About three or four weeks before he died, he called us all in and he told us he was sorry he didn't have a lot to leave us, but he said he was just in the wrong business to be honest.

I played on the high school baseball team for four years. In 1930 it was a good team. We won the State Championship. I batted lefthanded and threw right. I could run and I could bunt. I was an outfielder.

When I was caddying for Cochrane, he would send me down the driving range to shag the balls he hit. I very seldom missed one if he hit it any distance. When they're dropping they're soft. A lot of times he'd go to the ball park to see how the things they were renovating were coming along, and I'd go to the ball park with him. He might have an errand he wanted me to run or something. I did the best I could. I got along with him good.

When the team arrived, Cochrane asked Howell to be bat boy for the same $3 per day he had been receiving as caddie.

Some of my friends thought there was honor to it. I enjoyed it, I liked it. I just shagged the bats when they threw them down to go to first base. And anything else there they told me to do. A lot of times I would hang up clothes for them. One day there was a Chesterfield salesman in there, come in just after a ball game. He was passing out $100 bills if you endorsed Chesterfield cigarettes. He offered me one and I took it.

JoJo White gave me my first chew of tobacco. He was a bad guy. The ball park started swimming.

I never did have any argument with any player. They were mostly all good fellows. Greenberg was as good as they come. Gehringer was, too. He was very quiet. I guess my favorite was Cochrane. He was hard, but I think he was fair. Cochrane sure knew the game.

Spring training was run just like he wanted it. The guys would do as they were told. I think they all liked Cochrane because he was all for them. One time in the clubhouse he was mad about something. We were all in there and he told them, "Some of you are not going by what I say. I am running this particular ball club. Any of you SOB's think you can beat my butt, you can do that and take my job."

According to Detroit News *sportswriter John Carlisle, it was at such a meeting that Howell gained further favor with Cochrane, who had just announced that he was not used to playing on losing teams, and that the Tigers would win the pennant. "So up pops the Burrhead with the bright remark that he is the luckiest batboy anywhere, and that he had played ball for good old Lakeland and wasn't used to losing either. Whereupon our Mike took a fancy to Lakeland's pride."*

One day Howell got a chance to play in a spring training game because outfielder Gerald "Gee" Walker was in Cochrane's doghouse.

He was being punished for something and was sent with the B-team to Deland to play somebody. The main team was going somewhere else. And I went with the B-team to Deland. We was riding along in the bus, and Gerald told the bus driver to stop, he had to go in the woods. Gerald got out, walked out in the woods, [and] everybody told that driver, "Get on, let the son of a gun stay."

So that's one day I got to play a full game. I played left field that whole day. The seventh or eighth inning Walker came walking in with some old farmer who had picked him up out there. He wasn't mad. He was just as jolly as hell.

The Tigers had about 35 players in their training camp in 1934. On occasion, when they needed an extra player, they gave Howell the call. In one game he hit an inside-the-park home run.

It was a line drive off Vic Sorrell. It went between the right fielder and the center fielder. All the way to the wall. I didn't have to slide. It was pretty good.

Howell, who was given the nickname "Burrhead" by Tiger trainer Denny Carroll because "whoever heard of a ballplayer named Sidney," so impressed Cochrane that at the end of spring training he was offered a contract to play for the Charleroi Tigers in the Pennsylvania State Association. He quickly became a favorite of Charleroi fans, starting off with 10 hits in his first 17 at bats, and endearing himself to everyone with the story of how he broke into baseball, and with his "likeable boyish personality." Fans raised a "howl for Howell" when manager Dixie Parker benched him midway through the season, and gave him a gift at a special "Howell Day" near the end of the season. He was among the league's top hitters all season, and nearly won the batting title.

Tommy Henrich beat me by two points. I'd get the bunt sign, sometimes with two strikes on me, two outs, and a man on third. They could do that today [when] their third baseman is back past the bag. You can dump it down there and beat it out. It looks like a line drive on paper.

The ballparks were pretty tough. Most of them were just skin, clay. They were smooth. You'd hit rocks there sometimes. I played second base for three or four weeks when our second baseman got hurt. I didn't particularly like that on the hard clay diamond, and no grass, but I made out all right. The outfields were grassier. They didn't take such bad hops in the outfield. The crowds generally pretty well filled the grandstand.

It was a split season. We were tied for first in the first half, and we were playing Greensburg, and our manager liked to play once in a while. So he decided to play first base. I think there was a man on third, one man out, game tied, home team up in the last inning. And they hit a fast ground ball to Parker at first. That screwball. He ran and tagged first base, and threw home too late to catch the runner. It made the other players mad.

Most of us were staying in a little four-story hotel in downtown Charleroi, and the ball players were mad. And they got some Dixie Belle gin. They got enough to get rowdy and raise hell. There was a carpet on the floor of the hotel and somebody got a hose and wet the carpet down, and really messed up that hotel.

We went out the next day and beat the same team we lost to. Beat them 14-4. We went back to the hotel that night after the ball game and all our belongings were out on the curb.

I think I made $110 a month. Which you could sure get by on. We all stayed in a rooming house after we got thrown out of the hotel.

When the season was over in Pennsylvania, [it was] about 20 to 25 days before the season ended in Detroit, and I went from Pennsylvania to Detroit to see the World Series. I have two cousins that live in Detroit. I stayed with them. It didn't cost me nothing.

According to John Carlisle, Tiger players welcomed Howell when he showed up in his yellow Lakeland High

School letter sweater with a large black "L" on the front. With a sizable lead over the Yankees, they declared they would have no trouble winning the American League pennant now that their lucky batboy had arrived. However, the Tigers lost a doubleheader to the Philadelphia Athletics on Howell's first day in Detroit, and the dejected batboy declared he had "had an off day," and left the dugout for a place in the stands. Later he rejoined the team in the dugout and helped the regular batboy for the remainder of the season and the World Series.

I could've played a couple innings in Detroit if Goslin would have come out when Cochrane asked him to come out, but he wouldn't do it.

I never was an autograph seeker. I wish to hell I had been. One time Will Rogers was in the clubhouse. Cochrane told me to get a new ball and get Will Rogers's autograph on it. I fiddled around and got most of the ball players to autograph that same ball. I still have it.

I liked that Dizzy Dean though. I remember they were playing in Detroit in '34, the World Series. It was the seventh game and Dizzy was pitching for St. Louis. I forget what the score was, but they were ahead. It was a late inning and Greenberg came to bat, and Diz, he reared back and threw one right down the middle as hard as he could throw it. And Greenberg cracked that thing, looked like it was rising going out of the park. They asked Diz if he threw that ball on purpose. And Diz says, "I'm not going to say that I threw that ball on purpose, but I heard that big boy could hit one and I wanted to see it."

Despite his good performance in Charleroi, Howell left professional baseball after 1934, when Mickey Cochrane offered him a more lucrative alternative.

His brother was going to run an advertising team for Ford Motor Company. He said, "You can go there and play with him. I believe you'd make a lot more money going there. Or, if you want to go one step up in the system, you can go to Charleston, West Virginia."

I figured I needed the money, so I went and played with his brother. I was told that I made as much money playing on the Ford Motor team in '35 as JoJo White made playing for Detroit.

We travelled in the team bus for the Ford Motor team. They would charge wherever we played; we would get a cut on the gate, and I made a lot more money there than I made at the plant. If I wasn't playing that day, I got $5.80 a day at the plant, whether I worked or not. And sometimes I'd make $100 to $125 a week, splitting the gate. That was a lot of money then.

The biggest crowd we ever played for was Jackson Prison. I got a base hit to win that ball game, and after the game, the security guard come over and told me a prisoner wanted to see me. Well, I walked over there, he had his bosom all puffed out and he pulled out three cartons of cigarettes and gave them to me. I told him, "You smoke these? You keep them."

He said, "No, I want you to have three. I won ten cartons on that base hit you got."

It just lasted one year. The team was sponsored by the dealers of Michigan and northern Ohio. They got cars assembled in Dearborn. If they wanted the team in their town, they paid money to sponsor it. I think we played in 73 towns in Michigan, and around 20 in northern Ohio.

A lot of dealers didn't get the team in their town. So they didn't want to sponsor it again. I went to work for Ford Motor, and kept on working there till '39. I came back here [to Lakeland] then, and I built a filling station. When I first came back to Lakeland,I had bought the property with the money I earned playing for the Ford team.

The most fun I ever had in a ball game was after I came home from Charleroi. There was a fella who ran a hardware store here in Lakeland, he got a bunch of misfits together, and he wanted to go up and play a team in Palatka.

Well an ol' lefthanded pitcher was warming up for Palatka. He must've been 45 years old. And I don't think he could've broken a pane of glass. But he come over before the game started and wanted to make a bet with all of us. He said, "If you come up to bat and get a hit, I'll give you 50 cents, and if you don't you give me 50 cents."

Well, that's a damn good bet for any pitcher. So he kept jawing and jawing, and nobody was saying anything. I wasn't particularly interested in it. But he said, "You fellas are all feather-neckers. Can't any of you hit?"

I said, "Lefty, how much money you got?"

He said, "I've got $25."

"Well," I said, "I've got $20. I probably won't come up but four times in the game, but I will make a little bet with you. If I get a base hit, you give me $5, and if I don't, I give you $5."

He says, "You fool, you've got a bet."

He put the money up, and I ran out four bunts. One time, I guess second or third time, he threw the ball, he damn near beat the ball to the plate. And I swung at it kind of hard and missed it intentionally. He didn't run in fast any more.

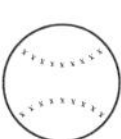

A football season in the sun

Jackie Robinson and the 1941 Honolulu Bears

Frank Ardolino

Jackie Robinson's career as the first black to break the color line in modern baseball is well-documented. Less well-known are certain events occurring before his first year with the Dodgers in 1947 which exerted significant influence on his subsequent career and political life as well. One of these important incidents, which has become better known through the 1990 teleplay produced by Ted Turner, is Robinson's Army court-martial in 1944, which he won and then was awarded an honorable discharge. The turmoil he experienced during this trial helped prepare him for the racial attacks he would endure when he joined the Dodgers. Another even less-publicized event concerns Robinson's anxious attempts after he left UCLA to find a job that would pay him for his athletic abilities.

Jackie temporarily found such a job in the winter of 1941 in Honolulu, where he played in the semipro Hawaii Senior Football League for the Honolulu Bears, who had joined the league in 1939 as the Polar Bears or the Hawaiian Vacation Team. Unlike the other three teams, the University of Hawaii Rainbows, the Na Aliis, or Chiefs, and the Healanis, the Bears signed their players to contracts, thus giving Robinson a paying sports job. He was hired by F. J. "Brick" Brickner, director of the Bears and former St. Mary's College football player, who traveled to California to sign Robinson. The contract included a $150 advance, which would be deducted from Robinson's subsequent salary; a fee of $100 a game, plus a bonus if the Bears won the championship; and, finally, a draft-deferred construction job near Pearl Harbor. Jackie was viewed as the prize signed by the league, and was hailed by the Honolulu *Advertiser* as the UCLA All-American halfback who would provide exciting open-field running.

Before transferring to UCLA in 1939, Robinson had starred for two years at Pasadena City College. In his first practice session there he had broken his ankle, but he returned, after the team had lost four games in a row, to star at quarterback and to lead his team to sixteen consecutive victories. At UCLA his athletic career established him, in the words of one sportswriter, as "the Jim Thorpe of his race." He became the university's first four-letter man—in baseball, track, football, and basketball—and received All-American honorable mention in basketball and football.

After exhausting his sports eligibility, Jackie decided to leave UCLA before attaining his degree, despite his mother's objection, because he wanted to repay her for supporting him during his college career. He intended to be a coach and he did not think he needed a degree for that. Robinson believed that a college degree would not provide him, a black man, with any more opportunities than his brother Mack had received. Mack, a vaunted athlete who had finished second to Jesse Owens in the 200 meters at the 1936 Berlin Olympics, had graduated from college only to end up as a street cleaner.

Determined to avoid Mack's fate, Robinson applied for and received an assistant athletic directing job in a National Youth Administration work project; however, this position disappeared when the war intensified in Europe. Jackie was without a job but not without resources. He played in the College All-Star game on

Frank Ardolino is a professor at the University of Hawaii, where he teaches Shakespeare and modern drama. He is a frequent contributor to Aethlon: The Journal of Sport Literature.

August 28, 1941, against the mighty Chicago Bears before a record crowd of 98,200 fans at Soldier Field, Chicago. The Bears had slaughtered the Redskins 73-0 in the 1940 title game, but the College All-Stars proved to be a tough opponent, staying close until the Bears scored three times in the final quarter to win 37-13. Jackie electrified the huge crowd by catching a 40-yard pass from Charley O'Rourke of Boston College and sprinting six yards for a touchdown.

National Baseball Library, Cooperstown, NY

Halfback Jackie Robinson kicking a field goal for UCLA.

After the All-Star game, Jackie played in a professional game at Hollywood's Gilmore Stadium before 10,000 people. The participants in this game were selected from among players on two barnstorming pro teams, the Hollywood Bears and the Los Angeles Bulldogs, with Jackie leading the Bulldogs and Kenny Washington, his former All-American running back at UCLA and one of the first blacks to play in the NFL, heading the Bears. Jackie left the game in the second quarter after spraining his ankle, and Washington's team went on to win the game. One week later, Jackie signed with the Honolulu Bears, because, despite the presence of black players like Kenny Washington and Woody Strode on semipro teams, he did not think he had a future in professional sports on the mainland.

"In those days," he remembered in his autobiography, "no major football or basketball teams hired black players. The only job offered me was with the Honolulu Bears....They were not major league but they were integrated."

Robinson decided to play in Hawaii, where he would be involved in an integrated, polyglot situation, have a steady, draft-deferred job, and be able to showcase his vaunted football talent.

Robinson arrived in Honolulu to great fanfare, with a full-length newspaper photo and banner headline announcing the coming of the "Century Express," describing him with hopeful exaggeration as "the great UCLA All-American halfback" who had starred in the All-Star game. He played his first game, an exhibition against a crack Army team that had won the military title six years in a row, and thoroughly outclassed them with his virtuoso performance. Jackie's winter in the sun seemed destined for the success predicted for him upon his arrival. But it never came to be. The favored Bears, who had won the championship in 1940, won only two games against the worst team in the league, and Robinson's performance, while exciting at times, ultimately was below par because of his recurring ankle injury. The team, known as the "Super Doopers," did not perform up to expectations at all. Although many of its members were seasoned college players, including Robinson's best friend and UCLA teammate, Ray Bartlett, who had introduced Jackie to his fiancee Rachel, and San Jose's star end Chuck Johnson, they were consistently outplayed by what seemed to be lesser competition of University of Hawaii players and former college players interested in prolonging their careers while working fulltime.

In an exhibition game at Schofield Barracks against the 35th Infantry team, known as the Cactusmen, Jackie starred as runner and passer, leading the Bears to a 27-6 victory. In their first league game on October 1, they faced the veteran Healani team, also known as the Maroons, which went on to tie the University of Hawaii for the league championship with a record of 5-1. Before an enthusiastic crowd of 20,000 people, who paid $1.10 for reserved seats, 55 cents for unreserved seats, and 30 cents for student rates, the Healanis handily defeated the Bears 20-6. Jackie gained a respectable 170 all-purpose yards, scoring on a three-yard run after completing a ten-yard pass. But he missed the extra point and had a number of his passes intercepted. As an *Advertiser* sportswriter put it:

> The Bears offered little in the way of an offense. A pass and a prayer and Jackie Robinson was all they had. Robinson, almost entirely on his own, reeled off some brilliant runs, but faltered in his passing, many of his attempts being intercepted by the Maroons.

On October 10 the Bears lost their second game to the University of Hawaii Rainbows, who had begun their college schedule with two mainland victories, by the identical score of 20-6. Again, Jackie's performance was a mixture of good and bad. He connected with his end John Wright on an 80-yard pass, but his next pass was intercepted on the three-yard line by the Bows. However, when the Bears got the ball back deep in Bow territory, Robinson threw for the short score. Overall, Jackie gained 103 yards, providing the only offense for the outclassed Bears. But he also committed two mistakes which led to scores for UH.

At this point in the season, the Honolulu *Advertiser* sportswriter, Red McQueen, argued in his regular column, "Hoomalimali" (Kid 'em along), that the Bears were using Robinson all wrong. Instead of running around end, Robinson should buck the line and gain big yardage. But the Bears obviously disagreed with McQueen, because at midseason they hired Henry Field, then Punahou School coach and former Healani coach, to install a new spread offense which would, ideally, free Jackie for more open-field jaunts. In turn, his heroics would prove popular with the fans, who were attending games in greater numbers than the previous year. Sixty thousand people paid $33,000 to see the first four games of the season.

In the next game, on November 1, the new strategy worked as the Bears defeated the Na Aliis 25-6, with Jackie showing his versatility. He scored on a punt return and a 65-yard run around end. On a third play, Jackie caught a pass and then lateraled to a teammate who sped for the touchdown, but it was called back because of a clipping penalty. However, in the next game, versus the powerful Rainbows on the day before Thanksgiving, Robinson hardly played due to his reinjured ankle, and the Bears were defeated 27-13 before a disappointing crowd of 5,500. In their next game, on November 29, the Bears defeated the hapless Na Aliis again 26-0, but without Robinson who remained on the sidelines with a chipped tibia.

Robinson reappeared in the Bears' final game of the season on December 3, when they were defeated again by the Healanis 19-13 before a minuscule crowd of 550 people. The game was played in a virtual gale which restricted vision and affected passing and kicking. Robinson threw two interceptions and attempted few runs. With this victory, the Healanis qualified to play Utah on Christmas day, but events on December 7 at Pearl Harbor led to the cancellation of postseason and bowl games scheduled in Honolulu.

The once-vaunted Bears ended their dismal season winning only two games against the winless Na Aliis. The Bears encountered personnel, coaching, and conditioning problems. Their star running back of the 1940 season, Charles "Babe" Webb, former New Mexico State backfield star, was upset about Robinson's replacing him and quit the team after the first game. Later, he tried to join the Na Aliis, but the management of the Bears prevented him from doing so by sending police to the dressing room to stop him from suiting up. Their coach, the esteemed Fred McKenzie, former Utah University captain and all-conference tackle, quit at midseason, upset at the way the team was being mishandled by a shifting series of assistant coaches and special advisors. The Bears were also accused of being in poor condition, of committing too many penalties, arguing excessivel,y and inciting the crowds to attack the officials' calls.

For Robinson, his football season in the sun must have been a rich, yet frustrating experience. He arrived to great fanfare as the league's all-star, had some superb moments, but succumbed to a recurring injury and faded in the last games. Perhaps the best part of the experience was his playing in a thoroughly integrated situation where his skin color was not controversial. His three-month stay in Hawaii gave him a vision of what a better America could be racially, and must have helped to inspire him in his attempt to integrate baseball and to fight for racial equality in his years after baseball.

Two days after the season ended Robinson sailed on the Matson *Lurline* for California. On December 7, the ship, somewhere in the Pacific, received news of the bombing of Pearl Harbor, and the captain ordered the passengers to don life jackets in case of an attack. Being superstitious and rebellious, Robinson refused, foreshadowing his future conflict with the Army and displaying the personality he would have to suppress during his season under fire in 1947 when he joined the Brooklyn Dodgers for the "great experiment."

Sources

Frommer, Harvey. *Rickey and Robinson: The Men Who Broke Baseball's Color Barrier.* New York: Macmillan, 1983.

Honolulu *Advertiser.* Sept.-Dec. 1941.

Robinson, Jackie, as told to Alfred Duckett. *I Never Had It Made.* Greenwich, CT: Fawcett Crest Books, 1972.

Tygiel, Jules. *Baseball's Great Experiment: Jackie Robinson and His Legacy.* New York: Oxford University Press, 1983.

Joss vs. Walsh

Ted Farmer

On a cool autumn day in 1908, two pitching greats of the dead ball era hooked up in a true classic, one that I think, because of the importance of the game and the enormous pressure surrounding it, remains unsurpassed as the greatest pitching duel in baseball history.

In 1908, the American League enjoyed one of its most peculiar and entertaining seasons. Thirteen pitchers had earned run averages under 2.00, while only three hitters batted over .300. Collectively, the entire league batted just .239. The combination of outstanding pitching and scant hitting made for many low-scoring, close games and a tight pennant race.

By October 2, Detroit was in first place, only percentage points ahead of Chicago and Cleveland, who were locked in a virtual tie. At 3 o'clock on that Friday in early October, the White Sox were scheduled to meet the Naps in what was to become a fitting climax to a season of brilliant pitching.

The White Sox and Ed Walsh—The performance of the 1908 White Sox was indicative of the league as a whole. The club batted only .224, with Patsy Dougherty leading the way with a .278 mark. Furthermore, the Pale Hose hit only three home runs, still the lowest total of the twentieth century. However tormented by this lack of offense, manager Fielder Jones kept the club in contention, just as he had done two years earlier when his "Hitless Wonders" had won the World Series. Jones' success was due primarily to the best pitching staff in the league. Frank Smith and "Doc" White were superb twirlers who had fine major league careers. For his starter on that fateful day, however, Jones selected the one man who stood head and shoulders above all American League pitchers in 1908.

Born May 14, 1881 in Plains, Pennsylvania, Augustine Edward Walsh was purchased by Chicago from Newark. Popularly known as "Big Ed" due to his 6 foot 1, 195 pound frame, he first appeared with the White Sox at their spring training camp in Marlin Springs, Texas in 1904. Blessed with an abundance of speed, but little else, Walsh realized that he would have to add to his repertoire of pitches if he was going to make the big club.

Also in Marlin Springs was Elmer Stricklett, a young spitballer whose career was eventually shortened because of arm trouble. His contribution to the White Sox was enormous, however, because it was from Stricklett that Ed Walsh learned the spitball. Walsh, fascinated by the wondrous possibilities the spitball offered, understood that the pitch represented not only the opportunity to become a big league pitcher, but the path to pitching greatness. In time, he became the greatest spitballer the game has ever known.

In a career that spanned 1904–1917, Walsh's earned run average was 1.82, still the all-time career record. His overall won-loss mark was an impressive 195-126, and he struck out 1,736 batters. It was the 1908 season, however, that made Ed Walsh a legend.

For in that majestic year, Walsh's performance was simply phenomenal. He led the league in games (66), starts (49), wins (40), shutouts (11), complete games (42), saves (6), and innings (an astonishing 464, which is still the twentieth-century high). His ERA was an

Ted Farmer is a historian who lives in Blacksburg, Virginia.

National Baseball Library, Cooperstown, NY

Ed Walsh, left, and Addie Joss shortly after their duel of October 2, 1908. A photographer's note on the back of this famous shot calls their matchup a "World's Record" performance.

outstanding 1.42, good enough for third in the league.

As the season came to a close, Jones started Walsh at every conceivable opportunity, including seven of the team's last nine games. On September 29, he pitched both ends of a doubleheader, winning the first game 5–1, while allowing only three hits. The second game was Walsh's twelfth shutout of the year, as he allowed only four safeties in a 2–0 victory.

For his Herculean efforts, Walsh was presented with a year-end bonus check of $3,500 by White Sox owner Charles Comiskey. This matched his salary.

The Naps and Addie Joss—In many ways, the 1908 Cleveland Naps resembled the White Sox. Blessed with a strong pitching staff, manager Napoleon Lajoie, for whom the club was nicknamed, guided his own hitless wonders to what was, until that time, their best season ever. The Naps' shortage of sticks was apparent to all who followed baseball. Even second baseman/manager Lajoie, a legitimately great hitter, batted just

.289. The team's leading hitter, George "Firebrand" Stovall, checked in at .292.

To oppose Walsh and the White Sox, Lajoie called on his ace, Adrian "Addie" Joss. Joss, from Woodland, Wisconsin, was a year older than Walsh and had been in the majors since 1902. At 6 foot 3, 185 pounds, he was one of the largest players of his time, and one of the best pitchers of the Dead Ball Era.

Addie was noted for an unorthodox spinning delivery and a pitch known as a "false rise." Judging by his career numbers, Addie's "false rise" and baffling delivery more often than not left batters helpless. His career statistics are mind-boggling.

In his brief career, which spanned 1902–1910, Joss won 20 or more games four times. He completed 234 games out of 260 starts, and his overall won-loss record was 160-97. Only once did his ERA exceed 2.26; five times it was less than 2.00. His career ERA (1.88) is second only to Walsh's (1.82).

For Joss, 1908 was a superb year even by his lofty standards. He led the league with a microscopic ERA of 1.16, and his won-loss record was 24–11. He completed 29 games, pitched 325 innings, walked only 30 batters, tossed nine shutouts, and appeared in seven games as a relief pitcher.

The game—Thus, the stage was set for a pitchers' duel. The weather was typical of Cleveland in October: damp, cloudy, and cool. Approximately 10,000 spectators jammed League Park. They weren't disappointed. After Joss retired the side in order in the top of the first, Wilbur Good of the Naps strode to the plate. He promptly struck out, the first of four whiffs for him on this day. Walsh's devastating spitter was working like a charm. Soon it became apparent that Joss was in top form as well.

Neither side could touch the pitching of the other until the bottom of the third. Joe Birmingham stroked a leadoff single off Big Ed, and proceeded to be picked off first. Or so it seemed. But first baseman Frank Isbell's throw to second struck the trapped Birmingham in the head and rolled into right field. By the time Ed Hahn retrieved the ball, Birmingham had raced to third. Walsh retired George Perring and Joss, but then crossed signals with catcher Ossee Schreck (AKA Schreckengost), and his pitch rolled to the grandstand, allowing Birmingham to score.

Both pitchers continued to master the opposing lineups throughout the next few innings. Batter after batter was retired, and the crowd became enthralled with Walsh's strikeouts. Good went down on strikes four times, Lajoie twice and Josh Clarke twice.

But even more impressive was Joss. Protecting a one-run lead with the pennant possibly riding on the outcome of the game, he refused to give up a hit or walk. He struck out three and induced so many ground balls that Stovall had 16 putouts at first base.

By the eighth inning, the Cleveland fans had begun cheering for Walsh almost as much as they were for Joss. Ed finished with 15 strikeouts, allowing only four singles and a walk.

Jones sent in three pinch hitters in the ninth, but to no avail. Nothing could thwart Addie's splendid effort, which lasted only 1 hour, 40 minutes, and was the second perfect game of the modern era. Although none of the players could have known, the game ultimately had no bearing on the pennant race. The Tigers held on to their lead and won the flag.

Afterward—For Ed Walsh and Addie Joss, the 1908 season, and specifically, the game of October 2, marked the pinnacle of their careers. After working 464 innings, Walsh was never again the same pitcher. He had several more good seasons, but never came close to the extraordinary performance of 1908. Nevertheless, he was rightly voted into the Hall of Fame in 1946.

Joss's record slipped to 14-13 the next year, and in 1910 he managed only 5 victories. Ironically, one of his victories was a no-hitter against the White Sox. Tragically, his career was cut short by spinal meningitis. Addie Joss died two days after his 31st birthday, on April 14, 1911. League stars played a benefit game which raised $13,000 for his widow.

To become eligible for the Hall of Fame, a player must play for at least ten years. For many years, Joss, who played just nine seasons, was therefore neglected by the voters. In 1978, however, the Veterans Committee waived this requirement and Addie Joss took his place among baseball's immortals; undoubtedly, his day of perfection was a crucial factor in the committee's decision.

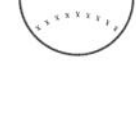

Elroy Face's magnificent 1959 season

The Baron of the Bullpen

Fredric E. Orlansky

In 1959 the Pittsburgh Pirates were coming off a surprisingly successful season. They finished in second place, eight games behind the pennant-winning Milwaukee Braves. Visions of the team's first pennant since 1927 flickered among the Forbes Field faithful.

Winning was an unusual event for the Pirates in the 1950s. Pirate teams during the decade were distinguished by their finishing either seventh or eighth (which in those days meant last) each year until 1958. The Pirates of the early 1950s were so bad that only by divine intervention could they be successful. In the 1951 movie, "Angels in the Outfield," manager Paul Douglas led the Pirates to a National League pennant with the assistance of angels and (newspaper household hints columnist) Janet Leigh.

While the 1959 edition of the Pirates was destined to finish in fourth place with a 78-76 record, nine games behind the Los Angeles Dodgers, Pirate fans were treated to a season-long drama by their diminutive bullpen ace, Elroy Face. The 5-foot-8, 155-pound righthander won 17 games in a row in relief, finishing the season 18-1. From Memorial Day, 1958, to Labor Day, 1959, the Baron of the Bullpen won 22 straight games.

As the season began, Manager Danny Murtaugh called his relief specialist the best in the game. The fulfillment of his prophecy was postponed by a typical Pirate streak of five losses (and a tie) to begin the season. Face finished three games during this stretch, giving up no runs in 5-2/3 innings.

Fredric E. Orlansky is an attorney living in Pittsburgh. He misses attending Pirate games at Forbes Field with his father, to whom this article is dedicated.

National Baseball Library, Cooperstown, NY

Roy Face. Think it's a forkball?

First baseman Rocky Nelson's first major league hit since 1956 drove in the winning run in Face's first 1959 victory. The Reds blew a 7-0 lead in the seventh inning as the Pirates came back to beat them 9-8 in Pittsburgh on April 22. After the Pirates had tied the game at seven, Face gave up his first run of the year on Gus Bell's eighth-inning home run. However, the Pirates came back in the ninth inning, aided by two errors by Frank Robinson. The tying run scored on a Roman Mejias walk with the bases loaded, followed by Nelson's single off Hal Jeffcoat.

The headline on the April 25 Pittsburgh *Press* sports section, FACE'S FORKBALL ACTS UP BUT PIRATES RESCUE HIM, was typical of those to come during the 1959 season. A ninth-inning rally by the Pirates brought Face his second win, as he pitched in his fifth game of the season. The Pirates beat the Phillies 8-5 in Philadelphia, despite Face giving up four hits, a hit batsman, a walk and two runs in 2-1/3 innings. Face admitted that his forkball "just wouldn't behave," leaving him "like a catcher without a glove." He entered the game with a 4-3 lead in the seventh, with a runner on and two out. Bill Virdon's spectacular running catch of a Wally Post shot prevented any damage in that inning. In the eighth, however, Carl Sawatski's double drove in Willie Jones and Gene Freese to give the Phils the lead. The Pirates regained the advantage in the ninth on four singles and a Smoky Burgess double. Face's trouble continued in the Phils' half of the inning. After retiring the first two batters, singles by Harry Anderson and Chico Fernandez brought the tying run to the plate. Face was able to induce Gene Freese to ground out to Don Hoak to end the game and preserve his seventh straight victory over the last two seasons.

A bases-loaded single by Bill Mazeroski in the tenth inning drove in the winning run as the Pirates beat the Cardinals 4-3 in the first game of a doubleheader on May 3. Future author Jim Brosnan took the loss as Face pitched three hitless innings to win his third game of the season. Although only 8-9, the Pirates moved to within 2-1/2 games of the National League lead.

The bullpen workhorse brought his earned run average down to 1.69 as he again beat the Phillies, 5-4. Face pitched a scoreless top of the tenth. In the Pirate half of the frame, Ted Kluszewski hit his first home run in almost a year, bringing Face his fourth victory in nine appearances. Jim Owens lost the May 7 game.

Six days later, Warren Spahn won his 250th game, beating the Cards 3-2. The Pirates and Elroy Face also had reason to celebrate. Don Drysdale became Face's fifth victim, as the Pirates won 6-4. Face finished the game, giving up three hits and two walks in three innings, while striking out five Dodgers. The Pirates took the lead in the eighth inning, as Dick Stuart homered with Smoky Burgess aboard. Bill Mazeroski's double drove in Bob Skinner with the sixth run. The Pirate reliever was in constant trouble during the game, giving up a double with two out in the seventh and allowing the first two Dodgers to reach in the eighth and ninth. Appearing in his third game in four days, Face admitted that he could use a bit of a rest.

In spite of his fatigue, Face won his sixth game of the season the next day, beating Clem Labine 7-6. It was another ragged outing, as the Pirates reached the .500 mark for the season. Bob Friend, who had six of the team's 14 losses, led 6-2 in the eighth inning. Face relieved, giving up a single to Rip Repulski and walking Jim Gilliam on a 3-2 pitch to load the bases. After striking out Charlie Neal, Face allowed a two-run single by Wally Moon to tie the game. Dick Stuart again powered the Face victory. For the second consecutive game, his late inning home run propelled the Pirates to a win.

The forkball—Throughout his career, Face's signature pitch was the forkball. He had developed it in 1954 while playing at New Orleans, the year after the Pirates drafted him out of the Dodger chain. (The Pirates were similarly successful in drafting Roberto Clemente from Brooklyn.) Face learned the pitch from ex-Yankee Joe Page, who had been signed in spring training. He watched Page warm up using the pitch and began working with it after learning the proper grip. Teammate Dick Groat described the forkball as similar to a knuckleball. He noted that when Face began using the pitch, batters complained that he was throwing a spitball. Face combined the forkball with the slider, fastball and curve to complete his pitch menu. He had good control of all his pitches, and usually struck out twice as many as he walked.

Injury, rumors, and more wins—Face's 1959 season was not without controversy. Following a one-inning appearance on May 17, when he saved Vernon Law's second victory of the season, he did not appear again until May 30, when he gained another save in a 3-1 victory over the Reds. The 31-year-old bullpen ace sat out two weeks with a cut right hand. Pittsburgh *Press* columnist Chet Smith reported that the cut resulted from a "fierce fight" between the pitcher and right fielder Roberto Clemente. Although nobody knew what started the argument, Clemente was supposed to have cut Face's arm with a knife or razor. Further damage was allegedly averted by the intervention of pitcher Bob Friend. A second story had Dick Stuart breaking up the fight by lifting Clemente and throwing him against a wall.

The truth, according to Face, was a lot less exciting. Getting up to get a glass of water, the glass slipped out of the reliever's hand, breaking on the basin, causing the mysterious cut. Face denied arguing with any of his teammates. In a tribute to Clemente's strength, Face speculated that Dick Stuart, strong as he was, could not pick Clemente up and throw him against a wall. He joked that he even had to deny a rumor heard by his wife that he hurt himself after being out after curfew and had been fined $500 by Danny Murtaugh.

Neither the injury nor the speculation surrounding its cause sidetracked Pittsburgh's victory machine. Face raised his record to 7-0, striking out five Reds in a wild 14-11 victory in the second game of a May 31 doubleheader. Smoky Burgess's seventh-inning homer broke an 11-11 tie. Bob Skinner had two homers (including a grand slam) and Don Hoak one, as the Pirates slugged four in each game. Face got into the act, with a single in his only plate appearance. Face's perfect record matched that of his American League counterpart, Hoyt Wilhelm.

The Stephentown, NY, native's eighth win came in his third appearance in two days, beating the Giants 12-9 in eleven innings. The Pirates battled back from a 9-4 deficit in the eighth inning to tie the game on Dick Stuart's homer. Pinch hitting for Face in the eleventh, Harry Bright hit a three-run home run, driving in Dick Groat and Bill Mazeroski for the victory. Face survived three singles by the Giants in the ninth. Unable to control his forkball, Face relied on sliders to retire the San Franciscans.

Face's heavy workload continued through the middle of June. Victory number nine came on June 11, again by a 12-9 score, again against the Giants. The Pirates were charged with seven errors in the game, in which Face admitted that he had little or nothing on the ball. Willie Mays tagged the Pirate reliever for a three-run homer to give the Giants an 8-7 lead. In the ninth, Danny Kravitz singled in the tying run. A sacrifice fly by Dick Stuart, a two-run single by Don Hoak, and an error completed the Pirate scoring. Vernon Law, usually a starter, finished what Dick Groat called "the worst game I ever played in," taking over from Face.

His fifteenth victory in little more than a year came three days later. Face beat the Dodgers for the third time in 1959, winning 6-3 in the first game of a June 14 doubleheader. He came in with the score tied in the eighth, striking out four and surrendering two harmless hits. The Pirates scored three runs off loser Clem Labine in the bottom of the eighth, with Stuart, Mazeroski and Hoak driving in the runs. Particularly hot was third baseman Hoak who raised his average to .313. He was on a 13-game hitting streak, batting .440, with four homers and 12 RBI.

The fourth of Face's five June victories came against the Cubs at Wrigley Field. In his longest outing of the season, he pitched five innings, striking out four, as the Pirates defeated the Cubs 4-2 in 13 innings. This improved the club's record to 34-30, 2-1/2 games behind Milwaukee. Face entered the game in the ninth and was never in danger, giving up only three hits. This was his sixth game in nine days and eighth appearance in eleven. A single by Bob Skinner and a Bill Virdon sacrifice fly provided the Pirates a two-run cushion.

Eddie Fisher was the victim of the twelfth Face victory, as the Pirates beat the Giants 3-1. Roy reduced his ERA to 0.87 with three shutout innings. He had given up no runs in his previous 15 innings, one in his last 29, and only 2 in his last 43. Roman Mejias hit a two-run home run in the top of the twelfth inning to put the Pirates ahead. Singles by Jackie Brandt and Willie Kirkland and a walk to Felipe Alou loaded the bases with two out in the bottom of the twelfth. On a 2-0 pitch, Eddie Bressoud bounced back to Face to end the game.

Halfway—At the first All-Star break, Face's stellar season stood as follows:

G	GS	IP	H	BB	SO	W	L	ERA
31	0	54	37	11	43	12	0	0.83

In June he had five wins, with 18 strikeouts in 23-2/3 innings. His ERA was 0.37. There were several members of the 1959 Pirates, including Dick Stuart, who had never seen Elroy Face lose a baseball game. His last loss had been in the first game of a May 30, 1958 doubleheader against the Braves at Forbes Field. Vernon Law started the game, leaving in the eighth with two out, a runner on first and a 4-3 lead. Face retired the side in the eighth, but in the ninth, a double error by Frank Thomas on Johnny Logan's grounder, Bill Bruton's safe bunt, a one-out single by pinch hitter Del Crandall and Felix Mantilla's single, led to a Pirate defeat, 7-4. From that game through the All-Star break, Face remained undefeated in 17 decisions.

According to Manager Murtaugh, "You have no idea what a feeling Face gives you when he takes over. He doesn't care who the hitter is or what the score is. He walks out there like he dares the batter to hit him. He's a real take-charge fella. You can see the whole team perk up when he comes in. They rely on him and he hasn't let us down yet." Dick Groat felt that "we're a different team when he comes into a game. Every time I see Face walk in I say to myself, 'We're in business.'"

Pittsburgh *Press* columnist Roy McHugh observed that Face was able to keep his success and fame in perspective. "No one is less impressed by the attention Face gets than he is himself. He's a down-to-earth country boy who wouldn't know how to put on an act, if he tried." Face would relax with friends at former Pirate Frankie Gustine's restaurant, a block away from Forbes Field. Away from the ballpark, Face would fish or do carpentry work. The Pirate reliever also played rock and roll guitar. While McHugh admitted that "Elvis Pressley [sic] has a slightly better touch... Elvis can't get the side out with three men on base."

All-Star disappointment—The first 1959 All-Star Game was played in Pittsburgh. Elroy Face was an obvious choice to appear before the crowd of 35,277 which paid $6.60 ($2.20 for bleachers), plus $.75 handling charge, to attend the contest at Forbes Field.

Face's appearance in the All-Star Game was a portent of the rougher treatment he was to endure during the second half of 1959. He pitched 1-2/3 innings, giving up three runs on three hits and two walks, while striking out two batters. Face retired the first five batters he faced. Then Nellie Fox, in the middle of his MVP season, lined a single past Face's head to start an AL rally. Harvey Kuenn walked on a 3-2 pitch. Fox scored on Vic Power's single to center. Ted Williams walked, batting for Rocky Colavito. Gil McDougald ran for the Splendid Splinter. Gus Triandos scored Kuenn and Power, doubling down the third base line on a high forkball. Face was relieved by John Antonelli, who retired the side. The National League All-Stars avoided Face's "first defeat" by scoring two runs in the eighth inning off Whitey Ford, winning 5-4.

The All-Star Game was Face's first 1959 appearance in which he was relieved in the middle of an inning. He blamed his troubles on a forkball that wouldn't behave. Instead of dropping, it stayed up. Face, who had brought his parents to Pittsburgh for the game, was disappointed in his performance. His only consolation was that his poor outing was not in a Pirate game.

The small righthander soon atoned for his All-Star performance. On July 9, Face won his thirteenth game of the season. The Pirates won 4-3 over the Cubs. Harry Bright's fourth pinch-hit of the year drove in the winning run in the 10th inning. Face came into the game leading 3-2, with Irv Noren on third base. Tony Taylor tied the game, singling on a 2-2 fastball. The Pirates came back in the tenth with Clemente and Bright singling around Mejias' sacrifice. Despite allowing Taylor's single, Face kept his 19-inning no-earned-run streak intact.

Face won his fourth straight extra-inning contest three days later, raising his record to 14-0. The Pirates defeated the Cards 6-5 in 10 innings in the first game of a doubleheader. He was brought in to protect a 5-4 lead for Harvey Haddix with two on and two out in the eighth. Face successfully completed the inning, but after a single and a sacrifice, Bill White's single tied the game, ending Face's scoreless streak. In the tenth Roberto Clemente singled in the winning run following two singles and an error. The Pirate reliever also pitched in the second game, retiring George Crowe on a strikeout before the game was suspended due to the local curfew.

Slump—It would be nearly a month before win fifteen was recorded. This was the longest drought for Face during the 1959 season. Between victories, he pitched nine times (including the completion of a previously suspended game). Face was ineffective, giving up nine runs in eleven innings. On July 26 he was warned about throwing a pitch over Henry Aaron's head. Face denied throwing at the Braves' slugger, since there were already two runners on base at the time and the Braves were ahead 2-1, but warned, "If I want to knock anyone down, I have good control and can do it."

During this time the Pirates lost nine straight games and 16 out of 19. Face's worst appearance occurred on August 1. He was brought in to protect a 5-4 lead with two on in the seventh. Willie Kirkland hit an 0-2 pitch for a single to tie the game. Following a wild pitch, Leon Wagner was intentionally walked to load the bases. Pinch-hitter Dusty Rhodes doubled down the left field line, clearing the bases. Rhodes scored on Jackie Brandt's single. Of the five runs scored in the inning, three were charged to Face.

Face also pitched the last two innings of the second All-Star Game of 1959 at the Los Angeles Coliseum. After giving up a solo homer to Rocky Colavito in the eighth, he pitched a scoreless ninth, as the American League gained a split with a 5-3 victory.

On August 8 the Pirates won their eleventh straight extra-inning game, raising their record in such games to 15-1. (Ironically, their only extra-inning loss was Harvey Haddix's 12-inning perfect game, lost in the 13th against the Braves in May.) The Pirates won 5-3 in ten innings as Pittsburgh's "Fort Knox" gained his fifteenth victory to go along with nine saves. Dick Groat booted a grounder leading to an unearned run off Face and a 3-1 lead for the Cubs going into the bottom of the ninth. Singles by Clemente and Nelson, a double by Groat, and Smoky Burgess's sacrifice fly tied the game. In the 10th the Pirates scored two runs. Mejias singled. Face sacrificed him to second. Following an intentional walk to Skinner, Groat singled, scoring Mejias. Clemente's infield single loaded the bases. Rocky Nelson's walk drove in the insurance run, as the Pirates won two games in a row for the first time since July 9-10. Face called the victory "a great lift for me," since he had been in a pitching slump for almost a month, although he was not charged with any of the defeats.

Face's pitching woes continued during the dog days of August, yielding two runs against the Phils on August 11 and three more to the Braves four days later. Face had surrendered 14 earned runs on 25 hits in only 12-2/3 innings through his August 15 appearance. He blew a save during the completion of a suspended game on August 19, leading to the Pirates' second extra-inning loss of the season. Play resumed against the Cards with the Bucs ahead 5-4, one on and one out. Face yielded a single to Wally Shannon and a triple to Curt Flood. The Pirates came back to tie the game in the ninth, preserving Face's streak, but lost 8-6 in 10 innings. The slump, which caused Face's ERA to jump to 2.54 was blamed on a tired arm.

Don Drysdale was again Face's victim, as the Pirates beat the Dodgers 4-3 in 10 innings in the second game of an August 23 doubleheader. It was a bad day for the intimidating Dodger righthander, as he lost both ends of the twin bill. A two-out single by Dick Stuart in the ninth inning scored Bob Skinner to tie the game. In the Dodgers' tenth, the bases were loaded with two outs when Face induced pinch-hitter Carl Furillo to hit a fly ball to Skinner. In the Pirate half of the frame, Drysdale intentionally walked a Pirate with runners on first and third and two out. Dick Groat then singled in the winning run. The fourth-place Pirates raised their record to 64-61, eight games behind the league-leading Giants.

Face called the victory "a great team effort." The Pirate reliever was excited that he had tied Philadelphia's Jim Konstanty for most wins by a relief pitcher (16) with his fourth victory of the year against the Dodgers. The victory also tied him with consecutive win streaks by Carl Hubbell in 1936 and Ewell Blackwell in 1947 (among others). On this night of his 21st straight victory, Face was given a trophy and clock by a local Elks Club for being the "greatest relief pitcher in history."

The Pirates' reliever came close to winning number seventeen as the Pirates scored four runs in the ninth to tie the August 26 game against the Giants. However, Ron Kline won his ninth game, as the Pirates scored a run in the tenth to defeat the Giants, continuing their amazing record in extra innings.

Given the amount of work by the diminutive righthander and his recent ineffectiveness due to a tired arm, it was surprising that Face pitched an inning of relief against a team of International League All-Stars in an exhibition game at Columbus. The Pirates lost the game 14-6.

It's a little-known "fact" that Elroy lost a second game during the 1959 season. He was brought in to relieve with two out in a one-inning game between KDKA television and radio staffers and members of the Pittsburgh press corps. He was awarded the loss in the 1-0 game when an error was made on a 40-foot ground ball. Taking the loss philosophically, Face rationalized, "If I had to lose, I'm sure glad it was to those guys."

Face defeated the Phillies on August 30. The Pirates won 7-6 in ten innings in the nightcap of a doubleheader. The Bucs came back from a 5-0 deficit, scoring the tying run in the ninth after two out. Clemente, who had walked, moved to second on a wild pitch and scored on Rocky Nelson's single. Face nearly lost the game when Ed Bouchee hit his 15th homer into the right field seats in the top of the tenth. However, the Pirates' comeback machine was not finished. Don Hoak singled in the tenth and, following a sacrifice, Virdon walked on four pitches. Once again, Dick Stuart came to Face's rescue, driving in both teammates with a double. With the victory, the Pirates had won five in a row and nine of ten. They moved to within four games of San Francisco.

The streak ends—Face gave up runs in two of his first three September appearances. In one of the games, coming in to rescue Vernon Law, with the game tied and two on, Face gave up a three-run home run to Willie Jones of Cincinnati.

Longtime Pirate broadcaster Bob "Gunner" Prince was famous for his colorful phrases. In addition to providing nicknames for numerous members of the Pirates, including "Baron of the Bullpen" (Face); Tiger (Hoak); Arriba (Clemente); Quail (Virdon); Dog (Skinner); and Deacon (Law), Prince developed the "hidden vigorish" theory. According to Prince, whether you were on a good streak or bad one, each successive victory or defeat brought the end of the streak closer. Whether it was hidden vigorish, luck or otherwise, Elroy Face's amazing streak of seventeen straight relief victories in 1959 (and twenty-two overall) would end in the Los Angeles Coliseum on September 11. Since he had defeated the Dodgers four times, it was somehow fitting that they would break his streak. (Face won seven in a row against the Dodgers. His last loss to them was in September, 1956.) Face was beaten by little-known Chuck Churn, who won his second game without defeat.

Face relieved Bob Friend in the eighth inning, leading 4-3, with a man on and one out. He retired the next two batters, but in the ninth Maury Wills singled and was sacrificed to second. Jim Gilliam hit a forkball to right for a triple. With the game tied at four, the next batter, Charlie Neal, rolled a single to left off a forkball and the streak was ended.

Face accepted the defeat stoically. According to the Pittsburgh *Press*, he "shed no tears, showed no remorse and didn't blink an eye" when he lost his first game since May 30, 1958. He took the loss in stride, chatting casually with reporters, drinking a soft drink. This was in contrast to the general atmosphere of gloom in the clubhouse following the loss.

"I felt badly because I couldn't save the game for Bob Friend and also the fact that we lost it. But after all, it's just another ballgame to me. I felt the same when I was winning, except I was happier. If you allow these things to get you down, you're no good." Face recalled Don Drysdale's recent losses, saying "Don Drysdale lost two games in one day at Forbes Field, so I guess I'm entitled to lose one game in one and one-half years. I should have lost before this. I've been very lucky. My teammates have saved me so many times. You've got to be lucky to win as many as I did in relief."

Face said the Rube Marquard (19 straight wins in a season) and Carl Hubbell (24 consecutive wins in two years) records never entered his mind. However, he was proud of winning more games in relief than any other pitcher, besting Jim Konstanty's record by one. Looking back on the streak, Face felt his best game was against the Cubs on June 18. In winning his 11th game, Face pitched five innings (his longest outing), striking out four, while giving up only three hits.

The loss completed a period of 28-1/3 innings in which Face surrendered 41 hits and 20 runs. The workhorse reliever had appeared in 54 games and warmed up almost every day in 1959. During the two-season streak, Face appeared in 99 games, winning 22 while saving almost 30 others.

One more time—Face's last victory of 1959 came, appropriately enough, in a 12-inning game against the Reds in his first appearance after the loss. He raised his record to 18-1, as the Pirates defeated the Reds 4-3 at Forbes Field on September 19 for his eighth straight win in extra-innings.

The Pirates again rescued Face, as he gave up the lead run in the top of the 12th inning on Johnny Temple's single. Don Newcombe retired the first Pirate batter in the bottom of the inning before Dick Stuart started the Pirates' rally with a double to left. He moved to third as Joe Nuxhall retired Smoky Burgess. Brooks Lawrence came in to relieve, hitting Don Hoak with his first pitch. After getting a one-ball, two-strike count, Bill Mazeroski hit Lawrence's fifth pitch just inside the third-base bag. Stuart scored easily. Hoak came in when Frank Robinson had trouble with the ball when it rebounded off the wall in left field.

Face pitched twice more in 1959, striking out three and giving up a hit in two innings. Despite his efforts, the Pirates were little better than a .500 ball club, finishing in fourth place at 78-76, nine games behind first place Los Angeles which defeated Milwaukee in a post-season playoff.

Thirty-five years later the righthander's .947 winning percentage remains the all-time record for pitchers with 15 or more decisions. The 18 wins are still the most by a relief pitcher. His 17 consecutive wins are the most by any pitcher since 1945.

In most other seasons in the 1950s, the Pirates' record would be cause for rejoicing. With hopes buoyed by their 84-70 record and second-place finish in 1958, the up and down season of 1959 was a great disappointment to the Bucco faithful. The long pennant drought would soon be ended by Bill Mazeroski's dramatic ninth-inning home run to win the seventh game of the 1960 World Series. However, during the winter of 1959-60, Pirate fans would have to content themselves with remembering the season-long odyssey of Elroy Face as he approached perfection.

Notes:

The Pittsburgh *Post Gazette* was the main source of day-by-day information for this article.

Roy Face in 1959

DATE	OPPONENT	IP	H	R	ER	BB	SO	SCORE	LOSING PITCHER	RECORD
4/22	Reds (H)	2	1	1	1	0	2	9-8	Pena	1-0
4/24	Phillies (A)	2.1	4	2	2	1	0	8-5	Schroll	2-0
5/3	Cardinals (H)	3	0	0	0	0	2	4-3 (10)	Brosnan	3-0
5/7	Phillies (H)	1	1	0	0	0	1	5-4 (10)	Owens	4-0
5/13	Dodgers (A)	3	3	0	0	2	5	6-4	Drysdale	5-0
5/14	Dodgers (A)	1.2	2	1	1	1	3	7-6	Labine	6-0
5/31	Reds (A)	3	1	0	0	0	5	14-11	Mabe	7-0
6/8	Giants (H)	3	3	0	0	0	1	12-9 (11)	McCormick	8-0
6/11	Giants (H)	1	2	1	1	0	1	12-9	Miller	9-0
6/14	Dodgers (H)	2	2	0	0	0	4	6-3	Labine	10-0
6/18	Cubs (A)	5	3	0	0	0	4	4-2 (13)	Henry	11-0
6/25	Giants (A)	3	2	0	0	2	0	3-1 (12)	Fisher	12-0
7/9	Cubs (H)	1.1	1	0	0	0	1	4-3 (10)	Henry	13-0
7/12	Cardinals (H)	2.1	4	1	1	0	0	6-5 (10)	McDaniel	14-0
8/9	Cubs (A)	3	4	1	0	1	2	5-3 (10)	Elston	15-0
8/23	Dodgers (H)	2	2	0	0	2	0	4-3 (10)	Drysdale	16-0
8/30	Phillies (H)	1	2	1	1	0	0	7-6 (10)	Farrell	17-0
9/11	Dodgers (A)	1	3	2	2	0	0	4-5	Churn (WP)	17-1
9/19	Reds (H)	4	5	1	1	0	0	4-3 (12)	Lawrence	18-1

Totals

G	GF	IP	H	R	ER	BB	IBB	SO	WP	ERA	W	L	S	PCT.
57	47	93.1	91	29	28	25	8	69	4	2.70	18	1	10	.947

Wins vs. Dodgers (4); Giants (3); Reds (3); Cubs (3); Phillies (3); Cardinals (2); Braves (0)

Home record: 11-0, Away record: 7-1, Extra inning record: 11-0

Source: Pittsburgh *Post-Gazette*

The 1949 Nashua Dodgers

Scott Roper

The 1949 Class-B New England League baseball season began with high hopes for the small mill city of Nashua, New Hampshire. Since the league recommenced operations in 1946 (after a 12-season layoff), the Nashua Dodgers had placed second three times in three years, winning the playoffs and the Governor's Cup in each of those seasons. Walter Alston, Roy Campanella, Don Newcombe, Dan Bankhead, and several other past or future major leaguers from the Brooklyn Dodgers' talent-laden minor league system had contributed to Nashua's success, and baseball fans in southern New Hampshire had little reason to believe that the team's fortunes would change in the coming season. However, 1949 was a disastrous year for minor league baseball in Nashua, whose Dodgers missed the playoffs for the only time in team history. The season proved to be the last for the New England League, and professional baseball has never been strong in Nashua or many of the league's other cities since.

The fall of Nashua as a baseball city coincides with the final demise of the New England League. The 1946 Dodgers are the best-known of Nashua's minor league teams, being one of the earliest professional clubs to integrate its roster. The team included future Brooklyn players Roy Campanella and Don Newcombe, as well as player-manager Walter Alston and general manager and future major league executive Buzzie Bavasi. Nashua developed a rivalry with both its closest neighbor, the Manchester (NH) Giants, and with the team it defeated in the 1946 championship, the Lynn (MA) Red Sox.

Nashua's success continued in each of the next two seasons. In 1947, Manager John Dantonio led the Dodgers to a second-place finish and a defeat of Manchester in the championship. Among the future major-league players on the roster that season were pitchers Newcombe (19-6, 2.91), James Romano (12-8, 3.23), and Bob Milliken (11-6, 2.70). In 1948, Manager Al Campanis, supported by the pitching of Dan Bankhead (20-6, 2.35 ERA, 243 strikeouts in 203 innings), led Nashua to another second-place finish and league title.

At the midway point of the 1949 season, Nashua found itself in first place. However, half of the league folded between late June and late July, and the Dodgers themselves seemed to collapse and lose interest in the race in mid-July. Relying mainly upon reports from the 1949 Nashua *Telegraph*, this article recounts the last season of the Nashua Dodgers and some of the factors leading to the demise of minor league baseball in much of New England.

Outlook Isn't Brilliant?—Hopes were high for the Nashua Dodgers in April, 1949. In spite of the fact that five ex-Nashuans were embroiled in contract disputes, the "Gate City Bums" were greeted on April 12 with the news that Brooklyn would assign $25,000 pitching prospect Billy Loes to Nashua. Loes, a native of Astoria, New York, had pitched six no-hitters in high school, five in his senior year. Other players expected to impact the ball club were first baseman Wayne Belardi, who was touted as another DiMaggio (presumably Joe) by the Nashua *Telegraph*, pitcher Marion

Scott Roper grew up watching the Nashua Pirates and Angels. He is a Ph.D. student in geography at the University of Kansas.

Fricano, and outfielder Gino Cimoli. Manager Greg Mulleavy seemed cautiously optimistic about the team's chances for the season, but management was optimistic enough to option a young player named Tom Lasorda to Greenville of the Sally League.

Three other teams promised to challenge the Dodgers for league supremacy. The Portland (ME) Pilots had placed third in 1948, losing to Lynn in the playoffs. The club, which was saved from bankruptcy in 1946, had gained the support of the Philadelphia Phillies and finished third in 1948, leading the league with an attendance of 117,606 people despite its ranking as the league's second-smallest market with a population of 73,643. The Pawtucket (RI) Slaters, under a working agreement with the Boston Braves, finished fourth in three straight seasons, making the playoffs in each of those years. The Slaters set the league's attendance mark in 1946, attracting 135,384 people. Finally, the Springfield (MA) Cubs, which in 1948 had finally found a receptive home after two disastrous seasons in the Massachusetts mill cities of Lawrence and Lowell, promised to be competitive with its infusion of new talent from the Chicago Cubs. Chicago had "liquidated" all but one of its Class B minor league teams, according to the *Telegraph*, so all of its "B" talent was concentrated at Springfield.

Elsewhere in the league, problems began to surface. In Manchester, according to columnist Leo Cloutier of the Manchester *Union Leader*, the Giants had lost $16,500 in 1948. When the New York Giants did not renew their working agreement with the farm club, Manchester obtained an agreement with New York's American League team and changed its name to the Manchester Yankees. Still, Manchester was left with an outstanding $3,000 debt, and the parent club was left to pay for the team's transport from Florida to New Hampshire after spring training. Lynn, too, found itself without a major league sponsor when the Boston Red Sox withdrew their support for a team which, in spite of a first-place finish in 1948, had drawn only 49,088 fans—sixth best in the eight-team league. Without Boston's minor league players, the club changed its name to the Lynn Tigers, although prospects for a successful season were dim at best. The two teams with worse 1948 attendance figures than Lynn, the Fall River (MA) Indians and the Providence (RI) Grays (which changed their name from the Providence Chiefs before the 1949 season), continued to operate without the support of major league clubs, and the Grays had to play in Cranston, Rhode Island, for lack of an acceptable stadium in Providence.

In order to boost interest in the circuit, representatives of the New England League voted to increase the prize money for the pennant-winning team from $1,000 to $2,000, and voted to give the first two runners-up $900 and $600, respectively. The distribution of playoff money also would change, so that the winner of the Governor's Cup would receive a flat $1500 (rather than 60 percent of the gate receipts, as had been the custom between 1946 and 1948). The championship runners-up receive nothing. In raising ticket prices by one cent, the eight New England League teams were expected to contribute $4,000 toward the prize money fund, and the league itself was to chip in the remaining $1,000.

For the 1949 season, ticket prices in Nashua remained at 80 cents per adult, 30 cents per child. For each adult ticket sold, Nashua made 52 cents; 10 cents went to the visiting team, five cents to the New England League, and 13 cents to the Federal government. However, wishing to improve upon the club's mediocre attendance of 1948 (63,382, third highest in the league), the club also began to offer 10-game and five-game books of tickets for $7.25 and $3.65, respectively, a move that promised to net Nashua 10 cents less per ticket. This move may have doomed the Dodgers from the start, as at regular rates the club needed to attract 138,000 paid admissions to meet normal operating expenses. The best the team had drawn up to that point was 70,813 in 1947.

Under these conditions, the defending Governor's Cup champions arrived in the Gate City on April 23. Upon seeing Nashua's Holman Stadium, Greg Mulleavy was reported to have said, "Boy...you don't find ball parks like this in the South, even in the highest classifications." The stadium had been re-sodded and the scoreboard had been repaired for the coming season, and workers were waiting for Mulleavy's instructions on where to erect the fences. The manager must have requested that they be placed at quite a distance from home plate, for only Wayne Belardi (with his team-leading 14 round-trippers in 69 games) hit more than three home runs for Nashua that year. Mulleavy centered his team's offense around baserunning: the Dodgers led the league with 142 stolen bases in 123 games, and seven players finished the year with 10 or more steals.

The Fall of the Grays—After exhibitions with Pawtucket, Manchester, and the semipro New England Hoboes, the Dodgers opened their season on April 30 by defeating Lynn, 7-2 behind the pitching of Loes and the hitting of Belardi and Cimoli. Opening ceremonies foreshadowed the catastrophic season: the high school band never arrived at the game as it was supposed to, and 12-year-old Jimmy Hogan—who was crowned Nashua's "King of Fans" before the game—arrived late. The following day, the club traveled to Lynn's Fraser Field and again beat the Tigers, 6-1 behind Marion Fricano's pitching.

Nashua won four of its first five games, with Loes finally losing in Springfield on May 5. Then on May 6, the Nashua *Telegraph* ran a headline reading Dodger Pennant Hopes Hit By Vet-Player Increase. In 1948, the league rules specified that no team could employ at any time more than six players with three or more years of professional experience. However, the number of available professional players had decreased from a 1946 high. As a result, over the objections of Nashua, Portland, and Pawtucket, the New England League voted to allow clubs to include 10 three-year veterans on minor league rosters. Obviously, the move was intended to strengthen the rosters of the league's weaker teams, particularly since teams had to pare their rosters to 17 players before the end of May. Nevertheless, the Dodgers maintained their winning pace, winning 20 of their first 27 games and holding a three-game lead over Pawtucket on June 1.

Nashua's early fortunes resulted in part from the remarkable accomplishments of Billy Loes and Wayne Belardi. On May 30, 18-year-old Belardi hit the "longest home run...that Holman Stadium has ever seen." Two nights later, Belardi hit his seventh home run while Billy Loes pitched his first professional no-hitter, striking out 13 and walking three in defeating Fall River. The no-hitter was not the first in Nashua; Pete Giordano had pitched one in 1948, and Dan Bankhead pitched two that same season. Still, Loes was only 19 at the time, and his success led many to believe— correctly—that he would be in Brooklyn in 1950.

National Baseball Library, Cooperstown, NY

Billy Loes

However, more signs of trouble arose in the league. On May 24 the Lynn Tigers announced that the club might move to Lewiston-Auburn, Maine. Lynn was "hopelessly" mired in last place, allegedly attracted the fewest fans per game in the league, and the ownership felt that the club would benefit from a move to Maine. The Tigers ultimately remained in Lynn, promising to move to Lewiston-Auburn in 1950.

Then on June 2 the Providence Grays became wards of the league when the club's owners failed to meet its expenses due to poor fan support. The league refused to allow the Grays to play its games in Cranston, forcing the Grays and Slaters to share McCoy Stadium in Pawtucket. Soon after, Grays manager Frank Pytlak requested his release. Finally, when neither the St. Louis Browns nor the Cleveland Indians could be convinced to back the team, the league turned to the Philadelphia Athletics for support. The Athletics would not back the team unless the Grays could find a home within the Providence city limits, and the Grays folded on June 21.

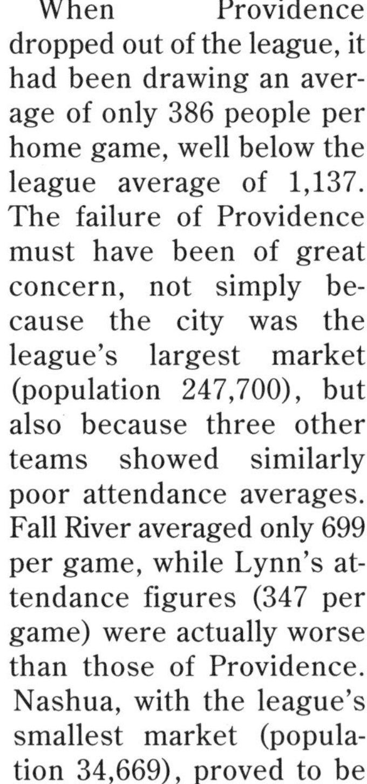

When Providence dropped out of the league, it had been drawing an average of only 386 people per home game, well below the league average of 1,137. The failure of Providence must have been of great concern, not simply because the city was the league's largest market (population 247,700), but also because three other teams showed similarly poor attendance averages. Fall River averaged only 699 per game, while Lynn's attendance figures (347 per game) were actually worse than those of Providence. Nashua, with the league's smallest market (population 34,669), proved to be the weakest major league-affiliated team, averaging only 891 people per game in spite of its competitive play during the course of the season. In fact, fourth-place Springfield (2,185 per game), third-place Portland (1,859 per game), sixth-place Manchester (1,292 per game), and first-place Pawtucket (1,187 per game) ranked ahead of Nashua, and Nashua had only one day earlier fallen behind the Slaters in the standings.

Bad News Comes in Threes—The decline of Providence and the vulnerability of the other teams forced New England League executives to consider emergency measures. In early July, Nashua business manager Bill Eberly presented a revised New England League schedule for the league's approval. The schedule would have divided the season into two halves, with the first-place team as of July 8 to be the first-half champion. The league would be reduced to six teams for the remainder of the year, with floundering Fall River—a club that had never made a profit in its three-plus years of existence—being asked to drop out of the circuit. Fall River and Providence were to be replaced by two new cities in 1950. Eberly's plan was not put into force, however, when Fall River appeared to find the backing of two unnamed major-league teams.

Rumors about the league's demise surfaced in the Nashua *Telegraph* on July 5, when columnist Frank Stawasz questioned whether the league would exist in 1950. He referred to the financial problems of Fall River, Lynn, and Nashua, and noted that even in the major leagues, attendance figures for July 4 doubleheaders had declined by five percent from 1948. Less than 10 days later, *The Sporting News* speculated that the New England League might merge with the Colonial League in 1950 to create a circuit consisting of Nashua, Manchester, Portland, Springfield, Pawtucket, and Fall River, as well as Bristol, Bridgeport, and Waterbury, Connecticut.

Despite Nashua's place at the head of the standings, Branch Rickey and the Brooklyn Dodgers seemed to prepare for the worst by sending three of the club's best players (all future major leaguers) to other leagues. On July 5, the club promoted Gino Cimoli, who led the team with a .370 batting average, to Montreal of the International League. Then on July 10, Billy Loes moved up to Fort Worth of the Texas League on the strength of his strong pitching record (11-3, 2.80 ERA, with a team-leading 95 strikeouts and four shutouts). The following day, power-hitting first baseman Wayne Belardi (.307 batting average, team-leading 14 home runs) was promoted to Greenville.

Then on July 14 came the news that three more of the league's teams planned to fold. Two of them surprised no one; neither Lynn nor Fall River were making any money. The third team, however, shocked everyone: the Manchester Yankees were considering dropping out of the league. The *Telegraph* claimed that Manchester was only twenty dollars in the red, and that the owners only wished to cease operations before the club—which was mired in the second division—lost thousands of dollars from lack of fan interest. Nashua itself had lost an amount of money "comparable" to that lost by the three financially unstable teams, but because of Brooklyn's support was able to continue its operations.

Columnists for the Nashua *Telegraph* and the Manchester *Union Leader* blamed their teams' financial problems on a recession in southern New Hampshire. "It's only now that jobs are beginning to pick up hereabouts," wrote one *Telegraph* reporter. In the *Union Leader*, Leo Cloutier wrote of the Yankees' 78-cent admission, "It must be remembered that this is a mill town and there aren't too many people who could afford to dish out that kind of cold cash three or four times a week." Other reasons listed for the Yankees' problems included the outstanding debt of $3,000 left by the 1948 Giants; the team's low position in the standings; the failure of the New York Yankees to bolster Manchester's roster with stronger players; the proximity of Boston's Braves and Red Sox to southern New Hampshire; and the competition added by the new medium of television, especially on nights when Red Sox and Braves games were broadcast.

On July 15, the New England League announced that it would continue as a seven-team league despite the problems of Manchester, Fall River, and Lynn. Such plans disintegrated three days later, when the three teams officially dropped out of the league. Combined with the withdrawal of Providence in June, this move stripped the league of four of its five largest markets. Apparently, the Brooklyn Dodgers considered disbanding its Nashua team as well, but then decided to field a team in southern New Hampshire "to give Nashua fans a final chance to show whether they are willing to support a Class B team in minor league baseball or not even though the losses for the first half of the season have been rather commanding." In a statement that now sounds ironic, considering the Dodgers' move to Los Angeles less than a decade later, Brooklyn management said it felt that it "owed an obligation to Nashua people to operate here for this year and to find out whether or not local citizens definitely wanted a team in organized baseball next year."

Memories of the Fall—Nashua had placed first in the first half of the season, but the team still had not won the pennant, nor had it guaranteed itself a playoff spot. The team with the best combined record overall would win the pennant; instead of awarding that team $2,000, the league voted to award the pennant winners $3,000. The last-place team in the second half of the season would be eliminated from the playoffs.

Nashua and Pawtucket started the second half of the season by winning two of their first three games, but then the Dodgers went into a tailspin from which the club never recovered. On August 2, Nashua had fallen to fourth place with a 4-8 record, 5 games behind the Slaters. Eight days later, the team had fallen to 6-13, 7-1/2 games back and fading fast. The team simply could not find suitable replacements for Cimoli, Loes, or Belardi. During the course of the summer the team signed several young players, but none could pull the Dodgers out of their descent.

The demise of four teams and steady fall of Nashua greatly affected the league's outlook. On July 25, as if evacuating a sinking ship, the Boston Braves promoted Slaters manager Earl Browne to Denver of the Western League in spite of the fact that his team was in the midst of a pennant chase, and two days later promoted Pawtucket's Joe Reardon to a team in the Three-I League. By the start of August, the Dodgers had transferred Marion Fricano to Pueblo of the Western

League. Fricano, who boasted an 11-3 record, had been leading the team with a 1.48 earned run average and 12 complete games in 17 starts; his departure stripped Nashua of its remaining dominant pitcher. As attendance continued at its lackluster pace, Nashua business manager Bill Eberly desperately attempted to fill the stands by reducing the cost of admission to 65 cents, but to break even the club needed to attract about 122,000 people in the remaining weeks of the season. Eberly's attempt was not enough. Nashua's final attendance was 38,979, down from 63,382 in 1948 and far below the club's regular-season mark of 70,813, set in 1947. The average attendance of 684 per game ranked fifth in the league, besting only Fall River, Providence, and Lynn; the mean was only slightly more than half of the 1948 average.

The remainder of Nashua's season saw no improvement in play; in early August, for example, the Dodgers lost an exhibition game to the semipro Keene (NH) Bluejays. Still, entering the last series of the season against Springfield, Nashua found itself only two games behind the third-place Cubs. Nashua dropped all three of its remaining games and missed the playoffs due to its second-half fourth-place finish. In the first round of the playoffs, Pawtucket lost its three-game series to third-place Springfield. Second-place Portland then defeated the Cubs in seven games, giving the Pilots the league's final Governor's Cup.

On September 7, 1949, the *Telegraph*'s Frank Stawasz penned wrote an article which amounted to an obituary for the Dodgers and the entire New England League. Stawasz wrote:

> Slightly more than 600 paid admission watched the Dodgers die...Yup, brother, that was the end of our New England league Dodgers. It wasn't the Cubs who proved to be fatal to the Dodgers but a slow strangulation at the turnstiles which also had a far reaching effect over the rest of the league as well, with the exception of the Springfield Cubs.

As expected, the New England League did not resurface in 1950. The Springfield Cubs, whose 102,387 attendance led the league in 1949, joined the International League in 1950. Pawtucket remained without a professional team for 16 seasons until an Eastern League franchise moved to McCoy Stadium in 1966. (Since 1973 it has been home to the Boston's International League club.) The New York Yankees finally placed an Eastern League team in Manchester's Gill Stadium again in 1969, but the club moved after three unsuccessful seasons. Providence has not been home to any minor league teams since 1949, and the city of Portland finally gained the Eastern League Sea Dogs in 1994 after a 45-year absence of baseball within city limits. Lynn eventually attained a team in 1980, but the club moved to Nashua after the 1983 season. Nashua's Holman Stadium has been home to two Eastern League teams since 1949: the Angels in 1983, and the Pirates between 1984 and 1986. Thanks in part to Nashua's recently developed geographical role as both a Boston commuter city and a tax-free shopping haven for Massachusetts residents, the second-division Angels were able to draw almost 140,000 fans to Holman Stadium in 1983, although the pathetic Pirates drew only about half of that number in their last two years. Holman Stadium still stands, and both the Nashua *Telegraph* and Manchester's *Union Leader* still occasionally print favorable reminiscences of the Dodgers, New Hampshire's most successful professional baseball team.

In his September 7 "eulogy," Stawasz reminisced about some of the memorable people and events that Nashuans had seen over the last four years, from Walter Alston ending his playing career due to injury against the Manchester Giants to the fabled exploits of some of the team's best-known players and executives, such as "Harvey Porter, loved by all Dodger fans, who used to daydream in his right field slot as an occasional ball whistled by him." Stawasz promised to cherish the memories that the Dodgers had provided:

> All this, in four fleeting moments of baseball history, was ours. It came to us after a long sleep, as we shall sleep again baseballwise, perhaps forever. Actually New England league baseball was not new to us when it came here in 1946. We'd had it before...That too, died and withered away. But the memory of it, old timers tell me, lingers on. The memories of four better than average Dodger sponsored Nashua New England league teams will stick with us and there may come a day when the national pastime, with all the fixings, will return here again.

Sources

The Baseball Encyclopedia, eighth edition. New York:Macmillan Publishing Company, 1990.

Peter Filichia. *Professional Baseball Franchises*. New York: Facts on File,1993.

Lloyd Johnson and Miles Wolff, editors. *The Encyclopedia of Minor League Baseball*. Durham, NC: Baseball America Inc., 1993.

Manchester (NH) *Union Leader*, July 5-July 20, 1949.

Nashua (NH) *Telegraph*, April 1-September 10, 1949.

Spink, J.G. Taylor; Ernest J. Lanigan; Paul A. Rickart; and Clifford Kachline. *The Spink Baseball Guide*. St. Louis: Charles G. Spink and Son, 1947-1950.

United States Bureau of the Census. *Statistical Abstract of the United States*: 1951 (72nd edition). Washington, D.C.: U.S. Government Printing Office, 1951.

(All quotes, unless otherwise stated, are from 1949 issues of the Nashua *Telegraph*.)

Eppa Rixey

David Driver

The state of Virginia has produced eight U.S. presidents, a ton of tobacco, and is home to thousands of Federal workers and installations. But when it comes to baseball Hall of Famers, the Old Dominion is not so generous. Its neighbor to the north, Maryland, has sent native sons Frank Baker, Lefty Grove, Jimmy Foxx, Babe Ruth, Judy Johnson, and Al Kaline to Cooperstown. North Carolina, due south, was home to greats Luke Appling, Rick Ferrell, Hoyt Wilhelm, Enos Slaughter, Catfish Hunter and Gaylord Perry. Not bad for a "basketball" state. Virginia? One of its three natives who made to the Hall of Fame is an overlooked left-hander who pitched 21 seasons, mostly for second-division clubs. (Negro Leaguers Ray Dandridge and Leon Day are the others.)

Eppa Rixey, whose career stretched from 1912-33, was the winningest left-hander in National League history until Warren Spahn came along and broke his mark in 1959. The man known to many fans as Eppa (Jephtha) Rixey was 266-251 with the Philadelphia Phillies and Cincinnati Reds. No lefty ever lost more. (The "Jephtha" was hung on him by Cincinnati sportswriter William Phelon, who reasoned that it made as much sense as the name Eppa.

The Culpeper native, who attended the University of Virginia, is the only former player from a current Atlantic Coast Conference schools (Duke, North Carolina, North Carolina State, Wake Forest, Clemson, Georgia Tech, Florida State, Maryland and Virginia) who is in the Baseball Hall of Fame.

Until Day recently and unhappily matched him, Rixey, born May 3, 1891, claimed another distinction. He was the only player honored in Cooperstown who passed away in the time between his election and his induction, according to Jack Lang, executive secretary of the Baseball Writer's Association of America, and vice president Bill Guilfoile of the Hall of Fame.

The pitcher was elected Jan. 27, 1963, three decades after his career had ended. An Associated Press photograph that ran the next day shows Rixey, who at time was a successful insurance executive, taking the obligatory phone call of congratulations from then National League president Warren Giles.

Rixey died a month later, Feb. 28, in a suburb of Cincinnati. The Hall of Fame ceremonies were Aug. 5 that year, and the pitcher with the herky-jerky motion who never walked more than 74 batters in a season was enshrined posthumously.

A Virginia thoroughbred—The Virginian, who was traded to the Reds prior to the 1921 season, was an intense competitor who hated to lose, according to one of his former catchers.

"He was one of a kind. He would break chairs in the clubhouse after he lost, and you wouldn't see him for a few days," Clyde Sukeforth, who played with Rixey on the Reds from 1926-31, said last year from his home in Maine.

Sukeforth, who turned 93 on Nov. 30, 1994, helped bring Jackie Robinson to the Brooklyn Dodgers and managed that team for two games in 1947. Like Rixey, he was nearing the end of his full-time playing career

David Driver is a sportswriter living in Hyattsville, Md. He played baseball at Turner Ashby High in Dayton, Va., a school that has produced one major leaguer: catcher Alan Knicely (1979-1986).

with the Reds in the early 1930s, though he did play in 18 games with the Dodgers in 1945 after an 11-year lull.

"He had a good assortment of pitches," said Sukeforth. "Like all good pitchers he had good control."

Despite his penchant for outbursts, Rixey was well-liked on the team and mingled well on the train during road trips, said Sukeforth.

"He was Virginia thoroughbred," said the former catcher. "He had been around a lot, so he had lost most of his (southern) accent" by late in his career.

In 1909, at the age of 18, Rixey entered the University of Virginia in Charlottesville, a town about 30 miles south of Culpeper. His family had moved there from Culpeper when he was 10. By his third year at UVa, 1911-12, the school yearbook listed his feats: member of the baseball and basketball teams and the singles champion in tennis. Of course, he pitched for the baseball team.

Rixey received a B.S.in 1912, and a M.A. in chemistry in 1914. In college the big (6-foot-5, 210-pound) pitcher played for Charles (Cy) Rigler, who was a National League umpire. After Rigler helped Rixey get signed by the Phils for $2,000, the National League prohibited umpires from serving as liaisons for other teams.

National Baseball Library, Cooperstown, NY

Eppa Rixey in his early years with the Phillies.

Rough start, rough Series—Rixey began his big league career with the Phillies and teammate Grover Cleveland Alexander in 1912, going 10-10, 2.50 in 20 starts and three relief outings for a team that placed fifth. The next year Alexander went 22-8, then 27-15 in 1914 and 31-10 in 1915. Rixey went 9-5 in 1913 and slumped to 2-11 in 1914.

After placing sixth in 1914, the Phils fired manager Red Dooin. He was replaced by Pat Moran, who became a supporter of Rixey on and off the mound.

The Phillies won the NL title in 1915, which would give Rixey (11-12 that year with 22 starts and a 2.39 ERA) his only World Series appearance in 21 big league seasons. In game five against the Boston Red Sox in Philadelphia on Oct. 13, with his team one loss away from elimination, Rixey came on in the third inning in relief of starter Erskine Mayer, who had won 21 games in the regular season.

The Phils went ahead 4-2 with two runs in the bottom of the fouth, and Rixey kept the Red Sox scoreless in the fourth, fifth, six and seventh. But Boston outfielder Duffy Lewis hit a two-run homer off Rixey in the top of the eighth to tie the game at 4. Lewis had hit just two homers in 557 at bats that year.

In the top of the ninth, Red Sox outfielder Harry Hooper hit his second homer of the game, which like his first bounced into the center-field stands (there was no ground-rule double at the time). Boston starter Rube Foster held the Phils in the bottom of the ninth for a 5-4 win and the Series title. Rixey was the loser in his only Series showing.

In 1916 Rixey went 22-10, 1.85, but was overshadowed by Alexander at 33-12. Rixey, the control pitcher, had a career-high 134 strikeouts and 74 walks that year, one of only three times he went over the century mark in whiffs.

In 1917 (at 16-21) and 1920 (at 11-22) Rixey led the National League in losses, an ironic twist for someone who would win more than 250 games.

In 1918, during World War I, Rixey was a first lieutenant in the Army's Chemical Warfare Branch. He didn't get out until May 1919, and was late for the start of the season. The Phils placed last, and Rixey went 6-12.

The Phils would finish last for the second straight year in 1920, though they were kept loose by the antics of a 30-year-old outfielder named Casey Stengel. Rixey struggled, and Philadelphia owner William Baker was losing patience with the Virginian.

Prior to the next season, Rixey was traded to the Reds for pitcher Jimmy Ring and outfielder Greasy Neale. Also in the off-season the Reds acquired pitcher Rube Marquard in a trade from Brooklyn. Rube went 17-14 in his only year with the Reds, but Cincinnati finished in sixth place.

Rixey went 19-18 in his first year in Cincinnati under manager Pat Moran, who had left the Phils while Rixey was overseas. The next season, 1922, he had the best year of his career. He was 25-13 to lead the league in wins for the only time, and he also paced the National League in games started (38) and innings pitched (313.1)—the second of three straight seasons over 300 innings and second of 10 consecutive over 200. The Reds were second, seven games behind John McGraw and the New York Giants.

Some bad clubs—In 1923, the Reds would have three 20-game winners: Dolf Luque (27-8), Rixey (20-15) and Pete Donohue (21-15). But they would finish second in the National League again, 4-1/2 games back of the Giants.

Rixey's salary in 1924 was $12,000, second on the team. He was 15-14 that year, and a few weeks after the season he married Dorothy Meyers of nearby Terrace Park, O. They would have two children: Eppa Rixey III, born a year later, and a daughter, Ann Chase, born in 1929.

In 1925, Rixey had the last of four 20-win seasons. He was 21-11, and for the third year in a row was among the top three in ERA in the league. In 1926 the Reds, with a first baseman named Wally Pipp acquired from the Yankees, finished second. It would be the last time in Rixey's career that his team would finish in the first division.

In 1928, he was 19-18. He hit his third and last career home run in the first series of the year against the Braves in Boston into the "Jury Box," which had been set up to make it easier for lefties to hit homers. Rixey, a right-handed hitter and lifetime .191 hitter, was the third Reds hurler in as many days to reach the short porch. After eight straight winning seasons, Rixey was 10-13 in 1929. He was 9-13 in 1930.

The Reds placed last in 1931 and 1932 (Rixey was a combined 9-12), and placing out of the money would become a Rixey trademark. He played on five last-place clubs, including the last three seasons of his career with the Reds. In 13 of his 21 seasons, his team was fifth or lower.

While his career winning percentage was just .515, the success rate of the teams he played on was even worse—.489 (1,563-1,635).

Despite the lack of support, Rixey kept his competitive fire to the very end of his playing days. Even in his last season, when he went 6-3 in 1933, he accused manager Donie Bush of only pitching him against the Pirates, whom he did well against. Pittsburgh was second that year, five games back of the New York Giants.

After the 1933 season Rixey complained to new general manager Larry MacPhail about Bush. MacPhail said he couldn't help Rixey, so the pitcher retired and built up his insurance business into an area leader in Cincinnati. Spahn, 26 years later, passed Rixey's win total, the most of any National League left-hander. "I'm glad Warren did it," Rixey said at the time. "If he hadn't broken my record, no one would have known I'd set it."

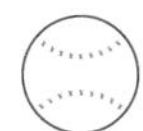

VIRGINIA LOSES IN NINTH

Pitcher Rixey Weakens and Princeton Pulls Out Unexpected Victory

Special to The New York Times

CHARLOTTESVILLE, Va., April 5.— Princeton defeated Virginia to-day, 6 to 3. Up to the ninth inning it was the prettiest game ever witnessed on Lambeth Field. Only two scratch hits, both made by Pendleton, had been made off Rixey up to the last half of the ninth, and it looked like Virginia's game. In this disastrous session, with the score Virginia, 3, Princeton, 2, and Pendleton, the first man up, the Southerners were a bit nervous, but when Rixey struck out the star shortstop, every one thought the game safe. Rixey passed the second man, and the next two got singles, filling the bases. He fanned Reed, but passed Berger, forcing in the tying run. Parker tripled and won the game.

—A.D. Suehsdorf

Adding a wild card

Hal Chase in Victoria

Geoff LaCasse

"Away hence in the dim futurity, say about in 1954, when Chase shall have earned the repose which comes to septuagenarians, he will often close his eyes and lapse into a day-dream of the glory galore which came to him in the days when he was a sun among lesser orbs on the field of play. To the grandchildren...who will cluster around his knees and hang on his shoulder, he will recite his marvelous feats on the diamond and arouse their speechless wonderment."[1]

The Chase in this quotation is Hal Chase—Highlanders–Yankees, White Sox, Buffalo Feds, Reds, and Giants—now loathed as much for his crooked baseball ways as he was revered in contemporary publications for his on-field abilities. The quotation, however, is not taken from any of those great cities, but 3,000 miles away on the west coast of Canada, from the small center of Victoria, British Columbia, where Chase played for the local baseball team. It is dated July 12, 1903. Chase's appearance in a Victoria uniform in 1903 was the result of an unlikely set of circumstances perhaps fitting in light of his later career.

This article has its origin in a couple of vague references to Chase in the local newspapers,[2] and a crumbling, yellowed poster dated 1904/05 of the Victoria Amity, a very good semiprofessional team based out of Victoria. The poster included a Hal Chase as a member of the team. A quick examination of the Victoria newspapers—they continued to follow his career long after he left the city—confirmed the Chase in the poster was the same Hal Chase of major league fame. The 1904/05 date (when Chase was in New York) on the poster was probably a marketing ploy for an important upcoming game.

Competition—How and why had Chase ended up in Victoria? Although the city was important in British Columbia and boasted a good semiprofessional team, Chase grew up 700 miles and several days' journey away, just south of San Francisco, near bigger cities, better climate, and a better class of baseball. Part of the answer lies in the nature and history of baseball in British Columbia.

Although the first recorded game occurred in New Westminster in 1862, Victoria teams, and the Amity in particular, would dominate Pacific Northwest competition over the next four decades. In British Columbia, between 1866 and 1901, only Kamloops in 1889 and Nanaimo in 1895 broke its string of (unofficial) provincial championships, and neither was a consistent challenger.

It took a newcomer to loosen Victoria's hold on the baseball crown. Vancouver was an insignificant settlement until it was selected as the western terminus of the Canadian Pacific Railway in 1885. From a population of 300 at incorporation in 1886, Vancouver fifteen years later had grown to 26,000, surpassing Victoria as the province's largest and most important commercial center. By 1901 its team, the Terminals, was also seriously challenging the Amity for provincial dominance.

Their rivalry pushed competition to greater heights

Geoff LaCasse is a computer consultant in Coquitlam, British Columbia and is currently researching baseball in British Columbia.

and, as a first step, led to the reformation of the BC Amateur Base Ball League in 1901 (which also included New Westminster and Nanaimo), based on a similar organization which had existed between 1890 and 1895, and briefly in 1898. After Vancouver won the first two championships with 6-0 and 5-1 records, the Amity were determined to do better in 1903.

Victoria had always had a pool of talented athletes to draw on, an important reasons for its successes over the years. Unfortunately, by 1903 this pool was becoming increasingly inadequate compared to the faster paced and stronger rosters elsewhere. In Victoria, locals did not play baseball as a vocation but in seasonal rotation with other sports. Baseball, in fact, ranked behind cricket, soccer, rugby, lacrosse, rowing, and possibly basketball and ice hockey in popularity, and it was becoming more and more difficult to get the best athletes and paying spectators to come out to the parks.

The search for talent— Victoria, instead, was forced to import talent to compete more effectively with rival Vancouver. This was not a new practice. Many teams in the 1880s and 1890s had attracted players with sinecure positions with the Canadian Pacific Railway (CPR) or other local businesses.[3] The flagrant excesses had, in fact, been partly responsible for the low public opinion of baseball during the 1890s. The practice had declined precipitously by 1901, killed off by the growth of fully professional baseball elsewhere, a consequent demand for players, and a rise in their wages. Victoria naturally looked south for additional players.

American baseball influence in Victoria was pervasive. San Francisco residents introduced baseball to British Columbia during the Fraser River Gold Rush of 1858-65. The sport received another boost between 1881 and 1887, when American railway workers fresh from the Colorado rail boom flooded the province during the building of the CPR. The game was revitalized in 1898, when thousands more passed through on their way to the Klondike Gold Rush. In fact, the long-term popularity of the sport in Victoria, despite the city's British origins, came from its large American population (20 percent), a residue of the 1858-65 period. Victoria, in fact, had developed a natural north-south rivalry, dating back to the 1860s and the days of sailing ships.

In Victoria, with scouting still in its infancy, recruiting players was generally by word of mouth or game experience. Once contacted, player signings took two forms: limited engagements and seasonal contracts. Seasonal contracts were more common among BC teams, although Vancouver did sign outstanding minor league pitcher Jesse Stovall for an important June, 1903, game against Victoria.

Victoria, like other Northwestern teams, generally tried to strengthen its roster at two positions: pitcher and catcher. The reasons are not hard to understand. Contemporary box scores show the better pitchers were dominant, striking out 15-20 batters per game. The 1902 Victoria team was fortunate in having an outstanding local pitcher, Jimmy Holness, but he was the exception (and left in mid-1903 to play in the Class C Pacific National League and then on to the Pacific Coast League). The catcher was the key to the infield defense. By 1903, this pitcher/catcher dominance was no longer paramount, but was still important. The Hal Chase signing, perhaps not surprisingly, given the unpredictability of his later career, fell into none of these categories. He was signed neither by word of mouth or game experience, nor as pitcher or catcher.

Young Hal—In early 1903, Chase was 20 years old, a second-year student, second baseman and pitcher at Santa Clara College, located just outside his home town of San Jose. Over the coming summer break he and teammate Elmer Emerson were planning to visit Emerson's relatives in Victoria, and then tour the province. Emerson had been in Victoria at least once before, as a pitcher for the Stanford alumni team against Victoria in June, 1902. By some process, his latest trip became known to the Victoria club management[4] and he was induced to play for the Amity.[5] He, in turn, may have convinced Chase to stay in Victoria and play for the team.

Chase's planned tour suggests he had not expected to play ball that year. Did he play with Victoria because it was amateur and would not harm his college standing? This is possible, because he turned down offers from professional teams during this period, but we are not sure Victoria was truly amateur. Did he like being a big man on a little team? Our sources give no indication. Was he a young kid with time on his hands and no sense of his future? It's impossible to say at present.

Whatever his reasons, Chase appeared at a pivotal moment, with Victoria baseball in transition from its outstanding amateur tradition to a more modern and businesslike game. His impact was immediate and dramatic. In 1902 Victoria had gone 16-14 in league and exhibition play with essentially the same team, and was not able to compete on even terms with Vancouver, much less the better touring teams. In 1903, with the addition of Chase (and Emerson), Victoria's record improved to 21-8-1 and attendance was excellent, averaging perhaps 1,000 per game.

Chase was arguably the most important factor in the team's success on and off the field. He began the year at third base, with an occasional stint at first base, was moved to catcher after an injury to Victoria's regular receiver, played another in left field, and pitched and won one game. In the 29 games with box scores, he hit .353 (42 for 119), slugged .563, scored 29 runs, hit doubles and triples, was the team's only home run threat (with three), and stole a lot of bases, although these weren't tracked in the press. His defense at third was not very good (seven errors in 24 chances), but he was phenomenal at catcher (177 chances, five errors, two passed balls), and he was considered an outstanding outfielder.

Although Emerson also had a superb season (he pitched a no-hitter and struck out 19 and 18 batters in two games), Chase was the new media star, so highly praised Victorians almost forgot about local hero Bernie Schwengers, out most of 1903 with a knee injury. Unfortunately, the contemporary newspaper accounts are directed solely at Chase the player. They give us no insight into Chase the person, as he was or would become. The only breath of scandal is a brief editorial in one of the local newspapers after the last game of the season, in which the editor discusses a long-ago throwing of a game involving Victoria. It's an odd editorial which takes on added meaning in light of Chase's later career.

A one-year wonder—At the end of the 1903 season, the newspapers reported that Chase had agreed to return to Victoria for 1904. He reiterated this in a series of wires to the club the following March, but a short time later signed a contract with Los Angeles of the PCL. Chase tried to explain his position, but would not play in Victoria again.

Victoria survived his passing and had a good season. It recruited seriously, re-signing imports Emerson and Whalen, adding a couple of new players from California (one recommended by Chase), and signing ex-major leaguer George Treadway as coach and first baseman. In 1905 the team and Vancouver, together with Bellingham and Everett, were inaugural members of the Class B Northwestern League.

Unfortunately, the BC Amateur Base Ball League was a mid-1903 casualty of the changes in the game. The weaker teams, New Westminster and Nanaimo, refused to play against Victoria and an obviously professional Vancouver.

The circumstances which brought Hal Chase to Victoria in 1903 were not typical of the times. He was not a regular pitcher or catcher, Victoria management had not seen him play before, and he had no outstanding reputation as recommendation. Chase, in fact, proved to be a once-in-a-lifetime acquisition, and a harbinger of the coming changes to the game in Victoria: the greater professionalism, the higher quality, the commercial product.

Notes

1. Victoria *Daily Colonist*, Sunday, July 12, 1903.
2. While researching the history of the Vancouver Beavers of the Northwestern League (1905, 1907-17).
3. This was clearly the case with the interior railroad town of Donald in 1886-88, Kamloops in 1889, and Vancouver in 1890. Even the pure-white Amity had stooped to such activities in the early 1880s.
4. "...a new player from California, who has lately decided to make Victoria his home." *Colonist* February 4, 1903.
5. It may have even been known as early as February (*Colonist* March 22, 1903), although another account says he was induced to play when he arrived in early April (Victoria *Times* April 15, 1903).

The job's not done yet

More Negro Leaguers for the Hall

John B. Holway

Burly Mule Suttles of the old St. Louis Stars was one of the greatest sluggers in baseball history. He slammed more over the fence than any man in the old Negro Leagues, even more than the legendary Josh Gibson. Mule's longest blast reputedly traveled 600 feet in Havana.

Why isn't he in the Hall of Fame?

Big Bill Foster of the Chicago American Giants was probably the best black left-hander who ever lived. He won more games than anybody in the black leagues, including Satchel Paige.

Then why isn't he in Cooperstown?

Their absence is one of baseball's most glaring vestiges of racial discrimination,but that is changing at last.

John Holway

Mule Suttles. That's Quincy Troupe behind the plate.

This year, the 50th anniversary of Jackie Robinson's signing, the Hall has announced a plan to let in five more Negro Leaguers—one a year for the next five years. Five more nineteenth-century stars will be admitted under the same plan. This will be in addition to the two vets a year now elected by the panel, one of which may also be a Negro Leaguer. The first Negro Leaguer admitted under this new policy was Leon Day.

This is an excellent start in recognizing these black stars of baseball history.

An all-star team of nine was originally admitted in the 1970s by a special group headed by ex-Negro Leaguers Monte Irvin and Judy Johnson. The job was then given to the veterans' committee, which named two more Negro League players over the next 17 years.

Those still outside looking in have faced a second

John Holway is co-editor of the Baseball Encyclopeda*'s Negro League section.*

bias in addition to race—geography. Negro baseball was divided into two fiercely competitive leagues, East and West. To cut travel costs to New York, Irvin's panel was composed entirely of Easterners, who elected a heavily Eastern slate. Suttles, Bill Foster, and other great Westerners were left out.

Here are some of the great players waiting to be admitted.

George "Mule" Suttles—An Alabama coal miner, Suttles holds Negro League home run records for a single season and lifetime. When he swung, said one player, "you could feel the earth quake." No wonder fans chanted, "Kick, Mule!" when he came to bat.

Mule slugged big league pitchers for 11 homers in 79 at bats, which comes to 79 for 550 at bats. Said Boston Braves outfielder Wally Berger of one blow off Larry French: "I just looked up and waved." Leo Durocher's advice to another worried hurler: "Just pitch and pray."

Suttles' most famous home run came in the 1935 East-West, or All Star, game in Comiskey Park. In the 11th inning he had a pitcher "pinch-kneel" in the on-deck circle so they'd walk Josh Gibson. Then Mule strode to the plate and blasted one into the upper deck to win the game off Hall of Famer Martin Dihigo.

Bullet Joe Rogan—Only Babe Ruth ranks with this little (5'6") ex-Buffalo Soldier as a double-threat at bat and on the mound. Those who saw them both agree that Rogan was better than Paige, the man who replaced him as the Kansas City Monarchs' pitching ace.

John Holway

Bullet Joe Rogan

Bullet also batted cleanup, and when he wasn't pitching, played center field and second base. He led the Monarchs to pennants in 1923 and '24, hitting .400 both years and leading all pitchers in wins.

And we don't even have his best years. Rogan was 30 years old when Casey Stengel discovered him pitching for the U.S. cavalry in Arizona.

"Old Rogan was a showboat boy," the Cardinals star, Dizzy Dean, chuckled. "Never gave you a good ball to hit. Should be in the Hall of Fame." Stengel himself urged Bowie Kuhn to put Bullet in the Hall, but nothing came of it.

Willie "Devil" Wells—Suttles' sidekick, Wells, tied Mule's single-season home run record and is fifth life-time. Says former Cubs coach John "Buck" O'Neil: "Ozzie Smith could field with Wells—but he couldn't hit with him."

Like Lou Boudreau, Willie had a weak arm but compensated by playing the hitters. "If you saw me dive for a ball, you know I misjudged it," he said. When he threw the ball, "you could run alongside it," Buck Leonard laughed. But he just nipped the runner at first.

As a manager, Wells sent Monte Irvin, Larry Doby, and Don Newcombe to the majors. What if Willie had gone himself? In a 1929 series against a major league all-star team in Chicago, he tripled and stole home to win the first game, tripled and stole home twice in the second game, and got three more hits, including the winning RBI in game three.

Jud Wilson—The husky, foghorn-voiced Wilson was built like a wrestler and was so tough he fielded hard grounders with his chest. "He could go bear-huntin' with a switch," the players said. "Didn't need a gun."

Paige, who faced Ted Williams, called Wilson and Charlie "Chino" Smith the two best hitters he faced. (Smith died too early to be eligible for the Hall of Fame.) "Paige tried to blur that ball by you," Wilson laughed. "I timed his blinding stuff and just raked him for base hits."

One night wakened by his tipsy roommate, Jake Stephens, Jud sleepily hung Jake out the window by one foot, lazily changing hands in mid-air. The quickly sobered Stephens couldn't walk for two days—"my knees kept buckling."

Willard "Home Run" Brown—Monarch pitcher Hilton Smith, who played with them both, considered

John Holway

Turkey Stearnes

Brown better than Jackie Robinson. "He was a better hitter. He was faster. And Jackie had a poor arm; Willard had a real good arm. And power! That guy hit one of the longest home runs I've ever seen in Kansas City off Satchel Paige in 1937. It was around 440 feet to center field, and it was still going when it went over the fence."

Though Brown flunked his only big league test in 1947 at the age of 36, he had earlier hit white stars for a .375 average. In 1947 in Puerto Rico Brown smashed 27 home runs in only 115 at bats—that would equal 129 for 550 at bats. It's still the Puerto Rican record. The next highest, Reggie Jackson, hit 20.

Norman "Turkey" Stearnes—Weighing only 168 pounds, Stearnes choked up on a short, light bat and swung from one of the oddest stances ever seen—front heel in a hole, toe pointed up. "But he could get around on you," Paige winced.

On the great Chicago American Giants of the 1930s, Suttles hit cleanup, Wells batted third, and Stearnes led off. He was probably the best leadoff hitter in history, even better than Ricky Henderson. Among Negro Leaguers, Turkey ranks first in triples, second in homers and doubles, fifth in batting, and eighth in stolen bases. In 1932 he led the league in doubles, triples, homers, and steals.

Stearnes was handicapped by two huge home parks, Chicago and Hamtramck, or his totals would be even higher. And he was considered an excellent center fielder.

"If they don't put *him* in the Hall of Fame," Cool Papa Bell said, "they shouldn't put *anybody* in."

Cristobal Torriente—In a head-to-head game against Babe Ruth in Havana in 1920, Torriente blasted three home runs and a double, and U.S. papers hailed him as "the Babe Ruth of Cuba."

Torri wore a red bandanna at bat, shook the bracelets on his wrist, and grinned, "Me get 'em." From 1920-23 he hit .400 twice to lead the Giants to three pennants in four years. His stats would be higher, but he played in Chicago's old Southside Park, a field so big that the 1906 White Sox could hit only two home runs there.

Raleigh "Biz" Mackey—Veterans compare Mackey to Mickey Cochrane, perhaps baseball's finest white catcher. Pitchers loved to pitch to Biz. "The way he handled you," said Hilton Smith, "the way he got you built up, believing in yourself. Ooh, I just felt on edge, and it looked like all my stuff was just *working*!"

Mackey's protégé was 15-year-old Roy Campanella.

When Campy was given a "night" by 90,000 fans in Los Angeles in 1959, he made Mackey take a bow. "This is the man who taught me everything I know," he said.

John Beckwith—Big, moody John Beckwith hit the ball as hard as anyone, including Josh Gibson and Babe Ruth, old-timers say. In 1921 he became the first man ever to hit the ball over the left-field fence at Cincinnati's Crosley Field. He was 19 years old at the time.

Beckwith's longest blast reportedly came in Washington's huge Griffith Stadium, when he hit a sign about 460 feet from home and 40 feet high. Senators owner Clark Griffith "almost ate his cigar!"

Big Bill Foster—The ace of his brother Rube's great teams, Bill did something in 1926 that no white pitcher has ever done. The Giants were trailing the Monarchs three games to two in the playoff with two games remaining. Foster and Rogan both pitched the doubleheader, Foster winning a double shutout 1-0 and 5-0. Then he won two more games in the black World Series, including another shutout in the finale.

The next year was Bill's best. He was 21-3 on the regular season, added two more against Paige's Birmingham Black Barons in the playoff, and two more in the World Series against Atlantic City, again clinching the finale with a shutout.

Bill would have won more games in his career, but he retired in the Depression to make a better living selling insurance.

J.L. Wilkinson—This white Iowa native formed the Kansas City Monarchs in 1920. After the Depression struck, he bought portable lights and played the first professional night game, in Enid, Oklahoma in 1930, beating Des Moines by two weeks. His traveling lights introduced night ball to several major and minor league cities and helped to save both the minors and the Negro Leagues in the Depression.

Wilkie gave a second chance to sore-armed Satchel Paige and a first chance to Jackie Robinson, Ernie Banks, and Lou Brock. The majors took them all, plus 23 other Monarchs, usually for nothing. Wilkinson said quietly he wouldn't stand in any man's way to better himself.

John Holway

Big Bill Foster

Many authorities feel that an all-star team of black Outs could defeat the team of Ins.

Inside Cooperstown

		BA	HR/ 550 AB*	(vs big leaguers)
1b	Buck Leonard	.328	24	(.358)
2b	Martin Dihigo	.319	25	(.246)
ss	Pop Lloyd	.353	7	(.321)
3b	Judy Johnson	.301	4	(.263)
lf	Monte Irvin	.345	21	(.293)
cf	Oscar Charleston	.350	27	(.318)
rf	Cool Papa Bell	.337	9	(.394)
c	Josh Gibson	.362	47	(.426)
dh	Ray Dandridge	.326	1	(.347)
Average		**.336**	**17**	

		W-L	Pct.	
p	Satchel Paige	124-80	.608	†
p	Leon Day	67-29	.698	†
Average		**95-54**	**.638**	

mgr Rube Foster (w)

Outside Cooperstown

		BA	HR/ 550 AB*	(vs big leaguers)
1b	Mule Suttles (w)	.329	34	(.374)
2b	Bullet Joe Rogan (w)	.343	16	(.389)
ss	Willie Wells (w)	.328	20	(.430)
3b	Jud Wilson	.347	13	(.360)
lf	Willard Brown (w)	.352	24	(.259)
cf	Turkey Stearnes (w)	.350	30	(.313)
rf	Cristobal Torriente (w)	.335	11	(.311)
c	Biz Mackey	.322	11	(.326)
dh	John Beckwith	.356	31	(.311)
Average		**.341**	**21**	

		W-L	Pct.	
p	Bill Foster (w)	137-62	.688	(6- 0)
p	Ray Brown	101-30	.771	†
p	Bullet Rogan (w)	113-34	.715	†
Average		**117-46**	**.718**	

mgr J.L. Wilkinson

(w) = played mainly in the west

(*Negro League seasons varied from about 35 to about 100 games a year. To equate homeruns with typical white major league seasons, the state HR/550 At Bats is used.)

†Not compiled.

Stats are from the Macmillan *Baseball Encyclopedia,* based on data compiled by many dozens of researchers Dick Clark and John B. Holway.

A team of deserving Hall of Famers could be fielded from still a third all-star squad:

Third Team

		BA	HR/ 550 AB*	(vs big leaguers)
1b	Ben Taylor (w)	.324	6	†
2b	George Scales	.309	18	(.245)
ss	Dick Lundy	.324	13	(.221)
3b	Oliver Marcelle	.304	†	(.251)
lf	Charlie Blackwell (w)	.324	16	†
cf	Wild Bill Wright	.336	13	(.375)
rf	Fats Jenkins	.335	4	†
c	Louis Santop	.321	†	(.316)
Average		**.322**	**11**	

		W-L	Pct.	
p	Smoky Joe Williams	78-47	.624	(22-7)

mgr Cum Posey

Some historical events just can't be captured in prose

Odwell's Run

Albert Flannery

Odwell checked the loaded bases,
trailing by a run
Pitching in a pinch beneath
the scorching Scranton sun
In eighteen-ninety-seven Odwell's
mean and stingy bosses
Spat and railed and cursed him
as he ran up twenty losses
The Eastern League for Wilkes-Barre
that summer was a grind
They staggered into August
more than thirty games behind
Shannon saw his shell-shocked
bench depleted as he feared
He asked his staff for outfield
help and Odwell volunteered

Ten years such as that poor
Odwell labored at the game
The Reach Guides as the seasons
passed did not have his first name
The diamond, as is often said,
is not a place for whiners
But Odwell passed his thirtieth year
still stranded in the minors
One afternoon a railroad train
came in from Cincinnati
A man fell off the boxcar
who got plastered at a party
He sought out Odwell at the ballpark,
battered and fatigued
And offered him a contract there
to join the National League

Two more seasons passed on by
till Odwell hit his peak
And then old Odwell took off
on a torrid batting streak
In the season's final game
the former bush league clown
Vied his teammate Seymour
for the circuit's home run crown
Odwell, in his last at bat,
attacked the autumn breeze
And socked a mighty blast
that traveled to the fence with ease
I'd like to say that Odwell
knocked the catcher down with style
The truth is that he beat
the outfield's throw home by a mile

Seymour toasted Odwell in the
locker room with pride
The senior circuit's home run
king of nineteen-hundred-five
The Reach Guide gave the ancient
gardener's team a silver cup
And every word I say is true
and you could look it up
I'd like to say that Odwell
left a mark that Babe Ruth passed
The truth is that the home run
in that game was Odwell's last
Frederick Odwell thought back
to more peaceful times he'd known
And bought a one-way ticket
to his boyhood country home

Albert Flannery is a mailman from Swampscott, Massachusetts with 10 years experience. This is his first published poem.

Walter S. Walker: Ballplayer, politician and tragic figure

One of Baseball's Odd Lives

Peter Morris

For a man who played only one major league game, Walter S. Walker has a number of claims to distinction. Few have had as peripatetic and ultimately as sad a life, and no one has ever made his major league debut under more trying circumstances. Walter was born on March 12, 1860, in Berlin, Michigan (renamed Marne during World War I), the fifth of six children born to immigrants from the British Isles by way of Canada. The family seems to have been moving about quite a bit at the time; they appear in the nearby town of Wright on the 1860 census, and Walter was baptized at St. Patrick's Catholic church in Ada, Michigan. In 1863 the family moved to Ionia, where they finally settled. Walter's father, Archibald, a station conductor, died soon after and Wallie's mother, Mary, supported the family by managing a hotel in Ionia.

After finishing high school, Walter went to Sandwich, Ontario, in January, 1879, to study for the priesthood. This ambition was put aside at some point, but Walter did graduate with a bachelor's degree in belles lettres. Upon his return to Ionia in 1882, Walter's play for the county baseball team began to draw favorable notices and soon earned him regular invitations to catch for other traveling teams. In the ensuing years Walter's life mirrored the transitory experience that was the baseballist's lot at this time. Along the way he passed up many chances at promising careers to play for teams that were almost invariably on the edge of bankruptcy. The jobs Walter got between baseball engagements included being a clerk in one of the state department offices in Lansing, acting as a traveling representative for a cigar company, and owning his own cigar manufactory in Ionia. But each was put aside when a new baseball opportunity beckoned. In April, 1883, Walter was elected as one of the seven umpires of the newly formed Northwestern Base Ball Association. This too proved abortive, and soon Wallie was back in Ionia, working as the City Clerk. Although his baseball activities for the remainder of the season seem to have taken a back seat to these duties, he did play a few games for the Muskegon club alongside Welday Walker, the black man whose record is next to Walter's in the *Baseball Encyclopedia*. He also found time to play for Detroit's Cass Club, where his play earned him a contract with the Detroit Wolverines for the 1884 season.

Into the majors—Detroit already had a superlative catcher in Charlie Bennett (who by coincidence would go into the cigar business after the tragic end of his career), but the need for a capable backup was great. Walter came to Detroit a month early to get down to his playing weight of 162 pounds on his five-foot, ten-and-a-half-inch frame. In informal workouts with his new teammates, Walker impressed with his speed, hitting ability and especially his strong throwing arm. Teammate Ned Hanlon marveled that Walter could throw almost as hard with his left hand as with his right. Bennett arrived in camp anxious to learn if all he had heard about his new teammate and rival was true. At first, it seemed that it might be. After Walter's first exhibition appearance, played at Richmond, Virginia, on

Peter Morris is an active member of the Biographical Research Committee who has tracked down numerous players, including Walter Walker. He was the winner of the first World Scrabble™ championship in 1991.

April 8, the Detroit *Free Press* raved, "Walker caught, and though he never saw [pitcher Dupee] Shaw previous to the first instant he caught him perfectly. Such a performance is wonderful...It will leave little doubt in the minds of the Detroit people that the club, for the first time in its history, has two efficient batteries." A few days later, another headline announced "SHAW AND WALKER DO UP THE WASHINGTONS IN A WAY TO PLEASE DETROITERS." At this point, however, the toils of his position began to catch up with him. After his next game, on April 22 at Indianapolis, the *Free Press* observed that "Walker, whose hands are very sore, had three passed balls and came very near losing the game." A week later he played again at Trenton and made a bad throw.

Family tragedy—As the regular season approached, Walter was suddenly confronted with more serious matters than his sore hands. His younger brother, James, had gone on a trip to Bois Blanc Island in northern Michigan with several other Ionians to look after some land holdings. While there James was taken ill, and in a deranged state wandered away from the group. Notices of James' disappearance were published in the newspapers on May 1, the opening day of the season, with the additional observation that "it was feared he had perished." As the week wore on without finding him, Walter's eldest brother, Archie, was severely injured on a logging road north of Saginaw. Mary Walker, their mother, traveled to Flint, where Archie was recovering at the Flint Surgical Institute.

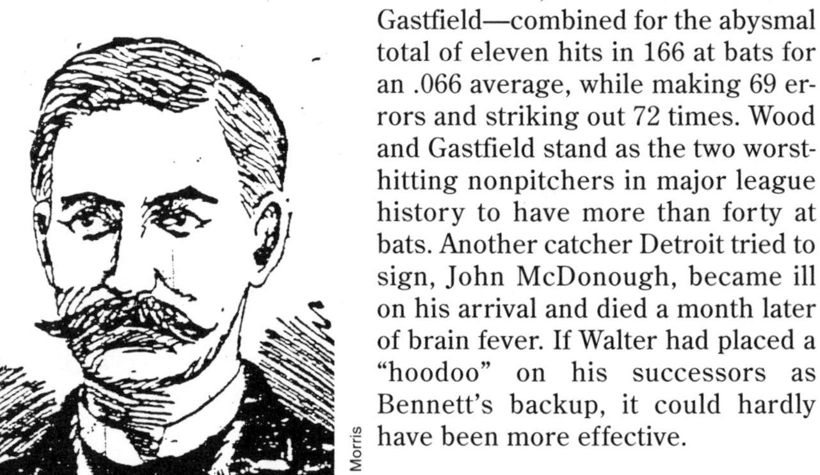
Peter Morris

Walter Walker

The National League schedule saw Detroit beginning with a twenty-six game road trip. They would lose the first eleven, most by lopsided margins, including a 25-3 thrashing. Walter Walker saw his first and only action for the Wolverines in an 8-4 loss on May 8, 1884, played in New York in a drizzling rain. Trying to catch Shaw's difficult curves, Walker was charged with two errors and seven passed balls. The account of the game, after waxing eloquent about the disheartening effect of poor fielding on a pitcher's morale, simply added "Walker's play behind the bat was frightful." Walter did manage one hit in four at bats and scored a run while facing future Hall-of-Famer John Montgomery Ward. This would prove to be his one and only major league game. A few days later he was sent back to Detroit by a club anxious to economize. The Ionia papers charged that Walter was being made a scapegoat for the team's ineptitude, and the Detroit papers defended the team. Walter told a reporter that he had told manager Jack Chapman he was not healthy enough to play, and that Chapman had played him only to have grounds for suspending him. While this was being played out in the press, Archibald recovered enough to be out of danger and Mrs. Walker decided to return home, only to discover that the train taking her home was also transporting the dead body of her son James. His body had lain in an area so concealed that it had not been discovered until May 13. The authorities determined the death to be accidental, caused by exposure after a fall had knocked him out. Walter returned home on the 15th for the funeral and while there was released by the team.

The Wolverines' efforts to replace Wallie were met with an extraordinary lack of success. Their six replacements—Fred Wood, Chief Zimmer, Ben Guiney, David Beatle, Dickie Lowe and Ed Gastfield—combined for the abysmal total of eleven hits in 166 at bats for an .066 average, while making 69 errors and striking out 72 times. Wood and Gastfield stand as the two worst-hitting nonpitchers in major league history to have more than forty at bats. Another catcher Detroit tried to sign, John McDonough, became ill on his arrival and died a month later of brain fever. If Walter had placed a "hoodoo" on his successors as Bennett's backup, it could hardly have been more effective.

The minors and politics—At the end of May, Walter joined the Minneapolis club of the Northwestern League, where he caught and played third base until the team disbanded near the end of the year. The following spring he signed on with St. Paul of the Western League but was released and caught on with Cleveland, which disbanded in May. In June, Walter was back in Ionia when he received another offer from the Detroit Wolverines and left to join the team. What came of this is not clear, but the team went on a winning streak and presumably decided it could do without him. Two weeks later, back in Ionia again, Walter decided to practice law and apprenticed himself to a local lawyer. Walter attacked his studies with characteristic energy and on February 20, 1886, was admitted to the state bar. A month later he and another new attorney, Fred C. Wallington, announced their plans to set up a practice in Mt. Pleasant. The partnership was not to survive very long, however; business was slow at first and when Walter received an offer to play for the Oswego, NY, in the International League, he accepted it. Walker returned to Mt. Pleasant in the fall and Wallington elected to buy him out. In September Walker received the Democratic nomination for prosecuting attorney of Isabella county, and in early October the Republicans nominated as his opponent his erstwhile partner F. C. Wallington.

The election campaign was contested with a zeal augmented by personal animosity, as Wallington implied that Walker might neglect his duties if a baseball team were to beckon. Walter nonetheless defeated Wallington by the narrow margin of 1,714 votes to 1,570, bucking a trend which saw Republicans elected in 18 of the 21 contests in the county. The Isabella *Enterprise*, in a very unusual move for a Republican paper in those days of doggedly partisan reportage, noted that "the 'ball' racket [had not] hurt the next Prosecuting Attorney of Isabella county" and went on to moralize that lying always boomerangs and hurts the party that begins it.

Wallington's supposition about Walker's commitment to his new duties proved unfounded. During his two-year term, the *Enterprise* was full of commendatory notes about his comings and goings and official duties. In September, 1887, he handled the county's first murder trial, resulting in a hung jury, and the following year he got a manslaughter conviction in a second murder trial. One of his less serious duties involved traveling to Dushville in July, 1887, in pursuit of a man claiming to be Christ. A number of his trips took him back to Ionia, a fact which began to attract speculation about an ulterior motive and, sure enough, on November 15, 1887, Walter Walker was married in Ionia to Jennie Kimball, an event which was heralded with warmth by the papers of both Ionia and Mt. Pleasant. In addition to his responsibilities as prosecuting attorney, Walter's private practice expanded to include work as a notary public and a collection agent as well as successfully instituting a major class-action suit. He also umpired local games and served as field captain of the Mt. Pleasant team, catching whenever his schedule permitted. All in all, these were two years of intense activity and personal fulfillment.

They came to an end in November of 1888, when Walter lost his bid for re-election as prosecuting attorney to the Republican candidate, Albert Coe. The defeat was the result of the county's predominantly Republican makeup, rather than a reflection on the job he had done. All 15 races being contested went to the Republicans, with Walter losing by the closest margin of all, a mere 70 votes. At first Walter intended to stay in Mt. Pleasant and carried on his usual flurry of activities, entering into a new partnership with the Hon. E. D. Wheaton in an office in a new commercial block, and becoming secretary of the Isabella Country Bar Association, but in March, 1889, he decided to relocate to Detroit and practice law there. Soon he was playing ball for a local amateur baseball team, the Detroit Athletic Club, for which he played off and on for the next three years.

League president and disaster—In 1891, when it appeared that Detroit would be without professional baseball for the first time in a decade, a bold new venture was announced. The Northwestern League, dormant since 1884, was revived with Walter S. Walker as president, secretary and treasurer of the league in which he had formerly played and umpired. The eight-team league was to include teams in Detroit, Bay City, Grand Rapids, Port Huron, Fort Wayne, Terre Haute, Indianapolis and Evansville. Walter would seem to have been the perfect man for such a task. He brought to it his abundant energy, his experience in law and business, and a personal charm which was frequently commented upon. Just as importantly, he brought the experience of having played for numerous teams and leagues on the road to bankruptcy. Two of the new league's innovations were informed by this experience—a strict salary cap and Sunday baseball. Both ideas seemed to be creative approaches to the challenge of making baseball profitable, but both backfired. The Detroit franchise, with Walker acting as secretary and treasurer, was the only team to adhere to the salary restrictions and as a result had a vastly inferior team. The first week alone brought losses by disheartening scores of 22-1, 19-4, 15-5, and 11-0 and must have reminded Walter of his days with the Wolverines. Just as crucial a setback was the city's unreadiness for Sunday baseball. A campaign by many of Detroit's churches forced the team to play its home games outside of city limits and, after drawing over 2,000 fans for the first-ever Sunday game in Detroit, the police broke up the second and final effort to play on the Sabbath. Walter traveled around the league tirelessly in the season's early days, addressing a myriad of problems, but as so often was the case, the league was only as strong as its weakest link. Within two weeks of the season's opening, the Bay City team was reneging on its financial commitments and soon afterward disbanded. Shortly thereafter, Detroit followed suit and, while the league did make it through the season, it was not a financial success.

No doubt this failure, on top of the election disappointment, was a great blow, but it is still difficult to fathom or explain what came next. On August 3, 1892, Walter Walker was placed in the Eastern Michigan asylum for the insane in Pontiac after a complaint from his wife. Diagnosed as sufering from alcoholism and monomania, Walter would spend the rest of his life there, dying on February 28, 1922; his body was brought back to Ionia for burial. The Ionia paper ran a brief notice that "Wallie" had died at his "home" in Pontiac, but none of the other newspapers that had chronicled his peripatetic life saw fit to bear the tidings of its sad end.

Signed by McGraw at 15

Remembering Waite Hoyt

Tom Knight

When he was a youngster his family lived on Hawthorne Street in Brooklyn and he used to walk over to Bedford Avenue and Sullivan Place to watch the construction workers building Ebbets Field. The same boy would one day pitch there, but his fame would come in another ballpark in another league. He built such a reputation as a high school pitcher at Erasmus Hall that John McGraw signed him right under the noses of the Brooklyn ballclub when he was just 15.

The kid temporarily dubbed "Schoolboy" Waite Hoyt did not make his major league debut until he was 18 years old in 1918. He pitched only one inning, gave up no runs and struck out two hitters. The Giants sent him to the minors and because of a foolish front office blunder, he became the property of the Boston Red Sox.

On December 15, 1920, the Red Sox dealt Hoyt along with catcher Wally Schang, infielder Mike McNally, and pitcher Harry Harper to the New York Yankees in exchange for catcher Muddy Ruel, second baseman Del Pratt, outfielder Sammy Vick, and pitcher Hank Thormahlen. In Brooklyn the following morning, Hoyt's father read about the trade in the morning paper. He went into the bedroom where his son was sleeping, woke him and said, "Waite, you've received a wonderful Christmas present—you've been traded to the Yankees!"

It was with the Yanks that Waite Hoyt had his greatest years. He won 19 games in 1921 and again in '22. To add insult to injury, he beat McGraw's Giants twice in the 1921 World Series. He pitched three complete games in that classic (won by the Giants 5-3), allowing the Giants no earned runs.

In 1927 he was 22-7 for "Murderers Row" and the next season went 23-7. On May 30, 1930, he and shortstop Mark Koenig were traded to the Detroit Tigers for pitcher Ownie Carroll, shortstop Yats Wuestling, and outfielder Harry Rice. Waite and Babe Ruth were good friends and had had some great times together. When Hoyt went around the clubhouse bidding the boys adieu, the Babe, notoriously bad with names, replied, "So long, Walter!"

On June 30, 1931, he was sold to the A's. He was back home in Brooklyn with the Dodgers for a while in 1932, then was with the Giants briefly before being traded to the Pirates in 1933. Some of the greatness returned the following year when he went 15-6 for the Bucs. He came home again to Ebbets Field in 1937 and won seven games for manager Burleigh Grimes' sixth-place club. After losing three games in 1938, Waite took off his Brooklyn uniform and ended his career where it started—in his home town. Outside the ball park after receiving his unconditional release, he looked up at the flags flying atop Ebbets and, remembering watching them building the park when he was a kid, he cried.

The talented righthander who stood just a shade under six feet and weighed 185 pounds, won 237 games and lost 182 during his 21-year stay in the majors. Hoyt was elected to the Hall of Fame in 1969.

A pretty good singer, he appeared at New York's Palace Theatre for a time. Hoyt was one of the first

Tom Knight was appointed Brooklyn's Official Baseball Historian in 1976. He authors "Diamond Reflections"—a baseball nostalgia column appearing in several weeklies.

Waite Hoyt as a youthful professional.

ballplayers to go into broadcasting. In the late '30s he had a radio program on a New York station called "According to Hoyt." He would tell stories and comment on baseball in general. He then went to Cincinnati as a broadcaster for the Reds, where he became a fixture for years.

Hoyt gets the punch line in one of baseball's great bittersweet stories. When the Sultan of Swat passed on in 1948, Waite Hoyt, along with other ex-teammates of Babe Ruth, was a pallbearer at the funeral. It was a hot, humid August day and as they were carrying Babe out of St. Patrick's Cathedral, the old third baseman, "Jumping Joe" Dugan, whispered to Hoyt, "I sure would enjoy a cold beer right now." Waite said, "So would the Babe!"

Waite Hoyt died just two weeks shy of his 85th birthday on August 25, 1984, in Cincinnati. He lies buried in that city's Spring Grove Cemetery, just a few feet from the grave of little Miller Huggins, his manager during the great Yankee years.

Head to head for the 1928 American League batting title

Goslin vs. Manush

Tom Simon

On September 30, the final day of the 1928 season, Hall of Famers Goose Goslin of the Washington Senators and Heinie Manush of the St. Louis Browns went head to head in perhaps the most exciting batting race in major league history. From newspaper articles and Goslin's and Manush's personal accounts, which appeared in Lawrence S. Ritter's *The Glory of Their Times* (1966) and an article by John P. Carmichael in the November 1946 issue of *Baseball Digest*, respectively, this article reconstructs the events of that memorable afternoon.

Goose's lame wing—By 1928 Goslin had established himself as one of the most dangerous hitters in the American League. He'd hit .334 and driven in 120 runs in 1927, the fourth consecutive season in which he'd batted better than .300 *and* topped the century mark in RBIs. At spring training in March 1928, however, the fun-loving Goose severely injured his throwing arm clowning around with a shot he'd borrowed from a high-school track team that was practicing nearby. The arm was so bad at times that Goslin could barely throw the ball 20 feet.

Switching to a 40-ounce bat, heavier than usual, and holding it somewhat differently, Goslin still managed to hit. His average stood at .397 on June 3, even though he'd already missed 16 games due to the injury. Player-manager Bucky Harris needed Goslin's bat in the lineup every day, so he devised a plan. Shortstop Bobby "Gunner" Reeves, whose arm was so strong that first baseman Joe Judge occasionally used a catcher's mitt during infield practice, would run into left field to take Goslin's weak tosses. Reeves would then relay the ball to the proper base, prompting Harris to call Goslin "the only outfielder in history with a caddy."

Goslin's strength at bat, however, by no means offset his weakness afield. The Washington *Evening Star* surmised that during the 1928 season "[m]ore than a dozen losses were directly due to Goslin's arm weakness." Moreover, Reeves, a promising third-year player, had to be rested frequently as the season progressed. When he failed to achieve the stardom that had been predicted for him, many attributed his failure to exhaustion caused by "caddying" for Goslin.

Harris's plan did result in one unexpected benefit for Washington. To spell Reeves occasionally, the Senators purchased a 22-year-old infielder by the name of Joe Cronin from Kansas City of the American Association. Cronin, who'd failed in a previous trial with the Pittsburgh Pirates, hit only .242 in 63 games after joining the Senators in midseason. In time, though, he would become the best shortstop ever to wear a Washington uniform.

The caddy system also benefitted the Senators in its intended way by keeping Goslin in the lineup nearly every day, and he made the most of the opportunity. Peaking at an amazing .441 on June 23 (all the more amazing considering his right arm hurt so badly at the time that he was experimenting with throwing left-handed), Goslin led the American League in hitting for most of the summer and remained over .400 until August 2.

Goslin was still leading the league with a .393 aver-

A resident of Burlington, Vermont, Tom Simon founded the Larry Gardner chapter of SABR in 1993.

age on August 5 when a new name appeared in the box most newspapers printed under the heading "American League's Five Leading Batsmen." That name was Heinie Manush, debuting at .356, and he would prove to be a worthy rival.

Manush comes on—While with Detroit in 1926, Manush had gone six for nine in a doubleheader on the last day of the season to beat out Babe Ruth for the American League batting crown, .378 to .372. The Tigers had traded Manush to St. Louis after he'd slumped eighty points to .298 in 1927, but the feisty line-drive hitter had rebounded and was having a career year for the Browns in 1928.

Manush gained steadily on Goslin in August and September. By the final series of the season, Goslin, whose right arm was strong once more, was leading the American League at .376 (166 for 441). Manush, who had not missed a single game all season, was close behind at .373 (233 for 624). Lou Gehrig, at .369, was a not-so-distant third.

The schedule called for the Senators to close the season with four games at Sportsman's Park in St. Louis. Most St. Louis baseball fans were focusing their attention on Boston, where the Cardinals were fighting for their second National League pennant in three years. Because the Browns had already clinched third place in the American League and the Senators fourth, the most important thing at stake in St. Louis would be the batting title.

"Before the series opened Dan Howley, our manager, asked me if I wanted him to throw lefthanders at them because Goose, like myself, was a southpaw hitter," Manush recalled in *Baseball Digest*. "I told him no. 'But I wish you'd do one thing,' I asked him. 'Play Oscar Melillo at second.' We'd been playing a kid named [Otis] Brannan, a fair hitter but not much of a fielder, and I figured I'd like Oscar out there to play Goose back on the grass."

Howley agreed to play Melillo, and it didn't take long for the switch to pay off. In his first at bat of the series, according to the Washington *Evening Star*, "The Goose finally socked one through the pitcher's box that would have been a real hit had there not been a mud puddle back of second base as a result of an early morning rain. The puddle slowed up the ball just enough to enable Oscar Melillo to make a nifty stop and flag the Goose at first."

In the first game alone, the slick-fielding Melillo, whose nickname was "Spinach" because he ate almost nothing but the iron-rich vegetable to combat a kidney inflammation known as Bright's Disease, handled three grounders off Goslin's bat and threw him out each time. "I'll say one thing," Manush remembered, "that Melillo made a couple of plays in the first two games that cut at least two hits off Goslin's total. You see, Goose was a dead-pull hitter, while I hit more or less straightaway, and I recall in that series Lu Blue, our first baseman, played way back even when they had a man on the bag if Goose Goslin was up."

Throughout the series the Washington sportswriters accused the Browns of bearing down harder on Goslin, and the St. Louis scribes made similar accusations about the Senators and Manush. For example, after the first game the *Star* reported, "And how they pitched to this Goslin. The first time he was at bat the Goose had to face everything the left-handed Walter Stewart had in his repertoire. Hooks, fast ones and a dazzling change of pace came Goslin's way." Even more direct was the St. Louis *Post-Dispatch*, which stated after the third game, "Manager Bucky Harris is doing what he can to help Goslin win the batting championship by using all the lefthanders he can against Manush, who is a southpaw swinger."

Even so, in the first three games, two of which were won by St. Louis, Goslin was 5 for 10 with two home runs, and Manush was 6 for 10 with one homer. Entering the final game of the season, Goslin's lead had been cut to two points, .379 to .377.

Gehrig, in the meantime, had kept pace with the front-runners. As the Yankees clinched their third consecutive American League pennant by taking three out of four games in Detroit, Gehrig had gone 6 for 12 with a home run, raising his average to .372.

Head to head—On the mound for the decisive battle were two righthanders, George Blaeholder for St. Louis and Washington ace Sam Jones. Formerly of the Browns, Jones had volunteered to work out of turn to attempt to deflate Manush's average.

Blaeholder struck out Goslin in the top of the first inning, lowering his average to .378. Manush failed to take advantage of the opportunity, though, grounding out in the bottom half.

Goslin's average fell to .37748 when he flied to center field in his second at bat. Manush virtually tied for the lead in the bottom of the fourth by slicing a single over Cronin at shortstop, raising his average to .37736. "One of the Washington players told me afterward that Goslin, after that hit, had suggested to Jones that he keep walking me and that Sam refused," Manush said in *Baseball Digest*. "'No sir,' he told Goose, the way I got it. 'I'm going to stop him if I can, but he's entitled to a chance to hit under the circumstances.'"

In the top of the fifth, Goslin helped himself by launching his third home run of the series and 17th of the season into the center-field bleachers. Manush remembered that at bat distinctly: "[Goslin] had nicked a foul off the end of his bat the previous pitch and the ball had glanced off the roof of our dugout, barely away from our third baseman's hands. I thought to myself out there by the left-field stands, He'll probably blast

National Baseball Library, Cooperstown, NY

Teammates with the 1933 Senators, left fielder Goslin and right fielder Manush pose with center fielder Fred Schulte

one now, and he did. The boys said later he must have guessed another outside pitch because he stepped right into it and Goose could get his bat around fast." The blast gave Washington a 5-1 lead, but more importantly, it raised Goslin's batting average to .3789.

Manush, however, tripled in the bottom of the sixth to raise his average to .3783. When Goslin grounded out to shortstop in the top of the seventh against the lefthanded Hal Wiltse, who, according to the *Star*, had been "rushed into the fray by the Browns in an effort to check the southpaw-swinging Goslin," his averaged dipped to .3780 (172 for 455). Manush had gained the lead.

But the lead was short-lived. In the bottom of the eighth Manush popped a soft sidearm curve from Jones into shallow left field. "I still can see [Bucky] Harris, at third that day, circling under and I thought, Even if he drops the ball, it doesn't mean a thing," recalled Manush, who apparently turned his head before Goslin, not taking any chances, called off Harris and made the catch himself. The out lowered Manush's average to .3777 (241 for 638).

To bat or not to bat—Entering the top of the ninth, the score was 7-1 in favor of Washington and Goslin was scheduled to bat second in the inning. By that point results from Detroit were in: Gehrig, who had left the game in the seventh inning, knocked cold by a bad-hop grounder, had gone 2 for 3 (including his 27th home run), finishing the season at .374. With Manush unlikely to bat again, Goslin knew that the batting championship was his as long as he didn't make an out. An out, however, would lower his average to .3772 (172 for 456) and give Manush the title.

"If I get up there and don't get a hit I'll drop below him," Goslin remembered. "I had that information before I went to bat. One of the sportswriters sent it down to me, with a note that said, 'If you go to bat and make an out, Manush will win the batting title. Best thing to do is don't get up to bat at all, and then you've got it made.'"

After Red Barnes opened the inning by walking, Manush waited in left field for Goslin to step up to the plate. "All of a sudden I looked up and saw Sam Rice starting out from the dugout with a bat in his hand and it was Goose's turn. For a second I just stood still and then I let out a yell and began running in. I don't know what might have happened, because I was mad, thinkin' what they were gonna do to try to protect his average. I was going to stop the game, I know that, and raise a fuss with the umpires and maybe Goslin and I would have wound up in a fight, but before I got there Rice had gone back and Goose came out swinging two bats. Somebody—maybe Bucky Harris—must have decided to make him play it out."

Goslin explains the delay in *The Glory of Their Times*: "Gee, I didn't know what to do. Bucky Harris left it up to me. He was the manager. 'What do you want to do, Goose?' he asked me. 'It's up to you. I'll send in a pinch hitter if you want me to.' 'Well,' I said, 'I've never won a batting title and I sure would love to, just for once in my life. [Actually Goslin had led the Sally League with a .390 average while with Columbia in 1921, his first full professional season.] So I think I'll stay right here on the bench, if it's OK with you.' Of course, everybody gathered around, wanting to be in on what's going on. 'You better watch out,' Joe Judge says, 'or they'll call you yellow.' 'What are you talking about?' 'Well,' he says, 'there's Manush right out there in left field. What do you think he'll figure if you win the title by sitting on the bench?' So this starts a big argument in the dugout; should I go up or shouldn't I? Finally, I got disgusted with the whole thing. 'All right, all right,' I said, 'stop all the noise, I'm going up there.'"

Wiltse nearly made Goslin regret the decision. "[D]oggone if that pitcher didn't get two strikes on me before I could even get set in the batter's box. I never took my bat off my shoulder, and already the count was two strikes and no balls. So I turned around and stepped out of the box and sort of had a discussion with myself while I put some dirt on my hands. I wasn't too much afraid of striking out, but a pop-up or a roller to the infield and I was a dead duck. Or a gone Goose, you might say. Well, I didn't know what to do. And then it came to me—get thrown out of the ball game! That way I wouldn't be charged with a time at bat, and it was in the bag.

"The umpire was a big-necked guy by the name of Bill Guthrie, so I turned on him. 'Why, those pitches weren't even close,' I said. 'Listen, wise guy,' he says, 'there's no such thing as close or not close. It's either *dis* or *dat*.' Oh, did that ever get me mad (I acted like). I called him every name in the book, I stepped on his shoes, I pushed him, I did everything. 'OK,' he said after about five minutes of this, 'are you ready to bat now? You're not going to get thrown out of this ball game no matter *what* you do, so you might as well get up to that plate. If I wanted to throw you out, I'd throw you clear over to Oshkosh. But you're going to bat, and you better be in there *swinging*, too. No bases on balls, you hear me?'"

On the next pitch Goslin lifted a pop to short right field that center fielder Earl McNeely, right fielder Frank McGowan, and Melillo all went after, but it fell among them and the Goose wound up with a double. The Senators added a pair of runs that inning to cement a 9-1 victory. "McGowan was playing right and he roomed with me all season and he felt terrible," Manush said. "He came into the bench moaning, 'Should have had it, Hein, it was my ball.'"

To show how close the ball was to being caught, Barnes, who had stolen second base while Goslin was batting, was able to advance only to third on the hit. "I guess that hit was the biggest thrill I ever got," Goslin told Ritter. "Even bigger than that single that won the World Series in 1935. Another lucky hit. Well, it was a great honor to win a batting title in those days."

Linked in history—On his return to Washington, the new batting champion, the Senators' first since Ed Delahanty in 1902, was feted with a testimonial banquet at the Wardman Park Hotel. At that banquet Goslin, whose left eye was blocked from seeing the pitcher by a nose that author Ira Smith described as "just about the largest thing of its sort seen on or off ball fields since the days of Cyrano de Bergerac," might have told a variation of a joke that would become one of his favorites in later years: "In 1928 I batted .379 as a one-eyed hitter. If I could have gotten two eyes on those pitches, I could have hit .500."

Manush was graceful in defeat. "Howley and the boys tried to cheer me up by saying the official records wouldn't be out until December and maybe I was tied or something, but I found out Eddie Eynon, the Washington secretary, had the figures all tabbed before gametime and knew that Goose had made it, .379 to my .378. When we got in the clubhouse McGowan came over and he was feeling pretty bad because if he'd caught that one in the [ninth] inning Goslin would have had one for five and I'd 'a won, .378 to .377, but I didn't let him say anything. What the heck, you do or you don't in baseball and I've missed a few myself in my day and that's part of the game."

The strange link between Goslin and Manush continued after the final day of the 1928 season. They were traded for each other on June 30, 1930, the only time in major league history that two former batting champions were swapped. After two seasons in St. Louis, Goslin was traded back to the Senators on December 14, 1932, and he and Manush played together in the same outfield in 1933. "Goose and I played on a pennant team for Washington five years later," Manush recalled in *Baseball Digest*, "but neither of us ever mentioned that game in St. Louis."

Manush died on May 12, 1971. Goslin died just three days later.

The Forgotten Pitcher

Herbert S. "Shan" Hofmann

A fine pitcher has been virtually forgotten. A U. S. Representative has taken his place. If he represents his constituents as well as he threw a baseball they must be very well served indeed. In politics he first won election to the state senate of Kentucky, lost a race for governor, and has since served in the lower house of Congress as Republican from District 4 in that state since 1987. He has not had any particular involvement with baseball since his retirement from the game. If you have guessed the name of Jim Bunning, move to the head of the class.

Bunning was at or near the head of the pitching class in most seasons in a career that lasted from 1955 through 1971. This 17-year career actually breaks down to just over 14 full seasons, because he was up for only short stints during his first two seasons and pitched only 110 innings in his last. The heart of his career was 1957-1967, and his pitching could be called outstanding in seven of these seasons. Excelling in both major leagues, he won more than 100 games, struck out over 1,400 batters, and threw a no-hitter in each.

By almost every standard of pitching success Bunning stood out. He won 224 games, which places him 56th on the all-time list. More important, during that 1957-67 prime, only Don Drysdale of his contemporaries won more, edging him by 185-184.

Bunning was a steady, reliable workman who almost never missed a turn in the starting rotation due to injury. His career total of 519 starts places him 30th on the all-time list, and he hurled 3,760.1 innings. Despite spending a month early in the season as a reliever in 1957 he led the AL with 267 innings; in 1967 he led the NL with 302.

Bunning's career earned run average was a solid 3.27. Although he never lead the league in ERA, he did finish second as a Detroit Tiger in 1960 and as a Philadelphia Phillie in 1967. In each year he pitched many more innings than the rival who bested him. The following chart shows that in seven of the prime years his ERA was far below his league's.

Yr	League ERA	Bunning ERA	Margin ERA	Rank (if in top 10)
1957	3.79	2.69	-1.10	3
1958	3.77	3.52	-.25	
1959	3.86	3.89	.03	
1960	3.87	2.79	-1.08	2
1961	4.02	3.19	-.83	8
1962	3.97	3.59	-.38	
1963	3.63	3.88	.25	
1964	3.54	2.63	-.91	5
1965	3.54	2.60	-.94	5
1966	3.61	2.41	-1.20	4
1967	3.38	2.29	-1.09	2

Jim Bunning was also a master of the strikeout. When he retired in 1971, he was second only to the great Walter Johnson on the all-time list, at 2,855. Today he is still 11th. Six times he fanned over 200. He led the AL in 1959 and 1960 and the NL in 1967. In five

Shan Hofmann is retired from teaching history at Muskegon (Michigan) Community College. He is currently working on a book on the great pitching seasons, year by year.

other seasons he was runner-up. He had 49 games in double figures during his prime period, with a high-point of 14 in each league. He averaged 6.83 "K's" per nine innings over his career.

Some of Bunning's strikeout feats were sensational. He fanned Ted Williams three times in a game, and did the same to Mickey Mantle in each of two straight starts. On August 3, 1959, he came on in the ninth inning to set down three Boston Red Sox hitters on nine consecutive strikes.

Unlike many strikeout pitchers, who sometimes tend to wildness and bases on balls, Bunning had excellent control. During his major league life he yielded only 2.39 walks per nine innings. In ten of his good years he was under three per game, three times under two, and led the majors in 1964 with a mere 1.46. He had 2.855 strikeouts to each free pass, an outstanding record, exceeded by only a very few other pitchers.

Forty of Bunning's wins were shutouts. He led the NL in 1967 and was tied for the league lead in 1966. Ironically, his best season effort, seven in 1965, earned him only a third place tie, such being the competition that year.

Early seasons—Coming up slowly through the Detroit Tiger farm system from 1950, Bunning did not reach the majors for good until he was going on 26 years of age. His minor league record was undistinguished. In 1955, he spent a part of the campaign with the parent club, and posted an unimpressive 3-5, 6.35. His card was much better in 1956, again late in the season, again in 15 games, where he was 5-1, mostly in relief. He was striking out some hitters, but up to this point neither his strikeouts/walks nor innings pitched/hits ratios were any harbingers of the future.

His spring training efforts in 1957, however, earned him the prized opening day starting assignment, which he promptly negated by getting bombed in the first inning against Kansas City, cuffed for four hits and runs in less than one round, although escaping the loss. Demoted to the relief corps, he made 11 appearances in the next month, generally quite effective, surrendering only 13 hits in 23 innings, with a win, a loss, and a save for his efforts.

As Tiger aces Frank Lary and Billy Hoeft were beset by a slow start and an injury, respectively, Bunning was pressed into starting again on May 16 in Boston. His response was a five-hit, complete game, 2-1 win. He had opened what was to be, in some respects, his career year. He won six more games in a month, and went 13 innings in a Detroit win for which he did not get credit. Such a game was an ominous sign of things to come, throughout his career. By the All-Star break he was 10-2, started and won the annual classic by allowing no base runners in three innings, and was the winning pitcher in a 6-5 AL triumph. His pace slowed a bit in the second half of the season, but he was still very solid and the Tigers would not have squeaked into fourth place without him. He tied Billy Pierce as the league's only twenty-game winners, pitched the most innings (267), finished second in strikeouts at 182 to Early Wynn, was second to Bob Turley in hits per nine innings (7.21), and finished fourth in K's per nine (6.13). In 30 starts, he yielded six hits or less in 10 of them. He was 10-2 against first division foes, with a winning margin over each. The Red Sox were his "cousins" as he took them by 5-1, the one loss a 1-0 two-hitter on a Ted Williams home run. Another two-hitter trumped the Yankees in New York, 3-2. Only seventh place Kansas City, which held him to 3-3, was a problem. Bunning had almost half of his wins and a better percentage in road games, was 5-1 in one-run decisions, and came through six times when his teammates gave him three runs or fewer to use. This effort produced a spot on the Major League All-Star Team for 1957.

First no-hitter—Although Bunning was not really a "rookie" in 1957, it was his first full season in the majors, and some observers were looking for, or hoping for, the so-called "sophomore jinx" to appear in 1958. To some extent, this happened, but it could hardly be called a *bad* season. He slipped to 14-12, aided by a wretched start which saw him only 1-4 by May 23 (Detroit was 13-21) and regular poundings by Cleveland all season (0-4). Still, he started moving up in June and did have some fine outings. Pushed around by other opponents, the Tigers seemed to save their quality play for games against the mighty Yankees. Indeed, they smashed the New Yorkers seven straight during parts of three different series in May and June, including a four-game sweep at Yankee Stadium June 13-15. The climax there came in a double shutout Sunday, June 15 before 54,817 as Frank Lary and Bunning scintillated, 2-0 and 3-0, respectively. Bunning repeated with another five-hitter the next Friday night in Tiger Stadium, thrilling the largest home crowd in four years, 53,168.

Bunning also decisioned the Yanks and Turley on September 17 in Detroit with a seven-hit, eight strikeout 5-2 job. The result gave the locals the season series by 12-10, the only one dropped by the champions. In Turley's 21-7, Cy Young, World Series MVP career year, three of his losses were to Bunning.

The highlight of Bunning's season, though, was the 3-0 no-hitter in Boston on July 20. In this contest he fanned 12 and gave only two free passes. The last hitter between Bunning and glory was Ted Williams, and he ended matters with a routine fly to right into the glove of future Hall of Famer Al Kaline, to finish an 0-4 day at the plate. Overall, Bunning fanned 177 (two behind Wynn again) and finished second in average K's per nine, at 7.25. He was seventh in hits per nine innings at 7.70, and he kayoed all rivals except the Indians.

Up and down—Bunning's 1959 season opened with a fizzle, much as had 1958. Blasted by Cleveland in his opener, he dropped his first three decisions. But he checked his slide, notching four consecutive wins before settling into a pattern that brought him to August 1 at 9-10. Then he reeled off six straight wins, and went 8-3 for the remainder of the season, finishing a respectable 17-13. His 3.89 ERA, a shade above the league's, highlighted the trouble he had during the season. He did move to the top spot in K's (201) and second in strikeouts per nine innings (again 7.25). He tied for fourth place in complete games (14) and also in games won. That the Tigers, even with a losing record, edged out Boston for fourth place might be traced to Bunning's 5-1 record against the Red Sox. Baltimore was his hoodoo at 0-3, the only adversary he did not clamp, but both the Indians and Yankees hit him harder as measured by ERA. His mark against each rival mirrored his inconsistent season.

In 1960, Bunning got off to his usual slow start, and finished at 11-14, largely because of weak support. He led the league in strikeouts (201), was second in ERA (2.79), and tied for second in shutouts (3). He was fourth in hits per nine innings (7.75).

For the Tigers and their fans, 1961 was almost a dream year. They had almost everything, but ran into a Yankee squad that had everything-plus. Norman Cash, having his peak career year, and Rocky Colavito did not match Roger Maris and Mickey Mantle in home runs, but they batted in more than the New York pair. Frank Lary had his best mark of 23 wins. Al Kaline had a very productive, injury-free season. The Tigers led all baseball in runs and the league in batting average. But they were also sixth in the circuit in fielding average and eighth in double plays.

In contrast the Yankees had the league's fewest errors, highest fielding average, and most double plays. They had baseball's best relief pitcher in Luis Arroyo. They had 60 more homers than the Detroiters. So, while the Bengals won 101 games, a greater total than garnered by any of Casey Stengel's champs, the Gotham City crew left them standing in the stretch as they grabbed 109. Most baseball historians rate this the best outfit of the great Yankee teams from 1949 through 1964. As for Bunning, his 17-11 was the second best among Tiger starters, but he was criticized because he was 9-0 against expansion Washington and Los Angeles. Still, he tied for second in shutouts (4), was third in whiffs (194), fourth in wins, and eighth in ERA (3.19), over both Ford and Lary.

If 1961 was frustrating, 1962 was one of the stranger of Bunning's prime years. For once, he got good support and he won almost every game he should have, along with a few where he was hit hard, and came in at 19-10. He was among the top ten in wins, winning percentage (9th, .655), complete games (tied for fifth, 123), innings pitched (third, 258), and strikeouts (second, 183). With injuries and slumps taking their toll, the Tigers took a nosedive into fourth place in a race for third that saw only one game separating third-place Los Angeles and fifth-place Chicago. Proving the debility of the Detroit relief crew, Bunning was sent in six times as a reliever and had a perfect record with as many saves. Except for the Yankees, against whom he pitched few but effective innings, he spread his con-

National Baseball Library, Cooperstown, NY

Jim Bunning

quests around, defeating all others at least twice each (six clubs), one three times. and finally kayoed the Baltimore whammy, going 4-0 over the Orioles backed with a fine 2.72 ERA for 43 innings. Indeed the Bengals could thank the Bird nine for cushioning their fall, as they pulverized them 16 games to two.

While 1963 wasn't a good year for the tall Kentucky right-hander, a closer examination of his game-by-game card shows it was hardly as bad as it appears on the surface. He was hit *much* harder in his bad efforts than he had ever been, and he had far more of these weak efforts than Tiger fans were used to. Yet he still pitched well in 22 of his starts, especially in the first and last months of the campaign. As usual, his best efforts were seldom rewarded in the "win" column. The month of September well illustrates this point. Five starts yielded only two victories for Bunning, though Detroit won all three no-decision starts, and he gave up only six earned runs in 41 innings. This brought his ERA down below 4.00 and he still managed to place second in strikeouts (196). It was his swan song as a Bengal, a disappointing 12-13.

On to the Phillies—The Tigers, thinking that Bunning's best days were long gone, sent him to the Philadelphia Phillies in December, 1963, along with catcher Gus Triandos for outfielder Don Demeter, their key object, and pitcher Jack Hamilton. With good young arms like Denny McLain, Mickey Lolich, and Joe Sparma coming along, the Tigers felt Bunning was expendable. For Detroit, the trade was a failure. Hamilton was gone in two years. Demeter was a reserve by 1966. Bunning, however, took a new lease on life and began the four finest seasons of his career.

From 1964 through 1967, Bunning was remarkably consistent. He was always overshadowed by someone else, including a few now in the Hall of Fame. His ERA dropped a bit each year. His luck and support also tumbled, from merely mediocre to bad. Indeed the depths into which both sunk will be treated in a separate commentary.

For the Phillies and their fans, 1964 was to be one of the most terrible, forgettable seasons in a long terrible, forgettable history. For some veteran followers of the franchise, nothing since—even a World Championship—has washed the taste of 1964 from their mouths. The Quaker City nine led by 6-1/2 games with just two weeks to play, went into a ten-game losing streak and opened the door for the Cardinals to snatch the flag.

Bunning was a part of both the upsurge and the collapse. Used only against AL teams in spring training, he was off to an uncharacteristic good start. When the skid began, he was 18-5, lost three during the nightmare, the last two when he was clobbered on just two days' rest. In the season's finale he blanked Cincinnati 10-0 to get the Phils into a second place tie with the Redlegs, each one game behind the Cards. Even San Francisco came back into the race and in fourth place was only three out. So Bunning finished with 19 wins and was named the righthanded pitcher on the NL All-Star team by *The Sporting News*.

The perfecto and beyond—On June 21 came one of the highlights of the entire season. That Sunday afternoon Bunning hurled the second no-hitter of his career, a *perfect* game over the Mets in New York. His brilliant 10-strikeout performance ended with a coup de grace in the last of the ninth as he nailed Charley Smith on a foul popup, then blew down lefthanded hitters George Altman and John Stephenson on strikes. He finished well in the league in most areas: wins (fourth, tied), winning percentage (fourth, .704), ERA (fifth, 2.63), complete games (ninth, 13), innings (fourth, 284), strikeouts (fifth, 219), strikeouts per nine innings (seventh, 6.94), shutouts (second, tied, five), and had the fewest walks per game average.

In 1965, he again was stopped at 19 victories but was still among the elite in wins (eighth), winning percentage (sixth, .679), ERA (fifth, 2.60), complete games (sixth, 15), innings (sixth, 291), strikeouts (fourth, 268—the most in his career), strikeouts per nine innings (fourth, 8.29), shutouts (third, tie, seven), and walks per nine innings (seventh, 1.92). He also had 12 games with five or fewer hits allowed, including four two-hitters.Of his first four years in Philadelphia only in this one did he not conquer each foe, as both St. Louis and Los Angeles denied him a victory. However, his team was a disappointing sixth, albeit nine games over .500.

Like a broken record, Bunning was stopped at 19 wins again in 1966, in spite of the team's jump to fourth place, eight games away from first. He also lost more games than in his two previous seasons, despite a lower ERA. Even an 8-1 log through June 7 did not, in the end, get him into the 20-win circle. A drought lasting to July 23 brought only one win, though three losses were by 2-0, 1-0, and 3-1 counts. He picked up again through early September before tailing off later in the month. Two of his September deficits were by 2-1 margins. A July 27 game deserves special mention. In Los Angeles Bunning dueled Sandy Koufax into extra innings. Each went 11 rounds and left with a 1-1 tie (LA won in 16, 2-1). Koufax yielded four hits, fanned 16, and walked three, while Bunning granted six safeties, whiffed 12, and passed only two.

The Philadelphia ace defeated all rivals. In key categories his league standing was: wins (sixth), ERA (fourth, 2.41), complete games (fifth, 16), innings (second, 314), strikeouts (second, 252), and walks/9 IP (fourth, 1.58), and shutouts (first, tie with five others, five). Although rotten support upped his defeats to 14, he silenced critics with a 10-5 edge over the top three teams.

In 1967 the Xavier University grad should have had a career year. Even modest fortune would have placed his wins in the high 20's. He pitched 26 games in which he went a minimum of seven innings and yielded two earned runs or less, yet had only a 17-15 record to show for it. Five losses were by 1-0, including three in September. He had no decision in seven games won by his team. Nevertheless, he was among the NL leaders in almost every standard: wins (third, tie), ERA (second, 2.29), strikeouts (first, 253), complete games (fifth, tie, 16), hits per nine innings (sixth, 7.15), shutouts (first, six), and innings (first, 302).

1967 was the last of Bunning's effective seasons. Traded to Pittsburgh over the winter, he slipped to a wretched 4-14 in 1968, although both his ERA and strikeout totals suggest he was not pitching *that* badly. In 1969, he pitched well enough for the Pirates that Los Angeles thought he might push them over the top in a close race. But his 3-1 from mid-August was not enough, as LA finished fourth, eight games behind Atlanta. Bunning ended at 13-10 for the two teams. Released, he re-signed with the Phils and finished on a 10-15 in 1970 and 5-10 in 1971. Significantly, even in 1969 and 1970 he was fanning over six batters per nine innings. Like many fine pitchers, he stayed aboard at least one, perhaps two, seasons too long, but they were enough to get him over the 100-win threshold in the national League

Assessment—Although fortune never placed Bunning in a World Series, he turned in a magnificent record in All-Star competition. Pitching in eight of these games, six in the AL and two in the NL between 1957 and 1966, he gave up no earned runs in seven of them. Facing the best hitters from each league, and probably a better offense than almost any possible World Series opponent could have mustered, his ERA was 1.00. In 18 innings, he yielded only seven hits, while notching 13 strikeouts to a single walk.

Unfortunately, over most of his career, Jim Bunning suffered from terrible support. He was shut out a total of 41 times, 15 by a score of 1-0. A further examination of his game-by-game records reveals even beyond those shutout statistics how often he was done in by the lapses of his teammates—where a relief pitcher blew a lead, or runs did not come while he was still the "pitcher of record," or a fielding lapse happened at the wrong time. The totals on the following chart are based on a higher criteria than that used today for a so-called "quality start", i.e., three earned runs or less in six innings. Here the measure is only two earned runs or less for a six-inning stint, or three deserved tallies for seven or more innings, with separate columns for both losses and no-decisions. For balance and justice, his fortunate victories are found in a third column, where the standard used is giving up five earned runs in an eight or nine round effort or four in the six to seven zone. Below are the tough losses, no-decisions, and lucky wins in the memorable Bunning years:

	Losses	**No-decisions**	**Wins**
1957	1	2	1
1958	5	0	0
1959	3	2	2
1960	8	6	1
1961	5	3	1
1962	1	0	3
1963	4	5	2
1964	3	6	0
1965	3	4	1
1966	9	4	0
1967	9	6	0
Totals	**51**	**38**	**11**

Despite such ill fortune, Bunning stacks up very well against contemporaries in both leagues. During his seven seasons in the Detroit regular rotation, only Whitey Ford of the New York Yankees, whose team won 108 more games than the Tigers, won more games, by a 119-110 margin. In his first four seasons as a Philadelphia stalwart, he won more games than any other NL pitcher except Juan Marichal, who benefitted from a much superior Giants team. From 1964 through 1967, the Kentucky righthander had more wins and a better ERA than such fine pitchers as Bob Gibson, Don Drysdale, Jim Maloney, and Chris Short. The Xavier University graduate also had more shutouts during those four seasons than any other major league pitcher, with 23.

Jim Bunning is one of those pitchers who was much better than his won-lost record indicates. He deserves to be remembered for a great career.

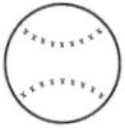

Think good ones are rare now?

A Bad Year for Catchers

Keith Storey

A lot of people complain about the lack of good catchers today. But it could be worse. Just look back at 1908, especially in the American League.

Perhaps one reason why the New York Highlanders lost 103 games and finished 39-1/2 games behind the Tigers was their catching. Their starter, Red Kleinow, hit only .168 with six extra-base hits. And their backups weren't any better. Walter "Heavy" Blair hit a whopping .190. Ed Sweeney, only managed to hit .146 with two RBI's in his 82 at bats. And this trio's game-calling skills didn't appear to be any better than their hitting, as the Highlanders ERA was the league's highest at 3.16.

The Senators had Gabby Street catching most of their games. Though known as a good defensive catcher he managed to bat a big .206.

The Athletics suffered through four catchers. Ossee Schreckengost hit a robust .222 before being dealt to the White Sox right before the end of the season. Syd Smith managed to bat .203 before being sent to the Browns during the season. That left them with Mike Powers, a fine defensive catcher who hit below the Mendoza line at .180 and would die tragically the next year. Jack Lapp managed to get into 13 games behind the plate and actually drive in a run while hitting .143.

The Boston team had Lou Criger, Bill Carrigan, Pat Donahue, and Ed McFarland as their catchers. Only Carrigan, at .235, and McFarland, at .208, hit above .200.

Among the contenders, the Browns actually had two catchers hit .200 or over (Tubby Spencer at .210 and Jim Stephens just making it at .200). Their trade for Syd Smith didn't help much, as he hit only .184 for the Browns.

The White Sox somehow managed to stay in the race to the very end with Billy Sullivan catching most of their games and hitting .191. They couldn't put their main sub in much, as Al Shaw hit .082 in 29 games behind the plate. Their trade for Schreckengost didn't help, as he hit only .188 with no RBI's in the final six games of his career.

Despite having two decent catchers, the Cleveland Naps finished a half game out. They had Nig Clarke hitting .241 and Harry Bemis .224 while splitting the catching chores for the team with the lowest ERA at 2.02.

Perhaps the Tigers won one of the tightest pennant races in history because of their catching. The solid Boss Schmidt caught 121 games and hit .265. Ira Thomas got in only 29 games behind the plate but hit an amazing (for catchers that year) .307. And for some reason, Freddie Payne got into 16 games as a catcher while beating out Al Shaw for the worst batting average among catchers at .067.

So, when people talk about how much better catchers used to be, remind them of 1908!

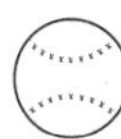

Keith Storey is a teacher who lives in Berkeley, California. He is a long-suffering White Sox fan who has become disillusioned with the change to three divisions and concentrates now on the history of the game.

<u>*A key to the Indians' 1948 pennant*</u>

Russ Christopher—Courageous Athlete

Joseph D. Tekulsky

In 1948 the Cleveland Indians defeated the Boston Braves in the World Series. Russ Christopher, their star relief pitcher, led the American League in saves with 17—an impressive number long before today's practice of a starter going six or seven "good innings," followed by a set-up man and a closer. Christopher's career was at its height, but he never played again, retiring because of a weakened heart resulting from a childhood case of rheumatic fever. He died six years later, aged only 37.

Born on September 12, 1917, in Richmond, California, the tall, thin (six feet, three inches, 170 pounds) submarine-style righthander was regarded by the 1948 champions as a loyal teammate and good citizen who, although in bad health, never complained. Described by sportswriter Red Smith as "the gentlest of guys" but with "a malevolent pitch, a sinking fastball," he was the classic closer for the 1948 Indians, appearing in 45 games, but pitching only 59 innings.

Infielder John Beradino (spelled "Berardino" in his playing days), a major leaguer from 1939 through 1952, interrupted by three years of military service from 1943 through 1945, was on the 1948 Cleveland team. He recalls, "His pitch was the true sinker ball," thrown "low and away and, sometimes, when called for," as a crossfire. It did not tail in or out. "It just did a lot of sinking."

Always aware of the risk to his health, Christopher had a seven-year career in the major leagues. In his last years he refrained from strenuous exercise, not even taking practice, except for his work on the mound during games.

Russ Christopher entered organized baseball in 1938, winning seven games and losing five for Clovis, NM in Class D, and playing seven games as an outfielder for the Class C El Paso, TX club. After an 18-7 record with El Paso in 1939, he moved up to Class B at Wenatchee, WA, breaking even at 8-8 in 1940. He won 16 and lost seven with a 2.82 earned run average for the 1941 International League champion Newark Bears, the New York Yankees' top farm club. But, evidently concerned about his heart condition, the Yankees did not bring him up to the majors, allowing the Philadelphia Athletics to draft him.

Christopher was with the A's from 1942 through 1947. He won 14 and lost 14 in 1944 and was 13-13 for a last place team in 1945. By late June of that year he had won 11 of the A's 20 victories and was considered the best pitcher in the American League by Shirley Povich of the Washington *Post* and J. G. Taylor Spink of *The Sporting News*. Although he won only two of his next 13 decisions, seven of his losses were by scores of 4-2, 2-0, 4-1, 4-3, 2-1, 3-2, and 2-0. During this lean period he pitched 13 innings of a 24-inning 1-1 tie with Detroit, giving up only five hits. Converted to relief, Christopher won 10 and lost seven in 1947, had an earned run average of 2.89, and was third in the league in saves, with 12.

A few weeks before the 1948 season opened, the Indians bought Christopher from the Athletics for a reported $25,000. Cleveland President Bill Veeck explained that the A's were willing to sell the pitcher since they "expected to lose him anyway after the end

Joseph D. Tekulsky is a retired lawyer living in Los Angeles.

of the season," when he planned to retire because of his weakened heart.

Veeck's judgment was quickly confirmed when Christopher pitched his first 14 innings of the 1948 season without giving up a run. Near the end of the season, when Christopher entered a game in the ninth inning with the bases loaded and one out, Cleveland Manager Lou Boudreau commented, "He's been my man in such spots all year."

National Baseball Library, Cooperstown, NY

Russ Christopher

The record bears out Boudreau's statement. Of Christopher's 45 appearances, 11 were for 1/3 inning, and 17 were for 2/3 to 1-2/3 innings. He pitched more than two innings only six times. Overall, his won-lost record was 3-2 with a 2.90 earned run average.

In 1948 the adage "Every game is important," was especially applicable. The Indians and the Boston Red Sox ended the regular season tied for first place. Cleveland won the pennant in a one-game playoff. Christopher had appeared in almost one-third of his team's games; he had saved 18 percent of its victories.

But Christopher's final game—his only appearance in the 1948 World Series—was a disappointment. Cleveland led the Braves, three games to one. Christopher entered the fifth game in the seventh inning with the Braves ahead, 8-5, men on first and third and one out. He gave up two singles for two runs and was relieved by Satchel Paige, who got the next two batters on a fly ball scoring Boston's final run and a ground out. The Braves won the game, 11-5. The next day, Cleveland won the sixth game and the Series.

In March, 1949, Russ Christopher retired from baseball, taking a non-strenuous job with an aircraft manufacturer in San Diego. After heart surgery in 1951, he considered returning to baseball, but he never attempted a comeback. On December 5, 1954, he died of his heart ailment in a Richmond, California, hospital.

Major League Relievers, 1947–48

	Games	Saves	Innings	Innings per game	Innings per save	ERA
1947						
Klieman	58	17	92	1.58	5.41	3.03
Casey	46	18	77	1.67	4.28	3.97
Christopher	44	12	81	1.84	6.75	2.89
Page	56	17	141	2.52	8.29	2.49
1948						
Christopher	45	17	59	1.31	3.47	2.90
Gumbert	61	17	106	1.74	6.24	3.48
Page	55	16	108	1.96	6.75	4.25

Down to the final day

The AL's 1935 Batting Races

Steve Krevisky

In 1935 the American League batting and home run titles were not decided until the final day of the season, and there were close races in many other AL offensive categories. In the National League, Arky Vaughan had a real shot at batting .400 until the last two weeks in September. It was a season of close races and close calls.

May 17—Charles Solomon (Buddy) Myer, the second sacker for Washington, went 3 for 3, with two runs scored (RS), four runs batted in (RBI) and two doubles (2B), in a 10-8 victory over Detroit. Hank Greenberg tallied 1 for 4 with two RBI. At this point, Gee Walker of the Tigers was the pacesetter in Batting Average (BA) at .433. Bob Johnson and Jimmie Foxx were second and third with .391 and .382, respectively. Charley Gehringer weighed in at .350.

Vaughan led the NL at .398, which marked the first time he'd been below .400 so far in the season (he also had 24 RS).

May 20—Greenberg doubled in two runs in the 11th inning, after Foxx advised A's pitcher George Caster to walk Gehringer in order to pitch to Greenberg. Foxx and Johnson both homered in this game, with Johnson going 3 for 6, two RS, two RBI. Foxx checked in at 3 for 5, one RS, two RBI. Greenberg went 2 for 5 with two RS and three RBI. Goose Goslin's muff of an easy fly ball in the ninth inning allowed the A's to tie the game, but the Tigers won 8-6 in 11 innings, thanks to Greenberg's heroics. Also on this day, Myer, batting cleanup, went 2 for 4 against the Browns in an 8-2 triumph for the Nats.

June 13—Greenberg blasted his fourteenth HR. Van Lingle Mungo shut out Pittsburgh 3-0. Indian outfielder Joe Vosmik drilled 2 for 4 as Oral Hildebrand pitched the Tribe over the A's by a 4-3 count. Earl Averill had a good day, going 3 for 5 with one 2B and one stolen base (SB). The Yankees led the AL race by 2-1/2 games over Chicago, with Detroit and Cleveland third and fourth, respectively. The second division saw Boston fifth, followed by Washington, Philadelphia and St. Louis.

June 21—A big nine-run fifth inning propelled the Chisox to a 10-6 win over the Senators. Myer tallied 3 for 4, one RS, with Luke Appling going 2 for 5 for the potent Sox. Schoolboy Rowe, whose wife had just given birth, whitewashed the Bronx Bombers, 7-0 at Navin Field in Detroit. This salvaged one win out of four for the Bengals in this series. Bob Johnson now led the AL at .370, with 49 RS. Buddy Myer stood at .345. In the NL, Vaughan maintained his .400 BA, with 50 RS.

July 13—Roger (Doc) Cramer went 6 for 6 with three RS and five RBI in the opener of a doubleheader against Detroit. Foxx belted HR No. 16, going 3 for 3 with three RS and four RBI. All of this helped lead the Mackmen to an 18-5 triumph. Pitcher Johnny Marcum chipped in with 4 for 6, three RS, three RBI. Greenberg

Steve Krevisky is associate professor of mathematics at Middlesex Community-Technical College in Middletown, Connecticut. He is the editor of the Left Field Baseball Book, *(1991, 1992), and has made numerous presentations at SABR and mathematics conventions.*

drove in two runs, going 2 for 4 in the process. In the nightcap, won by the Tigers 6-3, Tommy Bridges racked up his 12th win. Johnson went 3 for 6 and popped his 18th HR, with three RBI. Pinky Higgins went 4 for 4. Greenberg rapped out his 26th circuit clout, going 2 for 5, two RS, two RBI. In the batting race, Vaughan led the NL at .384, with Medwick second at .363. Johnson still led the AL with .353; Vosmik stood runner-up with .341.

After 92 games, Hammerin' Hank already had 118 RBI, which put him on a pace to break Hack Wilson's major league record of 190, set five years earlier. Hank was quick to give credit to his teammates, in particular White, Cochrane, and Gehringer batting in front of him and Goslin behind him in the batting order.

An example of this was a game where Greenberg went 4 for 5, with two RS, two RBI and a triple, as the Bengals pounded the Tribe in Cleveland, 14-6. Goslin was 4 for 6, with one RS, one 2B and five RBI. White checked in at 3 for 4 with four RS, and Gehringer 2 for 5, two RS, three RBI. Who would *you* pitch around?

Greenberg was well ahead in HR with 27, followed by Bob Johnson with 19, Bonura 19, Foxx 18, Gehrig 17. Johnson was second in RBI with 75, then Goslin 74, Gehringer 73, Bonura 71.

In the batting race, Vosmik led with .350, followed by Foxx at .337, then Gehringer and Cramer at .334. Gehringer had 85 RS. In the NL, Vaughan remained the pacesetter at .393, while Medwick weighed in second at .375 and 83 RS. Detroit led the pack in the AL with a 57-35 record. The Yankees stood second at 52-36. The A's had fallen to sixth place, 18-1/2 games behind Detroit.

August 6—Vosmik still led the AL in BA at .352, with Greenberg at .339 with 30 HR, Cramer at .334, Myer and Moses at .334. Vaughan still led the NL at .398, with Medwick .379 and no one else over .350. Vaughan climbed to .401 by Aug. 8 and to .403 by Aug. 18. By then the AL batting race had really begun to take shape. Vosmik led with .347, Greenberg .345 (with a shot at the Triple Crown), Myer .345, Cramer .344, Gehringer .328.

August 19—With the Tigers now eight games up on the Yankees, the actors in the AL batting race began to flip-flop. Myer now led at .345, followed by Cramer at .344, Greenberg .343, Vosmik .342, Gehringer .326. In the NL, Vaughan reached .407.

In the HR derby, Greenberg led at 31, followed by Foxx at 22, Johnson at 21, Bonura and Gehrig at 19. Greenberg now had 132 RBI; then came Goslin 86, Johnson 84, Gehrig 83, Gehringer and Foxx 81. Berger led the NL HR race with 26, followed by Ott at 24 and Camilli with 21.

August 27—The HR race in the AL had begun to heat up. The A's and Tigers split a DH in Detroit on Aug. 26. Foxx homered in each game, giving him 10 homers on the road trip and 28 for the year, only five behind Greenberg. Johnson blasted his 24th in the opener. Unfortunately for the A's, they stood 23 games behind the front-running Bengals. Meanwhile, player-manager Pie Traynor belted a grand slam, four singles and tallied six RBI for Pittsburgh in a 10-2 rout of the Giants in NY. Trosky drilled his 22nd HR, breaking up a pitchers' duel between Pearson and Walberg in Cleveland. Vosmik went 2 for 4 as the Indians topped the Bosox 4-3.

September 1—Myer took an 0 for 6 collar vs. Grove and the Red Sox, falling to .338. Vosmik remained the leader at .348 after going 1 for 5 in a losing effort against the White Sox. Greenberg at .342 and Gehrig at .340 stood ahead of Myer as well. Foxx pounded out his 29th HR in a defeat by the Yanks at Shibe. He now trailed Hank by only four HR. In the NL, Berger and Ott were tied at 29 HR.

September 7—Foxx broke up Elden Auker's no-hitter with an eighth-inning double in the nightcap of a DH, swept by Detroit. Gehringer went 4 for 6, Cochrane 3 for 4. In the opener, Foxx had popped HR's No. 30 and 31 against Tommy Bridges, with two RS and four RBI. Cochrane was 3 for 3, three RS, three 2B, three RBI.

Buddy Myer went 0 for 3, then 2 for 5 against the Browns, with game two called because of darkness. Vosmik now led the AL in BA with .353, followed by Myer at .342, Gehrig .338 (who thought he was having a bad year—he had 110 RS, 27 HR and 112 RBI at this point), Greenberg .336 (108 RS, 34 HR, 155 RBI), Cramer .334, Gehringer .328, Foxx .327 (99 RS, 31 HR, 101 RBI). In the NL, Vaughan remained over .400 at .402.

It seemed noteworthy that while Detroit was only 8-9 in games played against New York, they had fattened up on Philadelphia (14-5), St. Louis (15-4), Cleveland (15-5) and Boston (12-6). The Yankees held a 14-6 margin over the A's, but stood barely over .500 against Cleveland and St. Louis, and even with the Red Sox.

September 14—The AL batting race continued to be tight. Greenberg led the pack at .347 (112 RS, 35 HR, 163 RBI). Vosmik held at .344. Myer was at .342 (102 RS). Foxx re-entered the picture at .340, with 100 RS, 33 HR and 106 RBI. Gehrig weighed in at .336, 117 RS, 30 HR and 116 RBI. Cramer fell in at .334, Gehringer at .329 (115 RS, 98 RBI). Vaughan paced the NL at .393.

September 18—Harder shut out the A's in the second game of a DH for his 20th win. Foxx tallied 1 for 3 in game one, while Vosmik went 2 for 4. In game two, Foxx went 2 for 4, Vosmik 2 for 5. Vosmik and Foxx were now one-two in the batting race at .348 and .346 respectively—precisely the averages they would finish with. Jimmie now had an 18-game hitting streak. Myer weighed in at .341, Greenberg at .338, and Cramer at .334. Foxx and Greenberg each had 114 RS. Over in the NL, Vaughan led comfortably at .390 (105 RS) over Medwick (.357, 124 RS).

September 21—The Tigers clinched the pennant by sweeping the Brownies in a DH. Bridges and Auker collected the wins, Auker via a shutout. Foxx suffered an 0 for 9 collar in a doubleheader against the Senators, thus ending his 18-game hitting streak. Myer took an 0 for 4 collar in game one and sat in game two. Vosmik posted 1 for 2 and Trosky powered his 24th HR in a 7-3 Tribe victory over the Chisox.

Vosmik still led at .348, with 106 RS, 47 2B and 206 hits. Myer moved into the runner-up spot at .342, with 105 RS and 201 hits. Foxx checked in at .340, 114 RS, 34 HR and 109 RBI. Fourth stood Cramer at .337, with 207 hits. Greenberg held at .335, 46 2B, 117 RS, 36 HR and 170 RBI. Then came Gehrig at .332, 118 RS, 30 HR, 118 RBI, and Gehringer, .332, 120 RS, 100 RBI. The Tigers led in RS with 895, well ahead of the Yanks at 773. The Mackmen had only scored 683.

September 22—The Cubs won their 18th consecutive game, shutting out the Pirates 2-0. The Nats swept a DH vs. the A's by the lopsided scores of 10-2 and 11-1. Foxx again took an 0 for 8 collar, which ultimately cost him the batting crown. Myer meanwhile went 3 for 6. In game one of a doubleheader, Vosmik, batting cleanup, went 1 for 3. Entering the final week of the season, several players still had a realistic shot at the AL batting title.

The HR races remained close as well. Greenberg narrowly led Foxx, 36 to 34. Gehrig followed with 30. In the senior circuit, Berger had 33 round-trippers to Ott's 30.

September 24—At the beginning of the day, the AL batting leaders were: Vosmik .349, Myer .341 (he went 0 for 3 vs. Gomez and the Yanks), Foxx .340, Cramer .337, and Greenberg .335. Vaughan paced the NL at .389. The Tribe belted the Bengals 14 to 7. Trosky pasted his 25th HR, Vosmik went 2 for 5, Greenberg 2 for 3. The Bosox swept the Macks in a DH. Foxx tallied 1 for 4 in game one, then sat out game two. Johnson drilled 2 for 4 in each game. Now the AL leaders were: Vosmik .350, Myer .342, Cramer .338, Foxx .338 (he'd been slumping) and Greenberg .337.

September 25—Vosmik helped his cause by going 3 for 5 against the Tigers. Greenberg had 1 for 4. Wes Ferrell notched his 25th win of the season for the Sox, beating the A's in Boston. Foxx scored one run, going 1 for 3.

September 26—Myer enjoyed a big day, with 4 for 5, one HR, one RS, two RBI. The cast of characters in the AL batting race remained unchanged. Vosmik was top dog at .352, with 214 hits. Myer was second at .345, 109 RS, 209 hits. Foxx remained third at .338, 115 RS. Cramer followed with .336, 213 hits, then Greenberg at .336, 203 hits, 119 RS. Vaughan remained well ahead in the NL at .386.

September 27—The Cubs clinched the NL flag over the Cards by sweeping them in a DH, 6-2 and 5-3. This ran the Bruins' winning streak to an awesome 21. All AL games were rained out.

On the final weekend of the season, the pennant races had already been decided, but the batting, HR and other titles were still in doubt.

September 28—The Senators and A's split a DH, with the scond game shortened to six innings due to darkness. Foxx checked in with 1 for 4 in game one and 1 for 2 in game two, failing to gain ground on the leaders. Myer worked 1 for 2 in the opener and 1 for 3 in the nightcap. Greenberg took an 0 for 8 as the Tigers and White Sox split a DH. Gehringer went 2 for 4 and 3 for 5. The Tribe swept the Browns as Vosmik tallied 0 for3, then 1 for 4.

Vosmik's BA lead had narrowed considerably. He now batted .350, with 108 RBI, 215 hits. Myer, second at .348, had 211 hits. Foxx remained third at .338, with 115 RS, 34 HR, 109 RBI. Cramer stayed fourth at .334, 214 hits, followed by Gehrig with .333, 30 HR, 120 RBI, 124 RS. Greenberg had also "slumped" to .332, 119 RS, 36 HR, 170 RBI. Gehringer weighed in at .328, 123 RS, 104 RBI. (Wes Ferrell, who was 25-14, was also batting .401 in his limited appearances.)

Trosky drilled his 26th HR, but Greenberg still led the HR derby over Foxx, 36 to 34.

September 29—The final day of the season saw an exciting finish. Foxx powered two HR on this day against the Nats, thus enabling him to tie Greenberg for the HR title, after a long uphill climb. His 35th HR was a three-run shot, putting the A's ahead 4-2 in the third inning. His 36th four-bagger, a smash into Shibe's centerfield stands in the seventh inning, put the A's ahead, though the Senators regained the lead, 8-7. However, the Mackmen rallied to score four in the eighth and win their home finale, 11-8. Johnson's bases loaded double did the bulk of the damage. Foxx went 3 for 4. He had three RS and four RBI to go with his two HR.

In this same game, Myer went 4 for 5 with two RS and one RBI. This helped him to "steal" the batting title from Vosmik. Joe pinch hit in game one of a DH, going

0 for 1. He was going to sit out game two, but when the word was conveyed that Myer was getting hot, he changed his mind. He went 1 for 3 and thus lost the batting title by one point on the last day of the season.

Final figures—When the official figures settled in, Myer thus won the AL batting title with .349 to Vosmik's .348. Foxx finished a strong third at .346. Vosmik beat out Myer in hits, 216 to 215, with Cramer at 214. The doubles race was just as hot, with Vosmik again leading with 47, followed by Greenberg at 46 and Moose Solters with 45. Vosmik led in 3B as well with 20. Foxx edged out Hank for the slugging title, .636 to .628, and also led in HR percentage, with 6.7 to Greenberg's 5.8. Vaughan won the NL batting title at .385, and also led in slugging aveage with .607.

It was a remarkable season, with so many races going down to the final day. Myer became only the third Senator to win a batting title. Vosmik had a great all-around season. Greenberg posted an outstanding RBI total and would win the MVP award. Foxx, playing for a cellar team and getting help only from Higgins, Johnson and Cramer, had a fine season (even defensively—he made only three errors at first base all year, led all AL first basemen in fielding average, and became the first first sacker in major league history to participate in six double plays in one game.)

This remarkable season also marked the end of an era. Over the past seven years, four different teams—the A's, Yankees, Senators, and Tigers—had won the AL pennant. The next year would begin a stretch of unprecedented New York dominance.

New York Oddities

The second game of the May 31, 1964 twinbill at Shea Stadium between the Giants and the Mets is best remembered for establishing such records as game duration (seven hours, twenty-three minutes) and doubleheader length (thirty-two innings). There were, however, other memorable aspects of that twenty-three-inning marathon, such as the sight of Willie Mays playing shortstop for a stretch. Further, Roy McMillan snagged Orlando Cepeda's line drive in the fourteenth inning to start a triple play, surely the latest "trikilling" ever in a game. But another noteworthy event wasn't obvious at the time and, in fact, was not revealed until many years later—after Gaylord Perry finally retired. He then confessed that it was in this game, in which he pitched the last ten innings to gain the victory, that he first threw his infamous spitball in a major league contest.

In the long history of the New York Giants' occupation of the Polo Grounds (1891–1957), not to mention the years the Yankees called it home, there was only one home run slugged into the distant center field bleachers—that by Joe Adcock. Then the Mets were born and reopened the ballpark for 1962 and '63. In that brief two-year sojourn the total of center field bleacher homers was increased to three. But the amazing part of these two later blasts was that they were belted on consecutive days. The then-Cub Lou Brock did it on June 17, 1962 and the Braves' Hank Aaron duplicated the feat on June 18. Three center field homers over the course of sixty-nine years and two of them come on consecutive days. What are the odds?

—Jack Keeley

Chuck Klein's fabulous five-year run

Nobody Did It Better

Don Nelson

No major leaguer ever put together five consecutive years at the plate and in the field to equal Chuck Klein's five-year period from 1929-33, Klein:

1. Set the twentieth-century National League single-season standards for runs scored and extra-base hits.

2. Set a new NL record for home runs in a season.

3. Had more than 200 hits each year (averaging almost 224) and had more than 600 at bats every year except one, averaging 623 a season.

4. Won a triple crown and a Most Valuable Player award.

5. Led the league in home runs (including one tie) every year except 1930.

6. Led the league in total bases four times, in slugging and runs scored three times, in hits, doubles and runs batted in twice, and in batting average and stolen bases once each (the only time in NL history a player has led in homers and steals simultaneously. Ty Cobb did it in the AL in 1909).

7. Led the league in outfield assists three times and double plays by an outfielder once. He had an incredible 44 assists in 1930, the twentieth-century record for outfielders.

Beside his high hits-per-year average, Klein had seasonal averages of 36 home runs, 132 runs scored, 139 RBI, 46 doubles and a batting average of .359.

Klein won his way into the Hall of Fame entirely on the strength of these five great years. Even though he performed in 17 different National League campaigns, he was first a rookie (1928) and later a journeyman (1934-44), never leading in anything (except pinch hits in 1939), bouncing from team to team. In his five straight super years, he compiled more than half of his career totals for all offensive categories. He was a .359 hitter in 1929-33, a .284 batter otherwise.

A serious hamstring injury in 1935 may have been the reason Klein never excelled again.

Perhaps no other nonpitcher did so much in so short a time to earn a prized plaque in Cooperstown. You could chop out five consecutive years of Babe Ruth's career and still have combinations of other great five-year performances left over. The same would apply to immortals like Ty Cobb, Rogers Hornsby, Honus Wagner, Lou Gehrig, Jimmie Foxx, Ted Williams, Stan Musial, Mickey Mantle, Willie Mays and Hank Aaron. These men demonstrated sustained excellence year after year.

Klein's best year was 1930, when he set the runs-scored, long hits, and assists standards, and also registered four other performances that rank among

Don Nelson is a retired government worker living in Fairfax, Virginia. He is well-acquainted with losing teams, such as the one Chuck Klein played on: he's a lifelong Cub fan.

the top seasonal marks of all time in the NL: No. 2 all-time in RBI and total bases, No. 3 in doubles and No. 4 in hits.

In 1929 he set the NL record for home runs with 43. The next season Hack Wilson demolished that mark.

Of course, 1930 was that wild and crazy year in which the ball was a real bunny bopper. It was when Wilson of the Cubs set the all-time major league record for RBI (190) and the NL mark for HR (56), when Bill Terry batted .401, when 12 players rapped out more than 200 hits each and when Klein and his Phillies mates collectively batted .315, yet finished last.

In many ways, 1932, not 1930, was the year Chuck chalked up the most awesome stats. That year he deservedly was voted MVP. Without benefit of a carrot-crunching ball, he whistled out 226 hits, 38 home runs (good for a tie with Mel Ott for the league lead), scored 152 times and drove in 137 runs, batted .348, slugged .646, had 103 extra-base hits and racked up 420 total bases. Besides homers, he led the senior circuit in hits, runs, slugging, total bases and extra-base hits. His 1932 totals for runs, total bases and long hits rank among the top 10 all-time single season efforts in the majors. He was in the top three in the league in a dozen offensive departments. 1932 was also the year he pilfered 20 bases to establish his one-of-a-kind power-speed achievement.

National Baseball Library, Cooperstown, NY

Chuck Klein

Curiously, Klein captured the triple crown in 1933, which was, in effect, an off year for him. By then, the baseball used in the NL had not completely died, but certainly the rabbit had long since hopped out of it. Although he led the league in seven important batting categories, he had far from his best year in any of them. In fact, his league-leading 1933 totals for HR, RBI and BA would not have cracked the top five in any of these measures in 1930.

Looking back, it's easy to see circumstances that tend to rub some of the sheen off his accomplishments. Besides the lively ball in use in 1930, Klein had the advantage of playing his home games in cozy Baker Bowl, which had the easiest right-field fence in the majors (Klein was a left-handed batter). He had more than two times as many homers at home as on the road in 1929-33. Other Phillie lefty-swinging stalwarts, like Cy Williams and Lefty O'Doul, exploited the short barrier for offensive shows, too.

Also, unlike the performances of Ruth, Gehrig, Cobb et al., his tremendous hitting did not make his club a winner. The Phils never climbed higher than fourth in the 1929-33 period, finishing in the second division four times.

The limited dimensions of right field in the Phillies' home park helped his fielding statistics. That and the fact he had so many moving targets to throw at. Phillies pitchers were putting runners aboard at an alarming rate. The team from the City of Brotherly Love finished last in the league in earned run average every year in the half-decade under scrutiny. Phils moundsmen were shelled for more than 1,000 runs in 1929 and 1,199 in 1930!

But, going strictly by the numbers, Chuck really chalked 'em up, and baseball is and always will be a game of numbers.

Charles Herbert Klein was 24 years old and in only his second year in the bigs when he started his incredible five-year streak. By 1934 he was traded to the Cubs as a reward for his Triple Crown year and assumed his journeyman status. He didn't come cheap to the Cubs. He was traded for three players and $65,000. He was the regular right fielder for Chicago's 1935 pennant-winning team, but was traded back to the Phils during the 1936 campaign. In 1939 he was released by Philadelphia and signed by the Pirates. Following that season, the Bucs released him and he caught on with the Phillies again for the 1940 season. There he lingered through the '44 season, playing a little and coaching some.

In stark contrast to his superb 1929-33 years, his last five seasons saw him come to bat less than 500 times and bat sub-.200.

Chuck Klein, like two of the other great hitters of the '30s, Foxx and Gehrig, died prematurely. The end came for him in 1958, at age 53. He was named to the Hall of Fame in 1980, a half century after his assault on the record books.

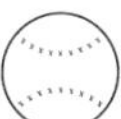

The "colored" team of 1866-1871

Philadelphia's Pythians

Jerrold Casway

When the African-American experience in baseball is discussed, the focus is usually on the twentieth century and Jackie Robinson. More detailed studies recollect late nineteenth-century black teams like the Cuban Giants of New York and the Orions of Philadelphia. But these clubs and their players represent the adolescence of African-American baseball. The roots of black baseball stem from post-Civil War ball clubs like the Pythian of Philadelphia.

The travails of this overlooked team reflected the changing patterns of postwar America. The Pythian in October, 1867, suffered the first recorded baseball act of segregation, it leased and played in white-used ball parks, and during the fall of 1869 it competed against white baseball clubs. Many of the Pythians were acknowledged by the baseball community for their athletic skills and sportsmanship. They also represented some of the most successful and best educated members of Philadelphia's small black middle class. Some of the players were politically active and were in the forefront of the Quaker City's post-war civil rights movement. Their story is as much social history as it is a baseball saga.

The number of "colored" people in Philadelphia after the Civil War was about 22,000, or four percent of the city's population. Only the border city of Baltimore had a larger urban African-American population. Most of Philadelphia's black inhabitants lived in the eastern inner-city wards near places of employment and economic opportunity. Contributing to the respectability of this mixed socioeconomic community were the Knights of Pythias Lodge and a Quaker-run high school for "colored youths." This was an old farm trade school relocated in 1852 to 7th and Lombard Streets. With the establishment of a library and a full academic curriculum, Liberty Hall, as the school was called, educated the city's aspiring black children and provided a meeting place for the community.

A leader emerges—One of the students was Octavius Catto. This free-born (1839) son of a Presbyterian minister from Charleston, South Carolina, was an outstanding student and exceptional athlete, who would become the captain and shortstop of the Pythian baseball club. Noted for his intellect and his oratory skills, Catto was appointed in 1859 to teach at his alma mater. Over the next decade he headed the boys' school and emerged as a local political activist. In 1864, Catto's school moved to 9th and Bainbridge Streets where it became a center of intellectual, commercial, and athletic endeavors. This new Institute for Colored Youth, renamed the Banneker Institute, gave Catto and his associates opportunities for personal growth and community influence. Playing baseball was one extension of their active lives.

Part of Catto's classical-style education involved athletics. During his high school years the dominant sport in Philadelphia was cricket. The game was particularly attractive to the socially striving people of the Quaker City. It was a sport identified with propriety and old-world traditions. Catto excelled at cricket, but the war interrupted the daily sporting routines of the new school. Eventually Catto enlisted with other black men

Jerrold Casway is a professor of history and division chairman at Howard Community College in Columbia, Maryland.

in a "colored" local militia. His leadership abilities led to his appointment as a major and inspector of the 5th Brigade. Stationed in the suburbs of Philadelphia, Catto was exposed to the popular bivouac game of baseball. After the war, like other returning soldiers, he began to participate in organized ball games. This sport was more than an athletic outlet. It provided Catto with a status that allowed him to circulate among the northeastern African-American communities that fielded baseball teams.

Club ball—By the summer of 1865 a number of black teams were already in existence. Among the first clubs organized were the Monitor Club of Jamaica, Long Island, and the Bachelor team of Albany, New York. But in May, 1866, a third team, the Excelsior of Philadelphia took the field. During that same season other black teams were spawned in the District of Columbia, Baltimore, Brooklyn, Chicago, and Camden. In Philadelphia the Excelsior gained competitors—the Independent ball team and a club from 9th and Bainbridge called the Institute. Later that summer, because a large number of Institute players were affiliated with the Knights of Pythias Lodge, the team was renamed the Pythian. Members met and stored their equipment at the Institute's former site, Liberty Hall.

Many of the players from these teams, including Catto's Pythians, received their early bat-ball experiences from town ball, an early baseball prototype, and cricket. Philadelphia had three black cricket teams, which played their matches "in a lot back of the Academy of Music and on an open square at the northwest corner of 16th and Pine." In spite of their enthusiasm for playing ball, the Pythian initially had trouble competing out of their neighborhood. Apparently, there was a turf boundary, and the Irish tried to keep the blacks of the inner-city wards from venturing south of Bainbridge Street. According to a reminiscence, Bainbridge was the "dead line" and any movement beyond "meant contention."

This prevented the Pythian from playing at the most convenient ball field, the Parade Grounds or Keystone Park, at 11th and Wharton Streets. Their alternative was to take the Camden Federal Street ferry and play ball on the old prewar cricket and town ball grounds at Diamond Cottage near Market Street. How they overcame the contentious Irish is not known for certain, but there is speculation that the Pythian took large number of players and followers out of the neighborhood to deter their adversaries. On October 3, 1866, at the Wharton Street grounds, the Pythian played and lost a match against the Bachelor Club of Albany, 70-15. This game is the only known regular match for the Pythian in their inaugural year.

The African-American community of Philadelphia had a great interest in baseball and ardently followed their white and "colored" teams. Eventually the growing importance of intercity rivalries led to the best players being drawn to one representative club. It was not inevitable that the Pythian would be that team, but their affiliation with the Banneker Institute and their own financial resources were hard to overlook. Beginning in 1867, the Pythian recruited players from the Excelsior. These raids caused much friction, and by the end of 1868 the Excelsior had trouble fielding a competitive team.

The 1867 season was the first full campaign for the upstart Pythian. It established a board of directors, (Jefferson Cavens, Henry Bascom and Joe Selsey) and elected officers (James Purnell, president; Raymond Burr, vice president; Jacob White, secretary, and Thomas Charnock, treasurer). They chose as their "field captain," Octavious Catto, who was described as a "brainy" and "consumate" manager. He was 28 years old and a 13-game schedule lay ahead of him. They won eight, lost three, and two games have no known outcome. What is most fascinating about these contests was the relationships between the rival teams. The secretary of each club, like Catto's close friend, Jacob C. White, would enter into correspondence for challenging and scheduling individual matches. Once a game was agreed upon, a ball field was contracted and arrangements set in motion for pre- and postgame festivities. Picnics, dances, and banquets were planned by the women, making these games community and family celebrations.

Two series played against the Alert and Mutual ball clubs of Washington D.C. were representative of these activities. In July the Pythian played both teams in Philadelphia, defeating the Alert in a rained-out four-inning game, 21-18, and losing to the Mutual in a disputed contest, 44-43. The return matches, in late August, were played before large and enthusiastic crowds in the nation's capital. Again the Pythian beat the Alert in a rain-shortened game and two days later avenged the earlier defeat by subduing the Mutual 50-43. Both series were celebrated with food, receptions, and celebrity watching. The greatest stir was caused by the appearance of Frederick Douglass, whose son Charles, a clerk at the Treasury Department, played third base for the Alert. The great abolitionist sat on the reporter's platform and cheered for his son's team. Douglass was joined by members of the Philadelphia Athletics, white sportswriters, and black leaders from both cities. A reporter from the Philadelphia *Sunday Mercury* described the Pythians as a "well-behaved gentlemanly set of young fellows ... [who] are rapidly winning distinction in the use of the bat."

All of these teams also had their own set of rules. The Pythian declared that liquor, card playing, and gambling were strictly prohibited. Neither would the team tolerate "unbecoming language or conduct" that might bring disrepute to the team or the Institute. Violators would be fined, suspended or expelled. Annual dues were one dollar.

Black and white—1867 was also a time of reckoning for the Pythian. By June the team had gone from semiweekly practices in Camden, New Jersey, to scheduled games at the Wharton Parade Grounds and the Athletics' park at 15th and Columbia. The Pythian even had players and officials from the Athletics serve as game umpires. These successes were dampened in October when their application for admission to the Pennsylvania Association of Amateur Baseball Players was rejected on the grounds of race. Although the Pythian had the active support of the Athletics and their vice president, E. Hicks Hayhurst, the Convention's presiding officer, they were advised after much debate to withdraw their motion rather than suffer the stigma of being "black balled."

Undeterred, Catto and White were determined to improve their club and expand their schedule to accommodate the challenges of all comers. To try the mettle of older teams and intercity rivals, the Pythian trained hard and enticed the last group of players from the Excelsior. The Pythian actually had four separate nines affiliated with the parent organization. The first team, led by Catto, had some exceptional players, like John Cannon and Jefferson Cavens. Cannon, their pitcher, leadoff batter, and power hitter, was considered by white admirers as "a baseball wonder." The other nines were composites of former Banneker students, businessmen, and club executives. During the 1868 season, Jacob White arranged for 11 matches. Of the eight games whose results are known, seven were victories and one was a tie. With the exception of games in Harrisburg and West Chester, the Pythian played its contests at the Athletics' ballfield, at the Parade grounds, and at an irregularly shaped field at 24th and Columbia, where the Phillies began to play in 1883.

The 1869 season was the zenith for the Pythian Baseball Club. It was scheduled for 14 games, but the results of 10 contests are not known. The available record was three wins and one loss. The year was also significant for two reasons—the extent of its traveling and its games against white teams. The Pythians had an overnight series in Washington, D.C., and ventured to New Brunswick, Camden, Chester and West Chester.

The most noteworthy contests of that summer were played against local white ball clubs. After the events of 1867, Catto and Jacob White were concerned about how the "white fraternity" would accept their success. Almost a year after their rejection by the Pennsylvania Association, Catto spoke about the "probability of our meeting our white brethren." With the Pythian's success and popularity, white clubs responded to their challenges. The first game of this kind was against the city's oldest ball club, the Olympics, who played at 25th and Jefferson Streets. On Friday, September 3, playing before the largest crowd "that has been on the ground for two years," the Pythian succumbed to the Olympics 44-23. Colonel Thomas Fitzgerald, the founding president of the Athletics and owner of the *City Item*, served as umpire. A return match was arranged for October, but probably was never played. Two weeks later the Pythian played and defeated Fitzgerald's white *City Item* ball club, 27-17, at the Athletics grounds on Columbia Avenue. But the scheduled game with the Masonic Club of Manayunk had no published results. The win against the newspaper team may have put off the challenges from white clubs. In 1912 a contemporary black Philadelphian chronicler, recounting Pythian exploits, commented how "Baseball did wonders in the way of levelling prejudice."

Although the Pythian players could not contend with semiprofessonal and more experienced teams, there was little difference between them and the city's other amateur baseballers. The team had an account with the A.J. Reach Sporting Goods Company, and the cancelled checks of Jacob White attest to the need for balls, bats, belts, uniforms, hats, and spiked shoes. Cross referencing the Pythians in census data indicates other similarities. African-American players, like their white counterparts, were artisans, petty proprietors, and clerks, but the data also shows they were less affluent than the white players. All the Pythians were born in America and were slightly older, at an average of 28, than their white contemporaries. By 1870 the composition of the team had changed, for only 40 percent of the Pythians were directly associated with the Banneker Institute.

Danger and tragedy—The next two years for the Pythian were a mixture of puzzlement and tragedy. There is no record of their playing in 1870, and it is not known whether they suspended competition or if their games were simply not recorded. There are several scenarios. First, after the ratification in February of the Fifteenth Amendment, the voting rights of African Americans were tested in an off-year spring election. Alarmed that the newly enfranchised black votes might jeopardize the city's entrenched Democratic leaders, a new wave of racial intimidation and violence surfaced. These conditions would have distracted men like Catto and kept them off the ball field. The situation also made it dangerous to invite other black teams to the Quaker City. These circumstances would have made it difficult to rent grounds for games. Another factor for their inactivity may have been the unexpected death of their star player and club director, Jefferson Cavens.

By the 1871 season, the Pythian resumed a moderate schedule and played four games at the city's leading ballpark, the newly renovated grounds at 25th and Jefferson. The use of that field was made possible by the Athletics, who had taken over the grounds when they joined the new professional National Association. The Pythian's only setback that summer was against the powerful Unique Baseball Club from Chicago. They lost 19-18, but two days later they avenged themselves by beating Unique 24-16.

This triumph seems to have been the last game played by the original Pythian of Philadelphia. Catto and many of his teammates were in their early 30s, and had done little to recruit or nurture younger players. Catto also spent a great deal of time in Washington and did not play that season with the Pythian. Whether he intended to relocate will never be known, for the dominant spirit of the Pythian, met an untimely death.

Less than a month after the Unique series, race riots broke out in Philadelphia. On election day, October 10, the Irish of Moyamensing, who remained hostile to the city's black population, became inflamed by campaign rhetoric and the closing of their volunteer firehouse. Incited by neighborhood Democratic politicians, the Irish, with police acceptance, assaulted the newly franchised black voters in the city's 4th and 5th Wards. Catto was attacked near his boarding house by a young Irishman, who had been injured in an earlier disturbance. Catto was shot three times, and killed. He was given a full military funeral, which progressed in a drizzling rain along Broad Street, before a huge crowd of mourners. An editorial in the *Philadelphia Bulletin* lamented,

> He was a good citizen, a pure and honest man, a ripe scholar and a consistent friend of the oppressed negroes. He was worth more to this community and the world than a million such men as the Democratic politicians who provoked the riots yesterday.

His murderer, Frank Kelly, was not arraigned until six years later. He was never convicted.

Catto was martyred for the cause of civil rights, and Philadelphia lost an articulate reformer. From the standpoint of baseball, Catto was mourned for what he had accomplished for the game and how he had used baseball to bring the city's diverse communities together. Missing their captain, the pioneering Pythians lost their will to compete on what Octavius Catto once described as, the "field of green." Without their heart and soul, the Pythian simply hung their spikes up and almost passed into oblivion.

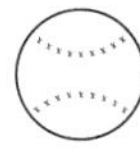

Dolly does the play-by-play

You Dear Darling Nan: Only think! I saw a real game of base ball yesterday, and when they all got ready and began, it was just too jolly for anything. Mr. Denny stood up with a stick in his hands—a bat Jack called it—and without a word of warning one rough-looking man threw a ball at him as hard as ever he could. The umpire jumped out of the way just in time to save himself, but another man—and he was the nicest looking of those on the other side— bravely stopped the ball or it might have struck some one. I asked Jack why they allowed the man who threw the ball to be so careless, but Jack told me not to parade my ignorance—Jack can be awfully rude when he likes—and I turned to see what the director of the game would have to say to such reckless behavior, but he didn't seem to mind it at all, and by this time the man who had stopped the ball before put on a front of some ash colored padded stuff, cut nearly V shaped. Then the excitement began and it was too perfectly delightful. I knew that other man would injure some one; the way he threw the ball at the umpire and he did. He struck one of our club and the poor fellow lay down on the ground, and I think he really cried. I felt so sorry for him that I asked Jack to take him my smelling bottle, thinking that it might perhaps revive him, and Jack heartlessly said that it was only a "fake"— whatever that may mean— and the poor man would get to first—whatever that was, quicker than if he waited to hit the ball. Only think. Yours in haste,

Dolly.

—Tony Kissel

This first appeared in the Philadelphia *Call* earlier in 1888, and was run by the Auburn *Daily Advertiser* on August 16 of that year. It was used as a filler then, too.

Joe Bauman

Bob Rives

Joe Bauman's words look harsher on paper than they sound when he says them. He still speaks with a quiet touch of his native Oklahoma, even after living 42 years in New Mexico. So mild is he that when he made his living as a baseball player, sportswriters called him "the gentleman first sacker."

But people don't call him now because he was gentle. It's his power that interests them. No professional player in history has hit as many home runs in one season as Joe did in 1954. In that one remarkable summer, he hit 72 for Roswell, NM, of the Class C Longhorn League. Baseball records date to the time of Little Big Horn, and only 11 of the 300,000 men who've played professionally have hit as many as 60 in one season. Only Joe has hit 70 or more.

"It used to be when some guy would get hot, go to hitting home runs, they'd all call and ask, 'Think he can do it?' Well, how do I know? I don't even know how I did it that one year out here," he says.

A native of Welch who grew up in Oklahoma City, Joe set his record the same year Henry Aaron hit the first of his career-record 755 major league home runs and Roger Bannister first ran the four minute mile.

For a while last summer there appeared to be a chance that the number of 60-plus hitters might grow. Even 70 didn't seem sacred. Three major leaguers appeared to have chances at 60 or more. Seattle's Ken Griffey Jr., Chicago's Frank Thomas and San Francisco's Matt Williams at various times were on schedule to tie or break Roger Maris's single-season record of 61.

Those hopes vanished in the haze of the baseball strike, and at their best, they all paled beside Bauman's output in 1954. His 72 home runs came in only 138 games. Over today's longer major league season that efficiency would produce 85 homers.

While Joe professes not to know why he hit so many, his size looks like one possibility. Even after more than seven decades of resisting gravity, he stands 6 feet, 5 inches tall. At 265, he is about 30 pounds over his playing weight.

But it obviously takes more than size to hit balls out of parks. From his shaded yard in Roswell, Joe today says good vision and the right kind of swing may be keys to his home run success.

"All that summer the ball looked this big," he says. As he speaks, two cats settle on and near him. One belonged to his late mother-in-law. He rescued the other from a snowdrift. His epileptic Spitz watches as Joe's hands outline a sphere as big as a cantaloupe.

That a ball could have appeared so big 40 years ago is miraculous. Joe played where lights were, at best, dim. Viewed from home plate an outfielder could almost disappear. Even worse was batting during the "gray time," just before and after sunset, when shadows covered home plate. The ball left the mound in bright sunlight, but near the bat slipped into darkness. Batting fourth, Joe usually hit at least once during that period.

Still, Joe set the home run record, batted .400, set another record with a slugging percentage of .916 and

Bob Rives was a sportswriter for two years before he turned to business, from which he retired in 1992 after a 35-year career. As a junior high student, he sold Cokes and hot dogs in the Woodward, Oklahoma, ballpark where he also watched Joe Bauman, then of Elk City, destroy his hometown's pitching and its fans' hopes. Rives has lived in Wichita, Kansas since 1959

became the first pro player to hit 50 or more home runs in three consecutive years.

Joe's swing was another source of his power. For a man so tall, his arms are not long. He wears a 35-inch sleeve, a size that fits many shorter men. But he extended the reach of his 35-inch, 34-ounce Vern Stephens bat by holding the knob in his palm. That unusual grip produced a callous on his right hand (he hit lefthanded). But it added "whip" to his swing.

"Most of my power was in my arms and wrists. You might hit the ball a pretty good ways without a lot of head wind if you pop it just right. Some guys take a gigantic fall-down swing and if they hit the thing, it may trickle back to the pitcher," he says.

"But others have a controlled, easy swing that drives the ball a long ways. You use a good, natural swing without trying to strain. You don't try to hit home runs. They just come."

Bauman described his swing as "bending under the ball." Jim Waldrip is a friend of Joe's who pitched both against him and on the same team at times. Jim says Bauman "golfed the ball."

Floyd Economindes once was mayor of Artesia, NM. He also was opposing catcher the night Joe set his record. He confirms that Bauman's "uppercut" was why he hit balls so far. "Joe didn't just hit balls over the fence. He hit them over the lights," he recalls.

Unbreakable?—Tom Jordan believes Joe's record is unbreakable. Now a farmer near Roswell, Jordan logged 17 seasons as a baseball professional. That included brief stints with the White Sox, Indians, and St. Louis Browns. He was Bauman's manager two years after Joe set his record, and later a scout.

"I can guarantee you that Joe's record never, never, never will be broken in a thousand years," he says with emphasis. "If it ever is broken, it will have to be out here in this country." Why? An almost nonstop 15-20 mile an hour wind. Architects placed most home plates so fly balls had the wind behind them.

Pitching was also why home runs flew in the Longhorn League. Teams had just six pitchers, half as many as major league clubs. Of the six, the best four were starters. "We usually left a starter in much longer than would be the case now. Back then, it didn't make sense to replace a starting pitcher with someone who probably wasn't as good," Tom says. As a result, batters faced more tired arms than hitters do now.

Selling shoelaces—Bauman was 32 in his record-setting year. For $100 a month, he went into pro baseball after graduating from Oklahoma City's Capitol Hill High School in 1941. He began at Newport, AK, before spending most of World War II playing baseball for a Navy team.

By 1946 he was among 5,000 professional players returning from the military. "There were so many in spring training in 1946 that there weren't enough uniforms to go around," he remembers.

In three postwar seasons, Joe advanced through Class A before a salary dispute with the Boston Braves, owners of his contract. Today he seems embarrassed at the memory. "I told them I could make more money selling 27-inch shoelaces on the sidewalk in Oklahoma City than they were willing to pay me," he said. Boston let him test the theory.

But shoelace selling was a short-lived notion. He signed for $500 a month to play semipro ball on an Elk City, OK, team organized to compete for the national championship at the national Baseball Congress World Series decided each year in Wichita, KS. He stayed three seasons in Elk City.

In 1952, finances forced Elk City to lower its baseball sights. Joe agreed to play at Artesia, in the Longhorn League. But first the team had to free him from the Braves, who still owned his contract. Joe had to arrange for his partner to take over the Texaco station they owned, and Joe wanted the right to buy his contract from Artesia for $250 after one season if he chose. He would get $1,000 to sign and earn $400 a month.

On to Roswell—It was a wise investment for Artesia. Joe set league home run records with 50 his first year and 53 his second. He also became manager. But when Artesia became a farm club for Dallas of the Texas League, leaving Joe uncertain of his future, he moved to Roswell for the 1954 season.

Even with the right field fence 20 feet closer to home plate in Roswell and hitting with rather than into the prevailing wind as he'd done at Artesia, the record did not come easily. With five games remaining in the season, Joe tied the professional baseball mark of 69 held jointly by former Amarillo star Bob Crues and Joe Hauser, who first set it in 1933 with Minneapolis of the American Association.

Joe grew increasingly frustrated over the following three nights at Big Spring, TX. "If I'd got the record there it wouldn't have been on a strike, but a ball. They wouldn't pitch to me, in other words." He swung at pitches outside the strike zone to keep from being walked, trying for another chance. But it didn't work. There were no home runs for him there.

That moved his last chance to the season-ending doubleheader at Artesia, against a team that had given up only five of his 69 homers. Bauman's manager, Pat Stasey, moved him from fourth in the batting order to first to give him more times at bat.

Artesia manager Jim Adair was once a Chicago Cub. "He told me he'd heard what happened at Big Spring and said they wouldn't walk me to keep it from happening. I appreciated that," Joe says.

But the Artesia manager's choice of starting pitchers

made Joe's task no easier. He was Jose Gallardo, 19, a Cuban rookie with a record of 4-1. His fastball would have at least equaled today's 86-mile-an-hour big league average, his catcher believes.

Jose wanted nothing to interfere with his promotion chances and giving up a record home run wouldn't help. He also was new. Artesia's older pitchers were well-known and it's easier to hit a pitcher the batter knows well, Bauman says.

The record—With Joe batting first, the showdown began with the first pitch. The count quickly was two strikes and two balls. Bauman fouled off two more strikes. Then it happened. He drove a fastball into the wind over the right field fence at the 345-foot mark. Artesia's was one of the few Longhorn League parks located so that lefthanded batters hit fly balls against the wind.

That early hit distressed some fans. Many were still driving from Roswell when the record was broken. But even latecomers got to see the final record set. Joe hit two more home runs in the second game off substitute pitchers Bobby Boyd, usually the backup catcher, and center fielder Mickey Diaz.

The record paid off, at least modestly. Fans often poked money through backstops to players who homered, maybe $50 for a routine one, but up to $250 for a game winner. Bauman recalls getting $500 that night, even playing away from home. Economindes remembers it as $800.

During the final games, Joe was acutely aware of pressure. His race for the record was attracting national attention. *Life* magazine followed him with a photographer, as did other media. The Associated Press reported progress on its national wire.

"I'll tell you one thing. I was glad when it was over. I can't imagine what it must have been like for Maris in New York. It'd be unbelievable; it'd be about enough to drive you nuts. It was bad enough out here in this little old league. Something like that with the amount of media hype in New York or any other big league city, it'd be brutal," he says.

But he left it at the ball park. Dorothy, a cheerleader and Joe's high school sweetheart, who has been Mrs. Bauman for 54 years, said the two talked about other subjects at home.

"I thought Joe handled himself real well. Of course, stress was there. When he was home, we didn't talk about it. I don't know how he did it. I don't know how anybody does it. Anybody. But Joe handled it," she recalls.

When he tied the record, it was like "a piano being lifted off my back," he said. Breaking it was a lesser lift, like getting rid of the piano stool.

That stressful record earned neither a promotion nor a raise for Joe. He would have retired, but fans urged him to play in 1955. His 1955 salary was the same $500 a month it had been in 1954. There was no big league offer, although the San Francisco Seals did call. But Joe was content to remain in Roswell. In 1955 he played in 131 games and hit 46 home runs.

Joe began 1956 with even more reluctance. He had reinjured an ankle over the winter. Refusing surgery, he started the season with Roswell in a new league. The Longhorn and West Texas-New Mexico Leagues had folded with ten of the cities forming the new class B Southwest League. In the first 56 games, Joe hit 17 home runs, a pace that would have again produced 46 over a full season. But on June 12 he yielded to the aching ankle and retired.

Today the ten commandments are on a monument on the Roswell courthouse lawn, but it's difficult to find evidence of the home run record that may last as long as they have.

In the local museum is a ball signed by Joe and teammate Stubby Greer. On it is written "72 home runs" but nothing explains his record. Golfer Nancy Lopez and rocket scientist Robert Goddard are the two Roswell residents most remembered.

A city library display includes a baseball signed by another Oklahoma-born player, Johnny Bench, but no mention of Joe. (No 1954 Rocket player made it to the major leagues, although one pitcher with a 7-1 record, Tommy Brookshier, became an all-pro defensive back for the NFL's Philadelphia Eagles.)

"Once in a while some kid will say, 'Mr. Bauman, did you know you're in the museum?'" Joe says now. "But I've never been over there and haven't seen it.

"Maybe one of these days I'll give them a bat or something."

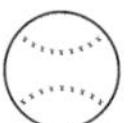

Maybe he had a lousy personality

Zaza Harvey began the 1901 season as a rotation pitcher with the eventual league champion White Sox. After being sold to Cleveland, Harvey became an outfielder. His .353 average in 170 at bats for his new team was bested only by Lajoie's .426. Overall he hit .333 on the season. Despite hitting .348 in limited action in 1902, Harvey was finished as a big leaguer with a .332 BA, .429 SA, and 17 stolen bases in 259 at bats.

—Cappy Gagnon

On the Hot Seat

Stew Thornley

Like their umpiring counterparts on the field, official scorers are an anonymous bunch. Fans usually pay attention to them only when a close call is made.

While this may happen more often with umpires than with scorers, the folks in the press box can find themselves the center of controversy, especially when a pitcher is working on a no-hitter. A hard ground ball that handcuffs a shortstop puts the scorer in the spotlight as fans and players alike wait for the decision: hit or error?

Three no-hitters in 1991—Bret Saberhagen's, Wilson Alvarez's, and the combined gem by three Atlanta pitchers—were dependent on a scorer's call of error on a borderline play.

Although most scorers won't allow the presence of a possible no-hitter to affect their decisions, some appear to subscribe to the philosophy that the first hit should be a clean one.

In 1979 Dick Miller of the Los Angeles *Herald-Examiner* used this argument in trying to justify his attempt to help California's Nolan Ryan complete a no-hitter against the New York Yankees.

In the eighth inning, Miller charged Angel center fielder Rick Miller with an error when he couldn't make a shoestring catch of Jim Spencer's low liner. Even Angel vice president Buzzie Bavasi disagreed with the scoring decision and is reported to have shouted at Dick Miller: "You didn't have to do that. You've embarrassed us!" The scoring call became academic when Reggie Jackson finally broke up the no-hitter in the ninth with a single too clean for even Miller to rule otherwise.

At times an official scoring decision appears to be all that stands in the way of a no-hitter. In June of 1992, the Mets' only hit off Ken Hill of Montreal was a fifth-inning grounder by Anthony Young that shortstop Tom Foley was unable to control with a backhand stab. Because he gave Young a hit on the play, scorer Bob Mann was on the hot seat after the game. (I think Mann made a proper call on this play; even if he had ruled it an error, however, it should be remembered that this is no guarantee that Hill would have completed the no-hitter.)

Scorers in these circumstances can be pressured, sometimes intensely, to change their calls. In an October, 1974, game at Metropolitan Stadium in Minnesota, Toby Harrah of the Rangers reached base in the first inning on a grounder that went through Twins' third baseman Eric Soderholm. Although it appeared to be a misplay by Soderholm, scorer Bob Fowler gave Harrah an infield hit. To Fowler's credit, he stuck with his call as it remained the only hit off Jim Hughes until two out in the ninth inning when, to Fowler's relief, Pete Mackanin tripled. In between these two hits, Fowler received a phone call from Texas manager Billy Martin, saying the Rangers would have no problem with a scoring switch, and repeated requests from the Minnesota dugout for him to change his decision. In one of the requests, Twins' coach Buck Rodgers asked, "Can you change the hit to an error?" Fowler's reply: "I can, but I won't."

A scorer who did yield to the situation was John

Stew Thornley joined SABR in 1979 and became the first president of the Halsey Hall Chapter in 1985. The author of several baseball books, he received the SABR-Macmillan Baseball Research Award in 1988.

Drebinger of the New York *Times* in a 1952 game at Yankee Stadium. In the third inning,, Drebinger gave a hit to Phil Rizzuto of the Yankees when Detroit shortstop Johnny Pesky bobbled his ground ball, then threw too late to first. The pitcher for Detroit was Virgil Trucks, who had already hurled a no-hitter earlier in the season. With Rizzuto's hit still the only one off Trucks in the seventh, Drebinger called Pesky in the Detroit dugout to get his version of the play. "I had the ball and it squirted loose from my glove just as I reached to take it out," said Pesky. "I messed it up." Drebinger then reversed the scoring call, charging Pesky with an error and wiping out Rizzuto's hit, a decision that brought a cheer even from the Yankee fans when it was announced and made possible Trucks's second no-hitter.

While such scoring changes and decisions cast doubt over the validity of a no-hitter, at least pitchers such as Trucks, Saberhagen, and Alvarez have been able to enjoy a hearty celebration on the field at the conclusion of the game.

A no-hitter by Ernie Koob of the St. Louis Browns against the Chicago White Sox on May 5, 1917, was different. Here the switch of a hit to an error did not occur until after the game.

This game took place among a cluster of notable no-hitters in the big leagues. Three days before Koob's no-hitter, Hippo Vaughn of the Cubs and Fred Toney of the Reds matched nine innings of hitless ball with Toney keeping his no-hitter and winning in ten innings. Seven weeks later, Ernie Shore relieved Babe Ruth, who was ejected after giving up a leadoff walk, and retired all the batters he faced. Shore for many years was credited with a perfect game although it is now officially ruled a combined no-hitter for Ruth and Shore. On top of this, the day after Koob's no-hitter, Bob Groom of the Browns pitched two hitless innings in the first game of a doubleheader against the White Sox, then no-hit the Sox in the second game, giving him 11 hitless innings for the day and producing no-hitters on consecutive days at Sportsman's Park.

The Koob game came less than three weeks after Chicago's Ed Cicotte had no-hit the Browns at Sportsman's Park in another gem marked by controversy because of a scoring decision. Sox first baseman Chick Gandil was charged with an error when he couldn't handle a wicked shot by Jimmy Austin of the Browns in the seventh inning.

Now back in St. Louis on Saturday, May 5, Cicotte was Koob's mound opponent. And while Eddie held the Browns to five hits and one unearned run, that tainted tally was enough for Koob, who held the White Sox without a hit after a first-inning single by Buck Weaver.

The hit by Weaver came on a high bounder to the right of the mound. Second baseman Ernie Johnson, according to the Chicago *Tribune*, "tore in and tried to pull a brilliant stop and throw, but failed."

W. J. O'Connor, in his game account for the St. Louis *Post-Dispatch*, although acknowledging that Johnson had given the grounder a "valorous battle," described the play this way: "He [Johnson] first fielded it with his chest, and knocked it silly at his feet. He then laid a prehensile paw on the pill and came up with ample time to assist [George] Sisler with the out. But he suddenly lost his prehensileness, and tossed the ball over his shoulder like a superstitious person throwing salt to avoid a fight."

Although official scorer J. B. Sheridan had credited Weaver with a hit at the time it occurred, he began second guessing himself as the game progressed. After the game, the *Post-Dispatch*'s O'Connor reported, Sheridan "sought sounder counsel from the umpires, the ballplayers and those who were better able to feel the pulse of the play in question.

"To a man the Browns and the enemy and the umps agreed that Johnson deserved an error and Koob a no-hit game. There was the suspicion of gang ethics, here; but the able and honorable official scorer yielded reluctantly under the preponderance of evidence and erased the hit, substituting the error."

Exactly how long after the game it took Sheridan to reverse his decision is not clear. The St. Louis *Post-Dispatch* headline read, No-Hit Game Nets Koob And Browns One-Run Victory: Weaver's Drive In Opening Inning Was Scored A "Hit," At First, But This Was Later Changed To An "Error." But the Chicago *Tribune* headline, Koob tames sox in one hit game, 1-0, indicates that the play was still considered a hit at the time the Chicago reporter filed his story.

The next day's Chicago *Tribune* referred to the Koob situation in its report on the Groom no-hitter: "There was no flaw in Groom's no-hit game. It was free from taint or suspicion which always will cling to the post-mortem thing handed Koob yesterday by expunging a hit that had already been recorded."

Meanwhile, in response to the scoring reversal in Koob's no-hitter, the St. Louis *Post-Dispatch* ran a story about a movement by St. Louis and Chicago baseball writers to "protect the official records of baseball from similar offenses in the future…to instruct all official scorers that their decisions cannot be reversed except in case of a misinterpretation of the rules. In other words, a hit scored in any inning cannot be wiped out any more than an umpire's decision can be reversed after the game."

But whether or not official scorers are prohibited from altering a decision already handed down, they will continue to make subjective judgments, sometimes difficult ones, in the course of their normal duties. Usually, only the scorers themselves will agonize over these calls.

But just wait until there's a no-hitter in progress.

Closer? Who needs a closer?

Ted Lyons's Complete Season of 1942

Lyle Spatz

In the three quarters of a century since the end of World War I, only one major league pitcher, Ted Lyons of the 1942 Chicago White Sox, has made at least 20 starts in a season and completed them all. Before Lyons, the feat had last been accomplished by Walter Johnson, who completed all of his 29 starts in 1918, thus becoming the first pitcher to do so since 1905.

With the decline of value placed on complete games, and the evolution of "situational relief pitching," it is unlikely that this will ever happen again. In 1993 (the last complete season), Terry Mulholland of Philadelphia went the distance in only seven of his 28 starts (25 percent) to lead the National League in percent of complete games pitched, while the American League leader was Chuck Finley with 13 complete games in his 35 starts (37 percent).

Lyons, who was 41 years old and in his 20th year with the White Sox in 1942, was the winner in 14 of those 20 starts, and his 2.10 ERA was the lowest in the American League. This for a Chicago team that finished sixth, 34 games behind the pennant–winning Yankees. He remains the oldest pitcher ever to lead a major league in earned run average.

Despite his adoption of a knuckle ball following an arm injury in 1931, Lyons was one of the game's great control pitchers. He finished second to Ernie Bonham of the Yankees in allowing the fewest walks per game in 1942, a category in which he had led the American League in each of the previous three years.

Lyons started twice against the Cubs in the annual Chicago City Series, and to no one's surprise, threw two more complete games, winning one and losing one. In the series opener on September 30, he pitched a three-hitter at Wrigley Field, beating Bill Lee, 3-0. It was Lyons's sixth consecutive win against the Cubs and gave him an 8-1 record in City Series competition. On October 5, in game five, Lyons allowed just five hits, but lost a 10-inning 2-1 decision to Claude Passeau.

With the 1942 season behind him, Lyons joined the U.S. Marines, where he spent the remaining three years of World War II. He retired as an active player in May, 1946, after being named to succeed Jimmy Dykes as White Sox manager. Pitching for a team that never finished higher than third (and that only three times) Lyons finished with 260 lifetime wins.

Lyons, who had not made a relief appearance since 1936, became over the next several years primarily a "once a week pitcher," almost always on Sundays. On April 17, in his first start of the 1942 season—the game in which Lou Boudreau made his home debut as manager of the Indians—Lyons beat Mel Harder 1–0. It was to be the final shutout of his career, and he followed it with his worst performance of the season. Pitching in Detroit six days later, he was battered for 16 hits in a 9–0 loss. The Tigers scored three runs in both the second and third innings, making it difficult to ascertain—even by 1942 standards—why manager Dykes never removed Lyons from this game.

Although he lost his next two games, Lyons pitched well in both. He held the Senators to four hits in Washington, but rookie Early Wynn beat him 1–0, and then in Boston he allowed home runs to Bobby Doerr in the

Lyle Spatz , a free-lance writer from Maryland, is chairman of the SABR Records Committee.

eighth and 10th innings and lost 3–1 to Joe Dobson. Thus far, in the four games he had pitched, the White Sox offense had scored just two runs for him.

In the opening game of a doubleheader on Sunday, May 17, Lyons made his first start of the season at home, defeating Bobo Newsom and the Senators 7–1. It was the first of eight consecutive outings in which he would pitch the first game of a Sunday doubleheader. Thirteen of his 20 starts in 1942 were on a Sunday, each one, as were two of his other starts, the first game of a doubleheader (a concept, like the complete game, now becoming only a memory).

After a 3–2 loss in Boston on June 7, Lyons's record stood at three wins and five losses. However, from that point on he was almost perfect, winning 11 of his last 12 decisions. His only loss came at Detroit on August 16 when he lost 3–2 in 10 innings to Hal Newhouser. Over those final 12 games the opposition scored more than three runs against Lyons only twice, and in six of the games, including the final four, he allowed just one run.

Included in Lyons's 14 wins were at least one against every club in the league, but his greatest success came against Cleveland. He defeated the Indians all four times that he faced them, limiting them to one run in each game.

He won the 250th game of his career at home against Boston on June 21, and a week later, again at Comiskey Park won number 251 as part of a doubleheader sweep of the Yankees. The win came against Red Ruffing, tying him with Ruffing for the most wins by an active pitcher. At the end of 1942, the count stood Lyons, 259; Ruffing 258, but Ruffing won 15 games between 1945 and 1947 to finish with 273 lifetime wins, 13 more than Lyons. Lyons was elected to the Hall of Fame in 1955, 12 years ahead of his longtime rival.

Ted Lyons: Complete in 1942

Day	Date	Opp.	At	W/L	Score	IP	Opp. Pitcher	Record
Fri.	4/17	CLE	CLE	W	1–0	9	Mel Harder	1–0
Thur.	4/23	DET	DET	L	0–9	8	Hal White	1–1
Thur.	4/30	WAS	WAS	L	0–1	8	Early Wynn	1–2
Wed.	5/06	BOS	BOS	L	1–3	9.2	Joe Dobson	1–3
Sun.	5/17 (1G)	WAS	CHI	W	7–1	9	Bobo Newsom	2–3
Sun.	5/24 (1G)	DET	CHI	L	2–6	9	Tommy Bridges	2–4
Sun.	5/31	DET	DET	W	9–4	10	Al Benton	3–4
Sun.	6/07 (1G)	BOS	BOS	L	2–3	8.1	Dick Newsome	3–5
Sun.	6/14 (1G)	WAS	WAS	W	9–3	9	Sid Hudson	4–5
Sun.	6/21 (1G)	BOS	CHI	W	6–5	9	Dick Newsome	5–5
Sun.	6/28 (1G)	NY	CHI	W	6–2	9	Red Ruffing	6–5
Sun.	7/05 (1G)	STL	CHI	W	14–2	9	Elden Auker	7–5
Sun.	7/26 (1G)	PHI	CHI	W	2–1	9	Roger Wolff	8–5
Tues.	8/04	DET	CHI	W	5–4	9	Tommy Bridges	9–5
Sun.	8/09 (1G)	CLE	CHI	W	11–1	9	Mel Harder	10–5
Sun.	8/16 (1G)	DET	DET	L	2–3	10.1	Hal Newhouser	10–6
Sun.	8/23 (1G)	CLE	CLE	W	3–1	9	Al Smith	11–6
Sun.	8/30 (1G)	PHI	PHI	W	2–1	9	Roger Wolff	12–6
Thur.	9/10 (1G)	WAS	CHI	W	7–1	9	Dutch Leonard	13–6
Thur.	9/24 (1G)	CLE	CLE	W	3–1	9	Al Smith	14–6

Bound for the Klondike

Tony Kissel

Canandaigua's first professional baseball team formed in 1888, as one of five members of the new Central New York League. The short season didn't begin until June 30, and Auburn won the pennant with a 22-10 record, followed by Penn Yan, Seneca Falls, Canandaigua and Waterloo. Canandaigua first baseman Frank Smith was a former major leaguer with Pittsburgh.

The following year, another minor league called the New York State League emerged, and Canandaigua joined, along with Auburn, Elmira, Utica, Seneca Falls and Oneida. Once again Auburn won the pennant in a heated race with Elmira. Canandaigua finished third and had a 27-24 record. The team averaged eight runs per game thanks to hitting stars Doc Kennedy .359, Halligan .353, Richard Knox .342, and T. Connor .335. When the league continued in 1890, Canandaigua and four other teams dropped out and new teams from the eastern part of New York State joined. A recession in the 1890s limited the number of minor leagues in the country.

The New York State League reformed in 1897, with the Auburn Maroons, Batavia Wahoos, Canandaigua Rustlers, Cortland Wagonmakers, Lyons Lyonese and Palmyra Mormons competing for the pennant. Teams had only 11-man squads with a spare pitcher or two, and they played five or six games every week (Sunday ball was illegal), with games starting at 3:30 p.m., just as the factories let out. General admission was only 25 cents, while grandstand seats cost 35 cents. The Rustlers played their home games at Watkins Field.

Club president, W. J. Coye, signed Hank Ramsey of Paterson, N.J., as his manager, and Ramsey quickly built a team around castoffs from the Class A Eastern League, then the top minor league in the country.

Auburn pulled ahead early, but injuries to two key pitchers ruined their chances. Canandaigua was back in fifth place, almost ten games behind as August approached. Due to bankruptcy, Batavia's team was transferred to Geneva to complete the season. On August 18, Palmyra held a 3-1/2 game lead over Auburn, and a 5-1/2 game lead over Canandaigua. The Rustlers soon caught Auburn, but on September 6, were belted by Palmyra 17-10. With just four games left to play, Palmyra had a comfortable 2-1/2 game lead over the Rustlers.

Two quick losses saw Palmyra's lead whittled down to a half game. On September 10, both front runners won, so the outcome of the chase for the "silk rag" would be decided on the last day of the season.

Canandaigua defeated the hapless Geneva club in Geneva, and then waited for the wire results of the Palmyra game. When the report came in that Lyons had nipped Palmyra 7-5, the jubilant Rustler players boarded the train heading home in first place for the only day all season (Lyons players insisted they were offered bribes by Palmyra players to throw the game). When the Rustlers arrived back at the Canandaigua train station, a huge crowd of 6,000 fans was on hand to greet the club. The players were escorted over to the Webster House amidst bonfires, firecrackers and assorted musical salutes. The players were given an all-night victory party before they finally returned to

Tony Kissel is a sales consultant for Nestle's Fundraising Division.

their hotel rooms and boardinghouses to sleep.

The Rustlers had a 52-35 record. They had scored more than 700 runs. Chris Genegal hit .364, Fred McFall hit .347, Jack Nelson hit .340, Jimmy McQuade hit .329, David Barber hit .319, Jack Lever hit .312, Bill Wittrock hit .308, Bill Hayward hit .304 and Bobby Cargo hit .302. Fred McFall finished with a fine 20-12 record, and Micky Mullen's record was 15-5. Despite the great personal achievements, not a single player would go on to the major leagues (although Cargo had played previously in the big time). After the Rustlers scored 94 runs in their final seven games, one reporter remarked, "They ran the bases as if they were bound for the Klondike!"

A new season—In the spring of 1898, Canandaigua's pennant winners were being called "Ramsey's Rustlers," the Red Jackets, and even the Giants. Only four players returned to the team, as the others found higher salaries elsewhere (the average State League player earned $50 to $100 a month).

Ramsey got his Rustlers off to a start of 17-7. The real story, however, was the brewing Spanish-American War, and every professional ball club had to pay a war tax of $10. Players' salaries were reduced by 10 to 20 percent since their fans had rushed off to join the army. The Canandaigua board of directors even put the Rustlers up for sale to any western New York town that wanted them.

On July 7 Canandaigua still held a slim 2-1/2 game lead over Lyons. A month later, the hot Oswego Starchmakers (they had replaced Geneva) moved to within 1/2 game of the lead. Both Lyons and Palmyra disbanded their struggling franchises and allowed their players to hook on with whatever teams they wanted. On August 25 Oswego swept two games from Canandaigua to take a 1-1/2 game lead with just two weeks to play.

In a final showdown the Starchmakers and the Rustlers squared off in a three-game series. "Wild Bill" Settley pitched the opener and defeated Oswego 7-2. Wild Bill pitched again the next day, and again beat Oswego by the same score. Who did Hank Ramsey pick to pitch the key third game? He picked Wild Bill Settley, who handcuffed Oswego for the third straight game as the Starchmakers fell behind, and then gave up and forfeited the game to Canandaigua. The pennant race was over.

No sane businssman—Canandaigua's record was 54-41, but the club did little celebrating due to the war and low finances. The club had lost $1,100 (equivalent to almost $20,000 today), and had barely survived the season. The team had only two .300 hitters, and Fred McFall again led in pitching with a 18-14 record. One difference in the 1898 team from the 1897 team was in the number of major leaguers who were on it. The 1898 club had two former big leaguers (Bobby Cargo and Charley Hamburg), and four others who would make the big leagues: Patsy Dougherty, a pitcher with a so-so 5-6 record who hit .400, would play the outfield for ten years in the majors and lead the AL in runs scored twice; Jack O'Neil, who would catch for five seasons in the majors, and who was one of four O'Neil brothers to play in the big leagues; Bill Hallman who was an outfielder for four major league seasons, and outfielder Bill Gannon (nicknamed Comedy Legs), who played for the Chicago Cubs in 1901, but was laughed out of the big-time for being bowlegged.

And what became of Wild Bill Settley? He played for many teams under names like Settley, Shaw and Snyder. He later umpired, and it was said that there were more than 100 stories about this wild character, including one that he threw out a runner at second with a peeled potato which he had hidden in the centerfield grass. And how about Micky Mullen? Micky kept pitching in the league, but in 1901, he suffered a tragic end to his career. A somnambulist, Micky was sleepwalking in his fourth-story hotel room, when his teammate awoke to see him do a victory slide right through the window and down four stories to the ground. He suffered a broken collarbone, but never actually woke up during his escapade. Fred McFall failed a big-league tryout in 1900, and became a journeyman pitcher, while "Honest Jack" Lawler failed a tryout in 1899, no doubt because he was one of the last outfielders to play without wearing a glove.

The Canandaigua board of directors unanimously voted to give up the franchise right after winning the second pennant. Fans had been supporting the club with $100 a week to cover player salaries, and the players were also contributing $2 a week apiece to help with expenses. It still was not enough. As one board member declared after the meeting, "No sane businessman would think of running his business this way!"

The New York State League continued until 1917, when another war put a halt to baseball for a while. Later, the NY-Penn League and the Eastern League filled the void for Central New York fans. Hall of Famers who played in the State League included Grover Cleveland Alexander, Johnny Evers, Joe McCarthy, and umpires Bill Klem and Tom Connolly. Canandaigua did give professional baseball another chance in 1905, but a franchise in the Class D Empire State League folded after just one week.

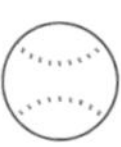

The 1942 Pennant Race

Stephen D. Boren and Thomas Boren

On the morning of August 1, 1942, the Brooklyn Dodgers enjoyed an 8-1/2 game lead over the second place St. Louis Cardinals. The Dodgers had surged to a 70-29 (.707) record, while the 60-36 Cardinals were actually closer to the third place Cincinnati Redlegs (53-45) than to Brooklyn. Later on that day, the Dodgers won 9-6 over their nemesis Johnny Schmitz of the Chicago Cubs. This gave them 71 victories in their first 100 games. The Cardinals split a doubleheader with the New York Giants and fell nine full games off the pace. The commissioner's office was studying a plan to play the entire World Series in Yankee Stadium, since its 70,000 seat capacity was double that of Ebbets Field. But the Cardinals were about to sizzle off two of the hottest months baseball has ever seen.

On August 2 the Cardinals and Giants split, as did the Dodgers and the Cubs. The next day the Dodgers extended their lead to 9-1/2 with a 7-4 eight-inning victory over the Giants. Because of World War II dimout restrictions, the lights could not be used.

On August 4 the Cardinals lost to the Redlegs and fell 10 games behind. The Dodgers appeared to have beaten the Giants when Pee Wee Reese hit a 10th inning grand slam home run. However, because of the dimout restrictions, the inning could not be completed, Reese's apparent game-winning hit was wiped out, and the game reverted to a 1-1 tie.

On the following day Max Macon's two-hitter over the Giants was matched by Johnny Beazley's three-hitter over the Redlegs. On August 6, five New York home runs, including two by Mel Ott, led the Giants to an 8-0 victory over the Dodgers. This was the start of the Cardinals' comeback. As they were idle, the deficit was now 9-1/2.

A gradual start—Poor managing by Leo Durocher led to a Dodger loss on August 7, as they dropped an 11-inning 2-1 game to the lowly Boston Braves. The Braves had a two-out triple by Nanny Fernandez in the 11th. Hugh Casey deflected a grounder by Max West, and Fernandez scored. Had the Dodgers stalled for a few minutes, the dimout regulations would have caused the game to revert to the 1-1 10th inning score. The Dodgers instead played quickly and lost the game. The Cardinals were defeated by the Pittsburgh Pirates 12-6.

The next day the Dodgers lost 2-0 to the Braves in a game marred by beanballs. The Pirates and Cardinals played to a 5-5 16-inning tie, and were 9 games out. On August 9, the Cardinals beat the Pirates twice and then won the rescheduled 5-5 tie, 6-4. The Dodgers beat the pathetic Philadelphia Phillies 6-0 to hold their lead.

The Cardinals took three out of four games from the Chicago Cubs from the 11th to the 13th of August. The Dodgers only played one game, beating the Phillies 1-0 when Rube Melton walked in the winning run in the ninth inning.

The Dodgers took three out of four games from the Boston Braves over the next three days, while the Cardinals took four straight from the Redlegs. The Dodger lead was down to 7-1/2 games. On August 18 and 19, the Cardinals beat the Cubs twice, and then took three

Stephen D. Boren is Assistant Madical Director at CNA Insurance in Chicago. Thomas Boren is a Chicago-based historian specializing in twentieth-century Americana.

out of four from the visiting Pittsburgh Pirates. The Dodgers beat the Boston Braves 11-1 on August 19. They swept the New York Giants from the 20th through the 23rd of August. In the first game of the series, Johnny Mize's second-inning home run deprived Whit Wyatt of both a no-hitter and a shutout. Dodger outfielder Dixie Walker offered to bet $100 that Brooklyn would win the pennant by eight games. Dodger boss Larry MacPhail replied, "I'll bet $100 you ought to win it by twenty games. Here's a club that has been in a slump and nobody worries about it except me. An eight-game lead in the middle of August isn't anything to sleep on. Leads like that have been lost."

On August 24 the Dodgers entered St. Louis for a critical four-game series. They held a 7-1/2 game lead, and a Brooklyn sweep would destroy the Cardinals. The home team took the first game 7-1 as Max Lanier won his 14th game. The next day, a 2-1 14-inning victory by Mort Cooper cut the Dodger lead to 5-1/2 games. When Johnny Beazley beat Max Macon 2-1 on the 26th, the Cardinals were only 4-1/2 back. Brooklyn was able to salvage the final game 4-1 to boost its lead back to 5-1/2 games.

August ended with the Dodgers splitting two games with the Cubs and taking two out of three games from the Pirates. The Cardinals had an easy time, sweeping three from the last place Phillies and two from the seventh place Braves. Brooklyn had played good baseball (18-11; .621) in August. The Cardinals, however, had played at a phenomenal pace, winning 19 of their last 22 games, and going 25-8 overall for a .758 percentage. They were only 3-1/2 out.

Late season maneuvering—On August 31 the Dodgers purchased pitcher Bobo Newsom from the Washington Senators for an unknown amount of money, plus Jack Kraus and Gene Moore. The colorful Newsom sent Leo Durocher a telegram stating, "Congratulations on buying pennant. Will report tomorrow in fine shape, rarin' to go."

The next day the Cardinals recalled infielder-outfielder Irv Dusak. Cardinal owner Sam Breadon countered, "They can have their Newsom, but I'd rather have Dusak. Dusak has extra-base hits galore. He has been one of the most sought-after players in the minor leagues." Unfortunately, Dusak hit only .185 with three doubles. Newsom didn't do much for the Dodgers either. He was 2-2 for Brooklyn.

September 1 saw Mort Cooper winning his 18th game as the Cardinals beat the Braves, while Kirby Higbe won his 14th against the Pirates. The Dodgers swept two games from Cincinnati as the Cardinals split two with the Giants. Newsom pitched a 2-0 shutout over the Redlegs. This temporarily increased Brooklyn's lead to 4-1/2 games. The Cardinals then took three games from the Redlegs as the Giants won two out of three from the Dodgers. The Redbirds had won 28 out of their last 34 games.

Down the stretch—On September 7 both Brooklyn and Boston split doubleheaders. A 4-0 Dodger victory by Ed Head over Lefty Wilkie and the Pirates extended their lead to three full games over the idle Cardinals.

On September 10 the Chicago Cubs' Lon Warneke beat Kirby Higbe as Howie Pollet beat Hal Schumacher and the Giants. Carl Hubbell was to have pitched, but was hit by an errant throw by Stan Musial during the pregame fielding drill. Now only two games out of first, the Cardinals invaded Brooklyn for a critical showdown.

Billy Southworth was optimistic, despite many experts' skepticism. He said, "Did you ever hear of the 1921 Giants winning after being 7-1/2 games behind in late August? The Yankees blowing a 13-game lead in 1928 and just barely limping home? The 1936 Giants coming from 10 games behind in August? The 1935 Cubs staging a 21-game late-season winning streak? The Pirates building a World Series press box in 1938 that was never used? And the Giants blowing a 7-1/2 game Labor Day lead in 1934? And you're trying to hint to me my outlook is dark! I've seen too much in my day, and we won't stop until they flash the mathematics on us, and maybe that won't be necessary."

On September 11 Mort Cooper wore Coaker Triplett's uniform with the number "20" on it. He pitched three-hit ball, as he won his 20th game of the season. The 3-0 victory was his eighth shutout. The next day, behind Max Lanier, the Cardinals won 2-1 to tie the Dodgers with a 94-46 record. On that day, the Cardinals ordered World Series tickets printed. Sam Breadon said, "I think we're in. We've won 29 out of 34 and those fellows have lost six of their last nine."

Leo Durocher thought the Cardinals would fold. "All right they caught up," he said. "It took them five months to do it. Let's snap out of it and get after them now."

MacPhail was not discouraged, either. He told his team, "I feel better now than I've felt in a couple of days. They're even with us and I know you can win. Something's going to happen soon—a break that will start our rally. Something like the bases full, two out and a dropped pop fly. And then an explosion—six straight hits."

Unfortunately for Brooklyn, Breadon was right. On the 13th the Cardinals split with the pathetic Phillies, while the Redlegs took two from the Dodgers. Bobo Newsom had planned to pitch both games of the doubleheader, but after he lost the opener 6-3, Durocher went with Curt Davis who lost 4-1. The Bums were now in second place.

The next day, a four-run ninth inning gave Howie Krist a 6-3 victory over the Phillies, and a single by

Jimmy Brown in the 14th inning beat Philadelphia again. The Cards led by two games.

Both the Dodgers and the Cardinals won on September 16. The next day the Dodgers lost to the Pirates 3-2 on Pete Coscarart's two-run single. The Cardinals won 6-4 over the Braves with a five-run ninth inning. The winning rally included a double oddity: Coaker Triplett pinch-hit for Stan Musial. After hitting a single, he was picked off base.

Between September 18 and 20, the Dodgers took two out of three from the Phillies. The Cardinals split a doubleheader with the Cubs. Over the next few days the Cardinals beat the Pirates and the Redlegs twice each. Mort Cooper's two-hit 6-0 victory over Cincinnati on September 24 was his 22nd win and 10th shutout of the season. This victory also clinched at least a Cardinal tie for the pennant.

As the season came to its final day, the Dodgers beat the Phillies and hoped for the Cubs to sweep the Cardinals. The doubleheader was a sweep, all right, but St. Louis took both games.

Billy Southworth was jubilant. "We won this one the hard way, and no one won it for us. We went out and won it ourselves. And we'll go out and beat the Yankees the same way. One thing this young club isn't afraid of is reputations." He was prophetic. His team beat the New York Yankees in a five-game World Series.

The Dodgers played 18-11 (.621) ball in August and 16-10 (.615) ball in September. The Cardinals were simply out of this world, playing 25-8 (.758) ball in August and 21-4 (.840) ball in September. After August 4 the Cardinals were 44-9 (.830). The Dodgers didn't collapse. They just were steam-rolled.

The Steamroller Develops

July 31, 1942

	Wins	Losses	PCT	GB
Brooklyn	70	29	.707	—
St. Louis	60	36	.625	8.5
Cincinnati	53	45	.541	16.5
NY Giants	52	47	.525	18
Chicago	47	55	.461	24.5
Pittsburgh	43	52	.453	25
Boston	41	62	.398	31
Philadelphia	28	68	.292	40.5

August 31, 1942

	Wins	Losses	PCT	GB
Brooklyn	88	40	.688	—
St. Louis	85	44	.659	3.5
NY Giants	71	58	.550	17.5
Cincinnati	64	64	.500	24
Pittsburgh	58	67	.464	28.5
Chicago	60	73	.451	30.5
Boston	51	79	.392	38
Philadelphia	36	88	.290	50

August record

	Wins	Losses	PCT
Brooklyn	18	11	.621
St. Louis	25	8	.758

September 27, 1942

	Wins	Losses	PCT	GB
St. Louis	106	48	.688	—
Brooklyn	104	50	.675	2
NY Giants	85	67	.559	20
Cincinnati	76	76	.500	29
Pittsburgh	66	81	.449	36.5
Chicago	68	86	.442	38
Boston	59	89	.399	44
Philadelphia	42	109	.278	62.5

September record

	Wins	Losses	PCT
St. Louis	21	4	.840
Brooklyn	16	10	.615

Combined August and September Record

	Wins	Losses	PCT
St. Louis	46	12	.793
Brooklyn	34	21	.618

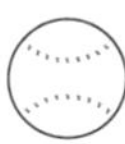

Building A Champion

Merl F. Kleinknecht

In the spring of 1941 Erie, Pennsylvania sportsman Ernest Wright drove to the city of Cleveland with the desire to establish a team in the Negro Baseball Leagues. Wright felt he had the necessary financial resources and was determined to find someone with the capability of utilizing these resources to build not just a team, but a championship team. To this end he decided to meet Cleveland sports promoter Wilbur Hayes.

Wilbur Hayes was a busy man. He worked for the city, ran his own business and operated the all-black Cleveland White Sox baseball club. Wright chose to meet Hayes at the Wilbur Hayes Sport Parlor on a Sunday afternoon. The busy Hayes was willing to talk but with a characteristic directness informed Wright discussions between them would have to wait until the next day.

As the owner of Erie's famous Pope Hotel, Ernie Wright was also a busy man. However, he was aware that Hayes had a reputation for accomplishment and felt he just might be the person to build a championship team. So Wright took a room in Cleveland's renowned Majestic Hotel and awaited the morrow.

Wilbur Filmore Hayes, son of farmer Doc Hayes and Ella Mae Daniel Hayes, was born August 25, 1898, in Owensboro, Kentucky. He came north as a child and attended Cleveland's Orange Elementary and Brownell Junior High. Wilbur possessed a strong work ethic and served as a city truck driver in addition to his business enterprises. He married Erma Brown in 1925. The couple had two sons: Wilbur, Jr. and Don Leslie, and four daughters: Betty, Garnett, Jeannine and Erma Dee. He had a daughter, Dorothy, from a previous marriage.

Hayes had begun promoting entertainment and sports events catering to the city's black population after World War I. He was the first to make a success of such promotions. He brought such talents to the city as bandleaders Noble Sissle and Fletcher Henderson.

Hayes, himself an all-around athlete, promoted sports into the '40s. He operated a boxing gym during the Depression, and is credited with establishing Cleveland's first all-black football team. His business, located at East 49th and Central Avenue, also served as a grooming and shoeshine parlor.

Hayes also entertained hopes of establishing a successful Negro League team. He had failed in an attempt to have his White Sox accepted as an associate member in the 1941 Negro American League, and he was aware that with resources such as Wright offered his opportunity to become a part of the Negro Leagues would greatly increase.

Getting into the game—The eventual meeting between Hayes and Wright resulted in a successful partnership. Wright purchased a half interest in the Negro American League St. Louis Stars. The pair worked to book Negro League teams to play in Cleveland that summer. Before the summer ended the Stars were being referred to as the Cleveland Stars by the local black press.

Following the 1941 baseball season Hayes and Wright made a decision to cut ties with the Stars and

Merl F. Kleinknecht is a 33-year veteran of the U.S. Postal Service, and has been involved in researching and writing about the Negro Leagues for a quarter of a century.

establish an entirely new franchise with a connection to Cleveland. The vigorous Hayes, with Wright's financial backing and a new Chevrolet, embarked upon an off-season sojourn into the south to sign players. Agreements to play games in both Cleveland's League Park and Cincinnati's Crosley Field were obtained. Wright and Hayes established the Cincinnati-Cleveland Buckeyes and prepared for the upcoming 1942 season.

Wright initially hoped to gain entry into the Negro National League, which operated mainly along the Atlantic seaboard. Rebuffed by that tightly-knit circuit, the Buckeyes joined the far-flung Negro American League, which operated throughout the midwest and south. They replaced the same St. Louis Stars Wright had held interest in during the 1941 campaign.

Wilbur Hayes proved both a successful baseball scout and persuasive signer in putting together the 1942 Buckeyes. Signings of particular note included a sandlot catcher from the St. Louis area in his mid-20s named Sam Jethroe. Hayes talked talented pitcher Eugene Bremmer out of a self-imposed retirement from the Negro Leagues. Willie Jefferson, a star hurler in the Mexican League, was also talked into the Buckeye fold and Archie Ware, a flashy young first baseman, was obtained from the Negro American League Kansas City Monarchs. The Cincinnati-Cleveland Buckeyes prepared for what would prove to be a most eventful maiden campaign in the 1942 Negro American League.

Triumph and tragedy—Walter Burch, a veteran catcher, was named Buckeye manager and began to mold the Hayes-built roster into a competitive unit. However, before spring's end Burch was replaced by Parnell Woods, an all-star third baseman. Hayes obtained Woods from the NAL's Jacksonville Red Caps and made him the youngest field pilot in the Negro Leagues. Woods proceeded to lead the upstart Buckeyes to the NAL's first half title, a stunning accomplishment that highlighted Wilbur Hayes' powers to recognize, acquire, and sign baseball talent. However, tragedy for the team was just around the corner.

While the eventual NAL champion Kansas City Monarchs were engaging the Negro National League Homestead Grays in the 1942 Black World Series, the Cleveland Buckeyes traveled into western New York for a series of games with the NNL New York Black Yankees. Early on the morning of September 7, a car carrying Hayes and five players home from New York developed a flat tire on Route 20 near Geneva, Ohio. Upon attempting to return to the highway after replacing the flat, the auto was struck by a truck. Catcher Ulysses (Buster) Brown, the driver, and pitcher Raymond (Smokey) Owens were killed instantly. Two remaining hurlers, Bremmer and Porter Moss, were hospitalized with serious injuries from which both recovered. Hayes and pitcher Alonso Boone also sustained injuries but avoided being hospitalized. Erma Dee Hayes still recalls how frightened she became upon first seeing her injured father's battered and swollen face.

Exclusively Cleveland—Hayes and Wright decided to operate exclusively out of Cleveland in 1943. The club's success continued as the indefatigable Hayes' efforts to promote the Buckeyes in his home town included involving Cleveland's black community. Friends, associations and contacts established over the years, coupled with his reputation and experience enabled Hayes to rally support of the community's black press and civic organizations. The *Call & Post*, the community's weekly newspaper, provided regular and in-depth coverage of the Buckeyes. The Forward Outlook League and Karamu House became involved sponsoring games. The end result was a five-fold attendance increase and recognition as the Negro American League's "Most Outstanding Club" at season's end. Sam Jethroe became established as a star center fielder for the Bucks and was named the league's "Second Most Valuable Player."

Hayes continued to piece together a championship club with the addition of all-star outfielders Al Armour and Lloyd Davenport to join Jethroe in 1944. The master builder had George Jefferson, Willie Jefferson's little brother, and Lovell Hardin added to the pitching corps and then proceeded to talk another player out of retirement.

Johnnie Cowan, a smooth-fielding second baseman, had struggled to hit Negro League hurling for a decade before retiring from pro ball. Hayes was able to convince the 31-year-old keystoner to join the 1944 Buckeyes. Cowan teamed with first baseman Ware, third baseman Woods and shortstop Billy Horne to give the club the NAL's best defensive infield. In Armour, Jethroe and Davenport they had the league's fastest and hardest hitting outfield. However, the 1944 Buckeyes were one player short of a pennant. That player would arrive in 1945.

Veteran catcher Quincy Trouppe joined the Buckeyes after six years of all-star play in Mexico. He signed not only to play but also to manage the Buckeyes. In what had to be a monumental effort of persuasion, Hayes convinced Woods to stay with the club as team captain to make way for Trouppe to manage. The tenuous setup held together for only a single season, but oh, what a season it was!

The 1945 Buckeyes swept to their initial NAL pennant with Trouppe at the helm. With a lineup including proven all-stars Trouppe (c), Ware (1b), Woods (3b), Armour (lf), Jethroe (cf), and Davenport (rf), the Buckeyes swept to the first half NAL title with a 31-9 mark. Cowan sparkled at second base and rookie Avelino Canizares, a Cuban, shone at short as Horne was drafted for World War II.

When the league decided to award the second half title to the 22-11 Chicago American Giants because the Buckeyes appeared not to have played the required 30 league games, Wilbur Hayes displayed his accounting ability by proving the 22-7 Buckeyes qualified. He presented a game-by-game accounting of the Buckeyes' second half results that included a nine-inning tie called due to darkness for a 22-7-1 log in 30 games. Hayes' record-keeping had prevented an unnecessary playoff series for the NAL pennant.

Wilbur Hayes waves a gift certificate entitling him to a new Chevrolet before a September 2, 1945 crowd at Cleveland's League Park. The car would replace the one he had put 250,000 miles on assembling his championship team.

A primary factor in the team's pennant run had been Trouppe's handling of the Hayes-built pitching staff. Trouppe called all the right pitches as the Jefferson brothers, Bremmer, youngster Frank Carswell and Harden paced the Negro Leagues' best corps of hurlers.

The Clevelanders then proceeded to play errorless defense behind the Jeffersons, Bremmer and Carswell in a stunning World Series sweep of the Negro National League Homestead Grays by scores of 2-1, 4-2, 4-0, and 5-0. In just four years Wilbur Hayes had used the financial resources of a generous Ernie Wright to build the premier team in the Negro Leagues. Hayes, Wright and manager Trouppe looked forward to a successful title defense in 1946.

A down year—The Cleveland Buckeyes opened the 1946 Negro American League schedule a decimated ball club. Davenport had jumped to the Mexican League during the summer of 1945. Canizares followed suit during the off-season. Following the World Series Woods and the Jeffersons traveled to Venezuela to play winter ball. Of the three, only George Jefferson returned to Cleveland for the 1946 campaign. Unfortunately he had suffered an arm injury in Venezuela and was finished as an effective pitcher.

Hayes had not allowed the winning of a championship to permit himself the luxury of a winter off. He scouted and signed a number of promising youngsters during the off-season. The group included infielder-outfielder Al Smith, catcher Tommy Harris and Panamanians Vibert Clarke and Leon Kellman. Clarke was a big lefthanded pitcher and Kellman could play any position. The pitching staff was further augmented with the acquisitions of veterans Chet Brewer and Alonso Boone. Boone rejoined the club after a tour with the NAL Birmingham Black Barons.

Despite Hayes' efforts the 1946 team slipped to .500. A quintet of shortstops was tried before Smith settled in to replace Canizares. Kellman replaced Woods at third and took turns behind the plate and on the mound as well. Both hit well, as did Harris. Nineteen different hurlers were utilized in efforts to rebuild the pitching staff. Clarke pitched regularly and well as a rookie. Hayes was also heartened by the emergence of a young outfielder in his fifth professional season.

Willie Grace, signed during the 1942 season, replaced the defecting Davenport in right field during the 1945 title run. Grace was particularly effective in the World Series hitting the Series' only home run and joining Cowan as the series RBI leader. Grace really hit his stride in 1946 and was named the Buckeyes' Most Valuable Player. Grace and the emerging youngsters gave Hayes hopes for another championship.

Wilbur Hayes had built the 1945 championship club from scratch. With the disappointing 1946 showing it now remained to be seen if he could rebuild the club and regain the title. Hayes had no doubt he could do just that. The experience gained by the rookies, the emergence of Grace and continued excellence from Trouppe, Ware, Jethroe and Cowan gave the Buckeyes a strong nucleus. Hayes would prove to be up to the task before him, quickly rebuilding the Buckeyes into champions.

Back to the top—Hayes was aware that no matter how strong a starting cast manager Trouppe fielded, it would take strong pitching to regain the crown. None of the 1945 pitching stars would return to form for the Buckeyes. To a staff paced by Clarke, Brewer and Boone, Hayes added youngsters Sam Jones and Ross Davis. This quintet would be the team's pitching mainstays in 1947.

The Cleveland Buckeyes (54-23) swept to the 1947 Negro American League pennant in a fashion reminiscent of their 1945 success. Clarke and Brewer were the club's pitching leaders. Jethroe, Trouppe, Ware, Kellman and newcomers Joe Atkins and Clyde Nelson paced the offense as Cleveland topped both Negro Leagues with a .301 team batting mark.

The big baseball news in Cleveland during the summer of 1947 was not the rampaging Buckeyes. It was Jackie Robinson. And Larry Doby with the hometown Cleveland Indians. The black press had long been pushing Negro League players for the major leagues. The Buckeyes' Sam Jethroe had joined Robinson and Marvin Williams in a press-promoted tryout held by the Boston Red Sox in 1945. Although the obvious abilities of the players were difficult to ignore, none of the trio was signed by the Sox.

Wilbur Hayes family

Wilbur Hayes, right, with manager Alonso Boone in front of Hayes's Sport Parlor at East 49th and Central in Cleveland.

Bill Veeck's signing of Doby signaled that the Cleveland Indians would be at the forefront of integration. Ten of the first 34 non-whites to play major league ball were introduced by Tribe management. This aggressive role of the Indians in erasing baseball's color line would be a factor in making the Cleveland Buckeyes an early casualty of the doomed Negro Leagues. Larry Doby and the Tribe stole much of the thunder in Cleveland that summer despite the Buckeyes' success.

The 1947 Negro Leagues World Series opened with the NAL Buckeyes facing the NNL New York Cubans. Between them the two clubs featured nine future major leaguers. The Buckeyes' Jones and Smith and Cuban third baseman Orestes Minoso were destined for long and fruitful major league careers. Sam Jethroe would experience a period of glory in the majors. Clarke, Trouppe and Cubans Lino Donoso, Rafael Noble and Pat Scantlebury would also play in the big leagues.

Pitching had been the key to the Buckeyes' 1945 triumph. In 194 7 the failure of the pitching led to their downfall as New York won the Series in five decisions. Minoso (.423) swung the hottest bat as the Cubans pounded Cleveland hurlers for 65 hits and 42 runs in winning the Series. Hayes, visibly upset over the team's series performance, made a tough decision.

Shake-up—In what had to be a questionable decision Wilbur Hayes fired Buckeye manager Quincy Trouppe. Trouppe was replaced by veteran pitcher Alonso Boone in December. On the change in field leadership, Hayes was quoted by *Call & Post* sports editor A. S. (Doc) Young, "We have always held Boone in the very highest esteem. After becoming dissatisfied with Trouppe's management we are giving Boone the job. He will have full charge of the players and the playing field". Trouppe was then sold to the Chicago American Giants.

Hayes continued to make changes. Johnnie Cowan was sold to the Memphis Red Sox. Joe Atkins, the NAL's 1947 home run leader, was shipped to the Kansas City Monarchs in exchange for veteran backstop Joe Greene and infielder Othello Renfroe. The team was poised for the 1948 campaign and a second title defense in three years.

1948 provided the last taste of glory the Buckeyes were to enjoy. After a slow 5-13 start they won 17 of 18 contests to gain a second place first half NAL finish. Then integrating Organized Baseball began to dip into the Buckeyes' ranks. Team sparkplug Sam Jethroe and the versatile Al Smith were the first to leave the team.

Hayes did not see the loss of the team's stars as the end for the Buckeyes or the Negro Leagues. He saw it as an indication that black teams and leagues would be developing grounds for future major leaguers. It was a role Hayes and other Negro League magnates were ready to accept. But there would be no accommodation of the black circuits by the major leagues.

It did not become unusual for major league clubs to

grab up Negro Leaguers with no payment to the losing club. Hayes was fortunate to get the $4,000 or $5,000 he received for Jethroe from the Dodgers and Smith from the Indians. The Dodgers later sold Jethroe to the Boston Braves for $100,000 or more. The Indians' Bill Veeck was among those owners willing to compensate the black teams for their players.

Without Jethroe and Smith the 1948 Buckeyes won but 10 second half games and plummeted into the second division. Vibert Clarke and Sam Jones were pitching mainstays. Rookie Earnest Long also pitched effectively. Jones was the NAL strikeout leader. Archie Ware, Willie Grace and Renfroe had successful seasons at the plate.

One of the qualities of a successful general manager is his ability to make trades advantageous to his club. By trading Atkins for Renfroe and Greene, Hayes accomplished just that. While Renfroe and Greene helped the Buckeyes, Atkins deserted the Monarchs to play ball in Canada. Hayes' 1945 acquisition of Trouppe came as the result of a swap to Kansas City of the rights to Mexican League twirler Theolic Smith. Smith remained south of the border while Trouppe was leading Cleveland to pennants. Clyde Nelson, an important cog in the 1947 title run, joined the team in a preseason trade of veteran Al Armour to the Chicago American Giants. Hayes' trading ability was just another reason for his success and the success of the Buckeyes.

Out of town, out of time—In 1948 Veeck's American League Cleveland Indians were the toast of the town, setting attendance records and winning the pennant and World Series. Former Negro Leaguers Larry Doby and Satchel Paige played key roles in the club's unparalleled campaign. It became apparent that there was little room in the Lake Erie city for the Buckeyes. Wright and Hayes opted to transfer the club to Louisville, Kentucky for the 1949 season.

In a move that Hayes later termed a mistake, the transplanted Buckeyes floundered at the bottom of a realigned Negro American League Eastern Division. Four teams from a disbanded Negro National League joined the six-club NAL as the circuit split into a pair of five-team divisions. Louisville's Buckeyes were last in the east during both halves of the schedule.

Prior to the 1950 season, Ernie Wright gave up his interest in the Buckeyes and Wilbur Hayes assumed ownership of the club. He returned the team to Cleveland and promised to burn the league with blazing youth. The result was horrendous. The Buckeyes went through some fifty players and lost 39 of 42 NAL games before withdrawing from the league in early July. The Buckeyes' brief and glorious run through the Negro Leagues was suddenly over.

Wilbur Hayes put miles and time and devoted effort into building a baseball team. With the generous support of Ernie Wright he had built a great team. Five of the young men Hayes helped launch their professional baseball careers played major league ball. This group includes Jethroe, Al Smith, Jones, Clarke and Joe Caffie from the ill-fated 1950 team. Trouppe and 1949 Buckeye Dave Hoskins also played in the majors. Smith, Jones, Caffie, Trouppe and Hoskins all played for the Cleveland Indians. Sam Jethroe and Al Smith have both been enshrined in the Ohio Baseball Hall of Fame. Jethroe was arguably the Negro American League's best player during his Buckeye tenure. He became the Boston Braves' first African-American player in 1950, when he won Rookie of the Year honors. He led the major leagues in stolen bases in 1950 and 1951.

With the 1950 demise of his Buckeyes, Hayes's days as a professional baseball executive were over. Just beginning to allow in nonwhite players, the major leagues were a quarter of a century away from an African-American field manager and over four decades away from an African-American general manager. A proven builder of champions, Wilbur Hayes' only brush with major league baseball came as a part-time scout briefly serving the Cleveland Indians.

Wilbur Hayes collapsed at the wheel of his car in Cleveland's Central Market area on February 9, 1957 and died. Ironically, this is now the site of Jacobs Field, home of today's Cleveland Indians. His death was front page news in the *Call & Post*.

During the heyday of the Negro Baseball Leagues 12 different teams represented the city of Cleveland in the black major leagues. Ten of these entries survived but a single season at black baseball's top level. An eleventh survived through two seasons. Only the Buckeyes were able to sustain and prosper as a Negro League member in the Lake Erie city. Only the Buckeyes were able to win a black World Series title for the city. But then, only the Buckeyes had Wilbur Hayes running the show.

Sources:

The Cleveland *Call & Post* (1941-50, 57)

Buckeye Briefs (Vol. 1, No. 2) 9/27/42

Negro American League Official Statistics (Various years from 1944 thru 1950), compiled by the Howe News Bureau, Chicago

Only the Ball Was White, by Robert Peterson

Encyclopedia Del Beisbol Mexicano, by Pedro Treto Cisneros

The Biographical Encyclopedia of The Negro Baseball Leagues, by James A. Riley

Conversations with: Jeannine Hayes Boone and Erma Dee Hayes Hairston (daughters of Wilbur Hayes), Willie Grace, Sam Jethroe, and Al Smith.

The Cubs pitching staff of 1904-1910 was the best in big league history at rationing hits to opposing batters

Kings of the Hill

Lawrence Tenbarge

The last few generations of long-suffering Cubs fans should have been around during the decade following the turn of the century, enjoying the most glorious era in the team's history.

In 1906 the Cubs pitching staff held opposing batters to a mere 6.6 hits per game, the lowest in modern history. This played no small part in the club's posting a record of 116-36, also the best mark of this century.

For the seven-year span between 1904 and 1910 this staff led the league in fewest hits allowed six times, finishing a close second to the Giants in 1904, then leading each following year. It had also led in 1903 with a mark of 8.6 hits surrendered per game, much higher than its later marks.

During this stretch, the Cubs posted an overall regular-season record of 715-356, a winning percentage of .668, four pennants and World Series titles in 1907 and 1908.

No other club in big-league history has been able to equal their feat of averaging better than 102 victories for seven years, including any of the great Yankee teams of the Ruth, DiMaggio, or Mantle eras, John McGraw's Giants or the Brooklyn Dodgers during the '40s and '50s reign of the "Boys of Summer."

The staff—This magnificent staff was headed by Mordecai "Three-Finger" Brown, who was ably supported by Jack Pfiester, Ed Reulbach, Carl Lundgren, Jack Taylor and Orval Overall.

Lawrence Tenbarge is a free-lance writer most interested in science, science fiction, and historical baseball statistics.

As for comparative unhittability, this crew had four of history's top nine seasons in limiting hits to opposing batters. Opponents' overall season batting averages were correspondingly low.

A further indication of the Cubs' pitching dominance during that stretch is team ERA: 1905-2.04; 1906-1.75; 1907-1.73; 1908-2.14, and 1909-1.75.

Brown had most of his great seasons during this time. He was 26-6 in 1906 with a phenomenal ERA of 1.04, the second lowest of this century, surpassed only by Dutch Leonard of the Boston Red Sox who posted an unbelievable 1.01 in 1914.

Brown won 20 or more games six consecutive seasons, from 1906-1911, with a high of 29 in 1908 and a league-leading 27 the following year.

Pfiester, in 1907, turned in an ERA of 1.15, the sixth best of the century. That same year Lundgren chipped in with a 1.17, eighth on the list. Thus, two members of this staff had near-record ERAs the season after Brown had his. No other team in history has had three pitchers simultaneously reach this level of performance—or even come close.

Reulbach also contributed some magnificent seasons during this span. He led the National League in winning percentage three straight years (1906-1908) with marks of .826, .810 and .774, respectively, posting records of 19-4, 17-4 and 24-7 in the process.

His ERAs also were excellent, going under 2.00 in four different seasons, the lowest a sparkling 1.42 in 1905. The following year it was 1.65 as he held opposing batters to a feeble .175 average.

Orval Overall is another name probably not well-known to modern fans. It can be assumed that many hitters of his time wished they hadn't heard it, either.

Joining the Cubs in 1906, he immediately began racking up some great numbers. With Chicago from 1906 through 1910 he chalked up a 82-38 record, good for a .683 winning percentage, including 23-7 in 1907. During this span he also posted ERAs of under 2.00 four times, with a low of 1.42 in 1909, when he led the league in strikeouts with 205 and opponents' batting average of .198.

Ed Reulbach

Jack Taylor, who played with the Cubs from 1898-1903 before moving on to the Cardinals, posted a feat from June 20, 1901, to August 6, 1906, that would be considered nearly impossible by today's standards. Although he pitched some in relief, when he started he threw 187 consecutive complete games!

Leonard "King" Cole, a late addition to the staff, climbed into the fray in 1910 to post a 20-4 record, a league-leading .833 percentage and a 1.80 ERA.

No other staff has ever had so many members of its crew post so many near-record and league-leading numbers. None is even close.

Modern competitors—1968 was justly referred to as the "Year of the Pitcher." The American League overall batting average dropped to .230 that season; the senior Circuit mark was not much better that year at .243. Individual pitching performances of that season included Denny McLain's 31 wins, Bob Gibson's ERA of 1.12, the third lowest in modern history and the best since the introduction of the lively ball, and Don Drysdale's 58 consecutive scoreless innings, including six straight shutouts.

It is possible, however, that the finest individual season of any pitcher that season, at least in the AL, went largely unnoticed.

Luis Tiant of the Indians held opposing batters to just 5.30 hits per game. For comparison, Gibson and McLain posted marks of 5.85 and 6.46. Tiant also led the AL in ERA with 1.60; McLain's 1.96 was a full 22% higher. Tiant held opponents to a collective on-base average of .233, exactly the same as Gibson.

In addition, Tiant led the league in shutouts with nine and came in second to teammate "Sudden" Sam McDowell in strikeouts per nine innings with 9.20 to McDowell's 9.47; McLain was fifth at 7.50.

Tiant also did just as good a job of squeezing out wins considering the team he had backing him as the others. His ratio of percentage compared to the rest of his staff was 1.41, McLain was 1.45 and Gibson was 1.24.

Led by Tiant the Cleveland staff limited opponents to 6.68 hits per game, the second best effort in history. Fireballing McDowell, who led the league with 283 strikeouts, was third, surrendering 6.06 hits per game, while Sonny Siebert was fourth at 6.33. With three of the four most efficient pitchers in the league at handcuffing hitters it can easily be seen why this crew came in second to the Cubs' earlier record.

Although Cleveland nearly equalled the Cub record, it must be remembered that for 1968 the AL hit .230 as noted earlier. In 1906 the NL hit .244; on a comparative basis, therefore, the Cubs' mark was clearly superior.

Also in 1968 a great Baltimore Orioles staff racked up the third-best mark in history, finishing just behind the Indians at 6.89 hits per game. As a coincidence, these two teams had the exact same ERA (2.66) and opponents' on-base average (.286). Had Jim Palmer not missed the entire season the Orioles' mark might have been even better.

McLain's world champion Tigers came in third in the league at 7.13, eighth best of all time. Thus, the league had three of the top eight team marks in history in one season.

It is interesting to compare the Cleveland effort that season with that of their more famous brethren of a generation earlier.

In 1954 the Indians won an AL record 111 games while ending Casey Stengel's string of five consecutive world championships with the Yankees. Early Wynn, Bob Lemon, Mike Garcia, Art Houtteman, Bob Feller, Don Mossi, Ray Narleski, and Hal Newhouser surrendered 7.74 hits per game; an excellent mark, to be sure, but more than one a game higher than Tiant and Company.

The 1927 Yankees are generally considered to have been the best team in history. How did the staff supporting Ruth, Gehrig, and the rest of "Murderer's Row" compare to the others?

Waite Hoyt, Herb Pennock, Urban Shocker and Wilcy Moore headed the staff. They did lead the league, but gave up an average 9.09 hits per game, a far higher ratio than those on the list.

When asked what was the greatest pitching staff he had ever seen, Branch Rickey was quoted in the book, *I'd Rather Be A Yankee* by John Tullius, as saying, "Raschi, Reynolds, Lopat and Ford." When asked why, he replied, "Well, to make it short and sweet, you name me another staff that won five straight pennants and five straight World Series. When it got toughest they always won."

Sure, five in a row is hard to argue with, but that squad's most efficient season was 1949, the first of their string, when they gave up 8.1 hits per game. The other four years, they came in second twice to the White Sox and twice to the Indians, who were busy consolidating the great staff mentioned above.

No discussion of great pitching staffs and individuals would be complete without mentioning the Dodgers of the early to mid-sixties and Sandy Koufax.

This staff was composed mainly of Koufax, Drysdale, Stan Williams, Johnny Podres, Claude Osteen and Ron Perranoski.

From 1960-66, this crew had a seven-year run of greatness similar to that of the earlier Cubs. They led the league five times, while finishing tied for second and third the other two years. Their best season, 1965, saw them hold opposing batters to 7.5 hits per game; exceptional, but not among the all-time leaders. Koufax, however, was another story.

Most baseball fans know that Koufax won three pitchers "Triple Crowns" in 1963-65-66, leading the league in wins, strikeouts, and ERA. Not surprisingly, the Dodgers won pennants all three years.

What is not so well known, however, was that from 1960 to 1965, six consecutive seasons, Koufax led the league in fewest hits allowed per nine innings, topping out in 1965 at 5.79, the ninth lowest mark in modern history. In 1966, his last season, he came in second, just a hair behind long-time rival Juan Marichal. It was unfortunate that chronic arthritis in the elbow of his pitching arm forced his premature retirement. His presence would have aggravated hitters' woes in 1968.

Back to the Cubbies—Were the 1904-1910 Cub pitchers really better than, say, the Indians of the early to mid-'50s? Times change. Rules, equipment, playing conditions, even umpires' interpretations of the strike zone vary from age to age. But judging purely by the numbers—ERA, winning percentage, fewest hits allowed—this group was without question the best in modern big league history. At snuffing out the opposing offenses over an extended period, they were truly "Kings of the Hill."

An autographed ball leads to a personal connection

Bosey Berger

Nat Rosenberg

In March of 1991 I found an autographed baseball on the shelf in the back of an old sports memorabilia store in La Grange, IL. On the beautifully white official Spalding were 28 signatures. I recognized Bob Feller and Al Schacht immediately. Bosey Berger did not come so readily to mind. Billy Conn the boxer was on the ball. So was Ray Bolger of Wizard of Oz fame. Ace Parker, the football Hall of Famer (and professional baseball player) was there, along with announcer Ted Husing. The ball was inscribed "N.Y. Sports Carnival 6/14/42."

For $50 the ball was mine, and my mission was clear. I wrote to all of the living athletes on the ball to see if they could share any recollections with me. Almost immediately, I received very nice short notes from Hugh Mulcahy and Bob Feller with mixed memories of the day and even the location. Both agreed that it was a charity game for the war effort. I was so pleased that they would consider writing to me. I had no idea what was in store for me next.

About two months later, I received a package from Mrs. Jean (Bosey) Berger. My father and I have been collecting autographs and writing to athletes for many years. Nothing I have ever received compared in personal caring to the response from Jean. Here is Jean's response to my letter.

Nat Rosenberg is always in spring training, is never on strike, and is happily married to wife Kathleen.

May 20, 1991

Dear Nat,

Since I handle much of Bosey's correspondence, I am answering your March letter. We have been married for 50 years and I can tell you much of what you want to know.

The baseball you bought was from a game played at the Polo Grounds for the Army/Navy relief fund and sponsored by *The Sporting News*.

Bosey (a reserve officer) from U. of Md. was called to active duty only 4 months before his army commission as an officer would have expired. One could hold the rank for only ten years by correspondence courses instead of week-end assignments and summer 2 week active duty stints. Because he played baseball summers, he had to keep up by paperwork assignments. He was the only officer in the game (an old second LT!).

He remembers signing *The Sporting News* check for a great dinner for the teams at "Toots" Shor's restaurant in N.Y.C. The players stayed overnight at a hotel in the city.

...Several players played for west coast teams. Back then, that was the AAA Pacific League—not the big leagues. Some of the young players were coming up from minor league teams—Bosey was coming down.

...Around Washington DC, old timers remember Bosey as a great basketball player.

Back in the 30's, pro basketball wasn't much and Bosey played baseball and felt fortunate to sign with the Cleveland Indians (Walter Johnson, a good friend of ours since till his death, was his first manager) during the depression when graduate engineers were lucky to be pumping gas!

National Baseball Library, Cooperstown, NY

Louis "Bosey" Berger, who was usually called "Boze" on the sports page.

Bosey loved his time with the White Sox—great friends. Ted Lyons, from Vinton, LA was a close friend till his death a couple of years ago.

Though Bosey gets no retirement from baseball (one must have ten years in the game to be eligible) and he never made much money, but he loved the game—had other skills that brought us a comfortable life-style and he'd not change a thing if he had his life to live over—except he'd be a switch hitter.

A college football injury has bothered him in recent years—has stenosis of the spine. He had good years after surgery in '78, but now doctors at John Hopkins say he is not a good candidate for further surgery.

He is 81, uses a cane but goes out daily with his remaining childhood buddies (old ball players), plays golf once a week (partners tee up ball for him), reads constantly—history and novels and enjoys games and old movies on cable T.V.

We run a tailgate group "20's crowd" of old athletes and families at the U. of Md. football games—and enjoy the company of our three grown children, all of whom live in the area.

Sincerely,

Jean L Berger

Bosey Berger passed away on November 3, 1992.

This is probably more than anyone thought they would ever read about an infielder with 13 career home runs. I feel very fortunate to have met Bosey and Jean Berger. It isn't surprising that a baseball brought us together.

Pittsburgh, 1887

Bob Fulton

Pittsburgh's first National League season began with a pregame ceremony in which outfielder Fred Carroll buried his beloved pet monkey—beneath home plate.

That was as close as the 1887 club came to normality.

Management and employees feuded like the Hatfields and McCoys through much of that inaugural season, creating an atmosphere that was more conducive to explosions of the temper than explosions of the bat.

The Alleghenys, as Pittsburgh's team was then known, were an acrimonious lot that engaged in backbiting and back-stabbing on a scale that would make the typical soap seem like a "Waltons" spin-off. Bad news on the field (a 55-69 record, good for sixth place in an eight-team league), the Alleghenys were sizzling news off, their exploits providing ample fodder for the gossip-hungry newspapers of the day.

The saga of the fledgling "Pittsburg Base Ball Club" (the "h" in Pittsburgh came later) dispels the image of the nineteenth century as something of an idyllic era in the game's history and features some juicy scenes worthy of today's tabloids: team-employed detectives shadowing star players suspected of "midnight carousing"; a nineteenth-century version of "Divorce Court," with shortstop Willie Kuehne ordering the arrest of his wife; management accusing Ed Morris of cowardice for refusing to pitch during a series in Detroit, and 17-year-old pitcher Bill Bishop blaming his fielders for nonsupport after manager "Hustling Horace" Phillips released him for being "too nervous."

Early hope—The Alleghenys were indeed "The Young and the Restless" of their day. And yet, despite the fact that their record and rapport deteriorated in equal measure as the summer wore on, the Alleghenys embarked on their first National League season brimming with hope.

Phillips' club had finished second the year before in the American Association, the other major league at the time. The AA had begun play in 1882 and initially outdrew the established National League at the gate with its willingness to play Sunday baseball (then banned in the other league) and its cheaper ticket prices (25 cents, half the NL admission fee).

But the National League was still considered the more prestigious circuit. So when Kansas City dropped out of the NL following the 1886 season, several Pittsburgh baseball officials resolved to seize this golden opportunity and switch leagues.

Their plan was met with less than unanimous approval. But William Nimick, a nefarious sort who was one of the team owners, discovered a way to circumvent that hurdle.

At his insistence, the Alleghenys declared bankruptcy, claiming debts of $30,000, and were put up at auction. Nimick then bought back the team for $30 and installed himself as president, effectively freezing out the opposition. He even ignored the wishes of his players, who groused about changing leagues.

"That there is much kicking in the ranks of the Pittsburg ballclub is an open secret," the Pittsburg

Bob Fulton , who has written extensively about Pirates history for various publications, practically grew up at Forbes Field, where his father was an usher. He lives in Indiana, Pennsylvania, home town of actor Jimmy Stewart.

Evening Penny Press reported. (Newspaper accounts in the 1880s were seldom bylined, even when the degree of editorializing warranted attribution.) "From the players' standpoint, they have been badly treated."

That was a common complaint by major leaguers of the time. A sense of powerlessness prevailed, owing largely to the existence of the reserve clause, which bound players to their respective teams and placed them at the mercy of management's whims. Indignant players denounced it as nothing more than legalized slavery and plotted to establish their own league.

But such weighty matters were momentarily shunted to the background on April 30, 1887, when Pittsburgh made its NL debut by whipping defending champion Chicago, 6-2. The leadoff man that afternoon for player-manager Adrian "Cap" Anson's team was 24-year-old outfielder Billy Sunday, who would achieve far greater acclaim as an evangelist than he ever did during an eight-year major league career.

Fred Carroll

Pitcher James "Pud" Galvin, a future Hall of Famer who was to win 28 games that season, earned the victory before a crowd of 10,000 at Recreation Park. The Alleghenys' batting star was 30-year-old first baseman Alex McKinnon, who died of typhoid fever less than three months later. He went 4-for-4.

"Saturday's victory was a glorious one, and reflects the greatest credit on the boys who so nobly battled for the honor of Pittsburg," the *Commercial Gazette* reported. "It was the league baptism and royally did they stand the test."

The victory served as a tonic for the newcomers, who longed to prove they were worthy of competing in the NL. The Alleghenys' opening day triumph raised eyebrows around the league and inspired a New York *Sun* writer to pen a poem titled "The Destruction of Chicago," the final verse of which read:

"And the Giants in Gotham are loud in their wail,
And the Straits City Sluggers grow silent and pale;
And the Bean Eaters tremble, the Phillies grow wild,
As they think of the strength of the League's infant child."

Allegheny fans remained in the grip of euphoria as their team toppled mighty Detroit (the Straits City) 8-3 in its second game before 6,000 fans at Recreation Park. Carroll slugged the team's first NL homer and also singled, doubled and tripled to complete baseball's "cycle." In this age of million-dollar contracts and lavish performance bonuses, it's revealing to note that Carroll's only tangible reward was a silk hat, courtesy of a local haberdasher.

"The excitement among the crowd was of the wildest kind," noted the Pittsburg *Post* in its account of the victory. "Hats were thrown into the air and men and women cheered wildly."

Trouble starts—But like those hats, the Alleghenys soon came back to earth. Reality struck in Detroit, where Pittsburgh lost three consecutive games—the last by an 18-2 score—to fall to 4-5.

The first fissures in a foundation that would ultimately collapse around the Alleghenys like Poe's House of Usher were now revealed. Morris, who refused to take his turn on the mound, was accused of cowardice, fined and suspended.

The pitcher's defense was that he was suffering from rheumatism of the arm. A teammate who did not wish to reveal his identity to management for fear of reprisal averred that he had rubbed Morris's shoulder with liniment and attached a galvanic battery to it.

"The serenity of the pitcher's mind has been exceedingly ruffled in consequence of the fine imposed on him," the *Post* reported. "He declares it a gross injustice."

Other Alleghenys would echo those sentiments

throughout the season. Dissension on the club was exacerbated by the dismal performances turned in by several of the team's highest-paid stars, who received annual salaries of between $2,500 and $3,000.

Apart from Galvin, the pitching staff was dreadful. Morris suffered through a 14-22 campaign after leading the AA with 41 victories the year before, and Jim McCormick, who had averaged nearly 31 wins through eight full major league seasons, finished 13-23.

Of course, those hurlers were often undermined by anemic offensive support. Carroll (.328) and the ill-fated McKinnon (.340) were the team's only .300 hitters, this in a season when bases on balls were counted officially as hits and pitchers needed four strikes to retire a batter. Left fielder Abner Dalrymple, a career .300 hitter and a mainstay with Anson's great Chicago teams (five titles between 1880 and 1886), batted a pitiful .212. The punchless Pittsburgers averaged .258 with a league-low 20 home runs.

"The players whom we expected to do heavy batting for us have done scarcely anything at all," Phillips lamented.

National Baseball Library, Cooperstown, NY

Alex McKinnon

Labor strife—As frustrations over the team's performance grew, so did the gap between management and players. Prior to a game with the Giants on June 21, Phillips delivered a lecture containing veiled accusations that the Alleghenys were guilty of playing for personal gain rather than the welfare of the team. He then warned "one or two players who have been indulging in lager and whisky a little too freely lately."

The latter issue came to a head in Philadelphia on July 5 when Phillips and Nimick hired detectives to trail Carroll, Morris and outfielder Tom Brown. Caught drinking, they were fined $50 apiece.

In media reports, Nimick painted a picture of players who "led a reckless life" and were guilty of "midnight carousing." The *Post* called for the immediate release of the so-called "boozers." (Brown would soon be dealt to Indianapolis; Carroll and Morris remained.) "It will certainly be more credible [sic] to lose with a team of gentlemen than with a number of debauchees," the newspaper concluded.

Brown, who resigned his captaincy over this latest flap (the Alleghenys went through captains that season the way Henry VIII went through wives), viewed management's actions as "unjust and tyrannical" and the public agreed. Fans sympathized with the trio and blasted the club's covert activities as reprehensible.

Other flare-ups further demoralized the team:

- Bishop, released after he was shelled in an 18-1 loss to last-place Indianapolis, claimed his fielders did not give him proper support. Phillips scoffed at the charge. "Bishop," he retorted, "is a failure. He is too nervous. When he went into the box his face was white as chalk."

- The Alleghenys tried to pry future Hall of Fame shortstop John Montgomery Ward from New York for the astronomical sum of $10,000 (in contrast, Detroit's championship team was paid $38,000 that season). But those skeptical of management's motives—especially in light of past underhanded maneuvers—dismissed the overture as a public relations ploy rather than a sincere effort to improve the club.

- Kuehne filed for divorce from his wife, whom he had once had arrested for "unpleasant demonstrations." His decision was triggered by the discovery that, while he was absent on a road trip, his wife's conduct was "of the most questionable kind."

With so much extracurricular activity taking place, it's little wonder the team's performance suffered. Even in triumph the Alleghenys sometimes alienated their fans. Following a late-season victory over Indianapolis, the *Post* noted that "if the Pittsburg club had not won yesterday's game there would have been sufficient cause for the 800 people present to clamor for the extermination of the home aggregation."

By then it was a miracle the Alleghenys had avoided *self*-extermination. They exchanged accusations and epithets with management and each other and seemingly expended more energy in those pursuits than in dueling opposing teams.

Consequently, the Alleghenys' hopes of winning a championship in their first National League season were buried early—not long after Fred Carroll's pet monkey.

Coupled in legend with the Babe

"Swish" Nicholson

Bob Mayer

Do you remember Bill Nicholson, who stroked 235 home runs during fifteen years with the Cubs and Phillies, whose prodigious swing inspired the nickname "Swish"?

It's been more than 50 years since Nicholson completed the first two-year home run–RBI quinella in National League history by leading the league in both categories in consecutive seasons, 1943 and '44.

In 1943, the first half of Nicholson's two-year reign, he hit 29 home runs and knocked in 128 runs. The following season would be his career year: 33 homers and 122 RBIs, while batting .287 and also leading the league in runs scored and total bases.

Nicholson's 1944 season was a longballer's dream year, highlighted by a remarkable and record-setting display of power one weekend in July that would indelibly couple him in legend with Babe Ruth himself. But…more about legend later.

Bill Nicholson wasn't merely a wartime baseball phenomenon. He struggled through 58 games with the Cubs in 1939, but followed that with 25 homers, 98 RBIs and a .297 average the following year, which was essentially his rookie season. This would signal his presence as a steady fourth, fifth or sixth slot hitter who was a consistent run producer.

Nicholson would enjoy a career that featured a number of 1940-like seasons, but was short-circuited by the onset of diabetes. He's needed twice-a-day insulin shots ever since.

Bob Mayer is an educational consultant in Westwood, New Jersey. He is a baseball dreamer…of players, places, and events before the advent of saucer-shaped stadia, artificial turf, and designated hitters. He bats and throws right.

During a recent conversation on his farm in Chestertown, MD, where he's affectionately known as "Mister Bill," Nicholson alluded to the diabetes and its effects during his finest season, 1944, when symptoms first appeared. He was markedly weakened, he said, until a correct diagnosis was made after many weeks and many doctors. "I should have hit 400 home runs," he said of his career total. Nicholson is sure the disease took a cumulative toll on all his lifetime totals and forced him to miss the 1950 World Series, when he played for the Phillies.

Nicholson's '44 season seemed a cinch for the league's Most Valuable Player award, but the great shortstop Marty Marion won it, receiving 190 votes to Nicholson's 189. Marion's offensive stats were anemic compared to Nicholson's. Asked how he felt about not winning the honor, Nicholson said, "Marty probably deserved it," adding, "and he was a helluva shortstop." It should be noted that Nicholson's Cubs finished the year in fourth place, 30 games behind Marion's Cardinals and their third straight pennant.

In 1945 Nicholson played a substantial role for the pennant- winning Cubs (equaling the record for World Series RBIs at that time, with eight), but his numbers dropped in 1946 before rebounding a bit in the next two years. He was traded to the Phillies for Harry "The Hat" Walker in 1948 and played five uneventful seasons in Philadelphia. He returned to his farm in 1953.

Despite a decade and a half in the National League, it would take just one dramatic weekend in 1944 to define the career, as well as the legend, of Bill Nicholson.

The Cubs were at the Polo Grounds, facing the Giants, in a series that typically included single games on

Bob Mayer

Above, Bill Nicholson at work. Below, the statue that Chestertown has erected to its favorite ballplayer.

Friday and Saturday, and a doubleheader on Sunday.

Here's what Nicholson did between July 21 and 23, 1944:

- set a National League record by hitting four home runs in a doubleheader;
- set a league record with home runs in four successive at bats;
- tied two league records with five homers in three games and six homers in four games.

Translation: Nicholson homered once in each of the first two games of the series, including his last at-bat on Saturday; he reached the seats his first three at-bats in Sunday's opening game; in the second game, which closed out the series, he managed one final home run.

That's when legend was introduced. When Nicholson came to bat late in Sunday's second game, having homered six times since Friday, the Cubs had the bases loaded, but trailed the beleaguered Giants on the scoreboard. Giants manager Mel Ott, himself a premier home run hitter, would allow no more Nicholson havoc. Defying the book, Ott ordered an intentional walk, taking the bat out of Nicholson's hands, but conceding a run. (Nicholson recalls that the Giants held on to win, 12-10, averting a four-game sweep.)

Bob Mayer

In Chestertown there's a large, awe-inspiring bronze statue of Nicholson's lefthand-hitting follow-through. Below the statue is a plaque which reads in part, "Legend has it that only Bill Nicholson and Babe Ruth have ever been walked intentionally with the bases loaded."

(Legends aside, research indicates that on May 23, 1901, Clark Griffith, then a first-year manager with the White Sox, ordered a bases-loaded walk to the great Napoleon Lajoie, who was on his way to a .422 season for the Philadelphia A's.)

Nicholson, who turned 80 on December 11, was asked about sharing a place in baseball lore with Babe Ruth. Without hesitation, he said, "Babe was a great ballplayer...I was just so-so. I'm not in the same class."

Indeed, Bill Nicholson is in a class by himself.

The College and the Semipros

Martin Payne

Washington College is a small liberal arts school located in the rural county seat of Chestertown, Maryland, which lies on the banks of a tributary of the Chesapeake Bay. With a student body of 70 to 80 young men, and given its rural location, the active role the college assumed when the use of professional players became an accepted practice in the area is somewhat unexpected.

When organized town teams began to appear on the Eastern Shore of Maryland in the fever season of 1867, the college club was already firmly established. The "Wissahickons" had existed as early as 1865, probably earlier, and in a short time the college squad came to dominate play on the upper peninsula. On the rest of the shore villages and rural district teams might begin their season in the spring, while the major commercial and political centers usually did not take the field before Independence Day. But in Chestertown the season began with the college campaign in March and rarely extended beyond commencement at the beginning of July. As the center of attention, the college assumed the role that the commercially and community sponsored teams played in other towns.

The college's position as the focus of the upper shore season culminated in 1883 with an undefeated 10-game campaign. In a series of smartly played contests that lasted but an hour and twenty-two minutes to two hours and fifteen minutes, the Wissahickons raised the expectations of their followers behind the pitching of little Albert Hopkins. The fans were somewhat disgruntled when the squad's fortunes fell the next year. Following a series of losses, including one to arch-rival St. John's of Annapolis, an alumnus voiced his displeasure to the Chestertown *Transcript,* observing that the boys seemed "just a little lazy." Before the season was over the college was accused of using an "imported" player, but the club justified his acquisition by the fact that he had been a member of the class of '80.

The use of imported players was not yet a common occurrence on local rural nines. The first mention of the college having to face such talent came in 1886, when the Wissahickons faced a team from Middleton, Delaware, that featured the Wilmington battery of McMann and Waverlain. There is no conclusive evidence that this McMann was the Sadie McMahon who went on to a significant major league career, but Sadie was from Wilmington and would have been 16 years old at the time.

Stronger competition—During the next few years the college continued its domination of the local season, but developments soon threatened its position of superiority. Improvements in transportation now brought Baltimore "amateur" teams to the campaign. The Maryland Intercollegiate Athletic Association, formed in the late 1880s, and along with similar developments in Delaware, college teams began to nudge local nines off the schedule. The local clubs that did remain were the better ones, and not inclined to take repeated losses lightly. Dr. Harold Seymour indicates that Philadelphia was a hotbed of semipro activity in 1900, but there is evidence in newspaper accounts that such an

Martin Payne is a participant in SABR's American Association Research Project.

environment was already thriving in the Philadelphia-Wilmington region by the 1890s. The college's proximity to this influence soon pressured their recruitment policies.

Recruiting—In 1891 the college faced the imported Delaware battery of Hawke and Hair. They were so impressed with Hawke's delivery that they "retained" his services for their game with St. John's of Annapolis. The next year, they signed 18-year-old local pitching phenom Al Burris, and a 25-year-old catching veteran Dave Zearfoss. But even this did not prepare them for what they were about to face.

Nearly every game they played against Baltimore, college, and local opponents now featured imported players. Teams often turned out to be far different from the ones originally scheduled. Centreville, for example, showed up as the Centreville-Hawke Combination Club, featuring the pitcher and a band of his friends. Bill (Dick) Hawke proved the most proficient and popular of the imports. He appeared for six teams during the upper shore season of 1892, and he may have played for more in the Delaware circuits. By mid-June he had made a "favorable impression," signing a $1,500 contract with the Reading, PA club, and posting a 4-5 mark with St. Louis before the season was over. Hawke, in fact, threw the first major league no-hitter from the modern pitching distance.

Their collegiate opponents were also giving way to the pressures of using outside players during this time. The New Windsor College featured an imported battery, and it was said that few of the members of the Deichman School nine were actually enrolled there.

With a limited enrollment, the college was forced outside the classroom to remain competitive. One technique was to accept written applications from aspiring young players throughout the Mid-Atlantic region in the spring. Through the 1890s there was always preseason speculation about who would be secured, and opening-day lineups were often temporary, and would be changed when a certain player "arrived."

Another method stemmed from the emergence of a strong, if somewhat informal, semipro circuit on the Eastern Shore of Maryland in the 1890s. Town teams recruited a mix of veterans, local talent, and regional teenage phenoms, and it was the latter that attracted the attention of the college club. It was not unusual for young players from this circuit to find their way onto the school's squad. At one point in 1897, the small town Federalsburg club put three future major leaguers in the field—Raymond "Chappy" Charles, Bob Unglaub, and Jack "Happy" Townsend—all of whom appeared for the college by 1900. Homer Smoot, later a Cardinal outfielder, was one of the many local talents to follow a similar path to the college.

Both parties found this arrangement beneficial. Washington was able to field a team better than most of its opponents, making themselves competitive with powerhouses like the Universities of Pennsylvania and Syracuse. Players were able to get up to 20 games under their belts before the college season ended and the rural semipro campaigns began.

Most of these young talents stayed only a year or two before moving on. To Zearfoss's credit, he completed his four-year term before signing a contract directly with the New York Giants as a backup catcher. Al Burris suited up an played many positions at the college for ten years, first as a student, and then while serving as a faculty member, coach, and athletic director. Burris, like many of the college players, routinely signed contracts with local semipro teams in the summer, and in 1894 he saw action with the Philadelphia Nationals. There are no known complaints of his crossing the line between amateur and professional.

Money—How compensation fit into this is only implied. It is unlikely that a player would "arrive" from a distance without some type of consideration. When Bill Hawke balked at his Oriole contract in the spring of 1894, the college fully expected to "secure" his services, suggesting that recompense could occasionally be significant. Unfortunately for the college, Hawke resolved his differences with Baltimore. "Old Reliable" Zearfoss was publicly presented with a purse of $30 in gold, and both he and Burris were given gifts of merchandise by the appreciative citizens of Chestertown.

There was only one attempt to restrict the club's activities during these years. Following Hawke's appearance for the college in 1891, the faculty passed a resolution that only students could play for the team. But within a week the second baseman went down with an injury and an outside player was allowed to take his place. This wavering of resolve on the part of the faculty found no support in the new Maryland Intercollegiate Association, which had not yet acquired the philosophical direction, or the power, to impose amateur baseball on its members. And the presence of Burris gave the club a strong voice in the school's administration.

This open environment lasted well into the first decade of the new century. By 1903 locals accurately boasted that one could not find better baseball in towns of similar size than on the Eastern Shore of Maryland. The college's players were routinely recruited for the Tri City series of 1900, the Eastern Shore League of 1904, and the many independent teams in the area. There they gained valuable experience playing alongside the former and future major leaguers of those circuits. Buck Herzog, John "Brownie" Foreman, Charlie Gettig, Sam Frock, Nick Maddux and Frank Baker were among the many who were on their way to or from the big leagues.

Changes—By the turn of the century the philosophy of progressive education had taken root in many colleges and school boards. One of its offshoots was the use of sports to impose the American values of hard work and fair play. In 1908, Burris left Washington College to pursue a medical degree, and he was replaced as athletic director by M. J. "Mike" Thompson. Thompson's impact was immediate, not only on the college, but also through his apparent influence in the Maryland Intercollegiate Athletic Association. Maryland colleges were now punished for using ineligible players. Washington no longer accepted spring applications, nor did they recruit from local semipro squads. The result was inevitable on the tiny school, as managers Raymond Moody, Ben Johnson, and Homer Smoot were saddled with some of the least competitive teams the school ever produced. The boys were encouraged to believe "bunting and rooting can win any game."

Thompson eventually moved on to a similar post at Mount St. Mary's College in Emmitsburg, and left the state entirely in 1914. In 1915, the college club was back to strength with a thirty-year-old veteran pitcher, Jack Enright, and several young players with experience on local town teams. This coincided with the formation of the semipro Peninsula League, with teams from Easton, St. Michaels, Cambridge and Salisbury. The Easton entry obtained the services of Frank Baker, who was sitting out the season in a contract dispute with Connie Mack, plus the college players Tom Kibler and Jack Enright. Even with this talent, the Easton squad could manage only a third-place finish, as most of the college's roster found their services in demand with other teams in the league.

The league realigned in 1916, and the college roster was again tapped for players. When the batting averages were published in late August, the circuit's three leading hitters—Erickson, Pearce and Spedden—had all started the season at Washington. This spoke well of the caliber of the college's squad in these four-team leagues that featured Home Run Baker in his prime, the young Eddie Rommel, local veteran Lee Ritchie, and the fringe major leaguers Doc Twining and Mike Cantwell. There is no mention of compensation to the college players, and if they weren't payed, they proved a boon to the usually spendthrift semipro managements. In June of 1917 Jack Enright signed a contract with the New York Yankees, but World War I was dampening the usual ardor for baseball. The sport was soon declared "nonessential."

When semipro baseball returned in 1919, it came back with a vigor never before seen on the Eastern Shore. Towns that numbered but in the hundreds brought in imported players, and home grown talents like Vic Keen, Jake Flowers and Dick Porter prepared themselves for solid major league careers on local grounds. Organized Baseball was acutely sensitive to the threat posed by these circuits. Baker had defected to the Delaware State and Peninsula Leagues in 1915, and Ty Cobb used the threat in his contract negotiations in 1917.

The major leagues responded by solidifying the minors with an increase of affiliation and money. The Class D level was created to make inroads into rural areas, the hotbeds of semipro activity, and such a league was formed on the Eastern Shore in the fall of 1921. College players were excluded from affiliated rosters and were forced to choose between amateur and professional. With the presence of organized baseball in the area, Washington College was alienated from its traditional role as the focus of the upper shore season, and it entered the era of modern collegiate athletics.

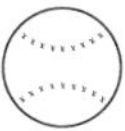

Wamby could've done it by himself.

What is conceded to be the most complicated double play in the history of baseball was made at Albany a few days ago. In a game against Syracuse. The play involved every player on the Albany team save the right fielder, and it was so peculiar as to attract attention throughout the east.

Syracuse had runners on first and third and one out, when the office was given for a double steal, the pitcher, suspecting, turned a new trick. Instead of pitching to the plate, he made a half balk motion and whipped the ball to third, drawing the runner off first. The man on third dived back to the bag, and the baseman threw to second, stopping the first and beat the throw [sic].

As the second sacker threw to first, the man on third streaked for home, but was turned back by the first baseman's throw to the catcher. As he was being run down by the catcher, the man on first continued around the paths. The left fielder finally touched out the runner between third and home, and turned to get the man between second and third. The ball was thrown back and forth several times, the putout finally going to the center fielder, who had hurried in to join in the play.

In all, the ball was thrown 18 times, every man but the right fielder had assists, and two outfielders were credited with putouts on an infield play. (From the Dayton Herald, *August 5, 1909).*

—Jack Carlson

A lost pennant

The 1950 Detroit Tigers

Marc Okkonen

Numerologists in early 1950 ordained that it was the Detroit Tigers' destiny to win the American League championship that summer. After pennant-winning seasons in 1935, 1940, and 1945, it seemed only logical that the five-year cycle would continue for the Bengals, based on a late surge in 1949 and some significant new additions to their roster for 1950. Owner Walter O. Briggs shelled out $100,000 plus promising young hurler Lou Kretlow to the St. Louis Browns for veteran second baseman Gerry Priddy in late 1949. Shortly thereafter the Tigers finally gave up on one-time bonus baby Dick Wakefield, trading him to the Yankees for first baseman Dick Kryhoski, a .328 hitter with Oakland in 1949. These two trades would beef up the right side of the Tiger infield—an obvious weakness in their '49 club.

Manager Red Rolfe, a humorless, hard-driving taskmaster, succeeded popular Steve O'Neill in 1949 and instilled a new commitment to winning baseball in the Joe McCarthy mold. Rolfe had been a questionable choice to lead the club, having had no real managerial experience. But he had done a masterful job in resurrecting the Tiger farm system and he was well acquainted with the player personnel throughout the Detroit organization. And his long association with winning Yankee teams gave him the inside track with General Manager Billy Evans. Rolfe's coaching staff included Hall-of-Famers Ted Lyons and Rick Ferrell plus the fiery Dick Bartell, a one-time Tiger favorite from the 1940 pennant-winners.

The Yankees and Red Sox were the preseason favorites to fight it out for the 1950 AL flag, just as they had done in the 1949 race. But many experts saw Detroit as vastly improved and seemingly a legitimate contender. "Fearless" Oscar Fraley of the Associated Press insisted that the Detroiters had the manpower to go all the way to the top. On paper, it seemed like a good bet. The starting pitching rotation of Newhouser (18-11), Trucks (19-11), Houtteman (15-10), Hutchinson (15-7), and Ted Gray (10-10) was as formidable as any staff in baseball. The only question mark was relief pitching. Veteran Diz Trout at age 35 had struggled to a 3-6 record mainly in relief in '49 and appeared to be washed up. Lacking a consistent relief ace in the mold of Joe Page, Rolfe had to rely on a combination of undistinguished veterans like Hank Borowy, Hal White, and Paul Calvert, plus marginal youngsters like Saul Rogovin, Marlin Stuart, and Ray Herbert to back up his starters.

Catcher Aaron Robinson, obtained the year before in an unpopular trade for promising home-town lefty Billy Pierce, provided adequate catching and some occasional power. Veteran Bob Swift and young Joe Ginsberg were behind Robinson The outfield of right fielder Vic Wertz (.304, 20 HR, 133 RBI), center fielder Johnny Groth (.293), and left fielder Hoot Evers (.303) was the envy of the AL. Groth had burst upon the scene as a rookie sensation in 1949 and was touted as the next Joe DiMaggio. Much was predicted for the young Chicagoan and he continued to live up to his promise with a fine 1950 season, but the Hall of Fame

Marc Okkonen is a self-employed artist, writer, and researcher living in Muskegon, Michigan. Marc has published several baseball books, including Baseball Uniforms of the 20th Century, *three books on major league decades, and a SABR publication on the Federal League. He has been a SABR member since 1985.*

expectations forever haunted him subsequently. Despite a fairly solid 15 years in the American League, he was never forgiven for not producing superstar statistics. Veterans Pat Mullin and Charlie Keller filled in on occasion for the Tigers' talented outfield trio.

The Tiger infield was anchored by baseball's finest third baseman, George Kell. Following a 1949 AL batting title, Kell had another all-star season at the plate and on the field in 1950. He hit .340, drove in 101 runs and led all third basemen in fielding at .982, committing only nine errors. Veteran Don Kolloway, backed up by young Kryhoski, provided creditable first base coverage and chipped in at the bat with a fine .289 average. Shortstop Johnny Lipon, inspired by his new keystone partner Priddy, had a career season with a .293 BA. Priddy hit a respectable .277 and, with Lipon, led the league in double plays executed by shortstops and second basemen (the Philadelphia A's led the AL in total DPs with 208, Detroit not far behind with 194). Neil Berry and Eddie Lake filled in in utility roles when needed.

Early days—The Bengals started the season with four straight wins, but their vaunted pitching staff was crippled by the baffling sore arm problem of ace lefty Hal Newhouser. Prince Hal was unable to contribute until the end of May, and the Tigers were temporarily overtaken by the Yankees but remained on their heels. Some fine outings by Houtteman and Trucks in the early going plus signs of rejuvenation by Paul Trout helped offset the absence of Newhouser. Tiger bats were booming and by the middle of June they surged back into the lead. They held a 1-game margin over their Yankee pursuers when the New Yorkers invaded Briggs Stadium on June 23 for a showdown four-game series. The opening game of that series offered a memorable slugfest of classic proportions—"the wildest ever seen at Briggs Stadium in our book," according to Tiger announcer Harry Heilmann, who had witnessed every game played there since the mid-'30s.

Tiger nemesis Tommy Byrne had been treated to a 6-0 lead when Detroit came up to face him in their fourth. Byrne loaded the bases for Diz Trout and the big pitcher unloaded them with a grand-slam homer to cut the lead to 6-4. Homers by Priddy, Wertz, and Evers followed, and suddenly it was an 8-6 Detroit lead. Those four shots set an American League record for home runs in one inning by one club. The Yanks regained the lead with homers by DiMaggio and Henrich, and Detroit came up in the ninth trailing 9-8. Vic Wertz doubled with one out and then Hoot Evers hit a dramatic inside-the-park homer to pull it out, 10-9. The game total of 11 home runs set a new American League record and gave the Tigers a 2-game lead. They took two of the next three from New York and the Bronx Bombers left town three games in arrears. Pennant fever was now in high gear in the Motor City.

Holding on, falling off—Virgil Trucks' season was already over due to arm troubles, but Art Houtteman, Hutchinson, Newhouser, Gray, and even Hal White gave the club consistent pitching to keep the Tigers on top through July and August. Tiger bats continued to sizzle as six regulars at times during midsummer were over the .300 mark. Detroit, despite the Yankees' winning pace, maintained a 2- to 4-game lead over second place New York through the months of July and August. Cleveland, which ended up in fourth place, six games out, proved to be the ultimate nemesis for Detroit's pennant hopes. The Tribe was the only club with a final winning record against the Bengals, taking 13 of their 22 meetings. The Yankees and Tigers broke even during the season. But the Yankees, sparked by the call-up of rookie pitcher Whitey Ford (9-1) in mid-season, caught up with Detroit by early September and the lead changed hands several times going into the two clubs' final face-to-face meeting at Briggs Stadium on September 14. The Bengals held a precarious 1/2-game lead entering the three-game set. The Yanks handed Newhouser his 10th loss, 7-5, in the opener, but Detroit stormed back to take a 9-7 slugfest despite a three-homer day by slugger Johnny Mize. Rookie Ford took the rubber game 6-1 with a fine six-hitter to put New York 1/2 game ahead. Ironically, Ford throughout his subsequent career had difficulty beating Detroit and was seldom used against them by Manager Stengel.

The Red Sox, with pennant plans of their own, followed the Yankees into the Tigers' lair and swept three to put them in second, pushing the Bengals back to third, 1 1/2 games out. The AL pennant chase had now developed into a three-way dogfight, with Cleveland poised to assume the role of spoiler. All three cities were accepting World Series ticket orders as Detroit entered Cleveland on September 22 for a crucial three-game set, now tied with New York for the top spot. At the same time, the Yankees were facing Boston with a chance to virtually eliminate the Bosox from contention. The Cleveland-Detroit series proved to be the heartbreaker for Tiger followers as the Tribe swept all three to push the Tigers 2-1/2 games out with only seven games left, including another final three with dreaded Cleveland at season's end. The opener of the September 22 series at Cleveland pitted the two ace hurlers Feller and Newhouser for their umpteenth confrontation and ended in dramatic fashion. Don Kolloway hit a clutch two-run blast in the top of the ninth off Rapid Robert to tie the game 3-3. But Joe Gordon took Prince Hal "downtown" in the bottom of the ninth to hand Newhouser his 12th defeat and push the Tigers back into second place. Mike Garcia dropped them another game back, 10-2, in the second game as New York was shutting out Boston 8-0. The stage was set for game three and the swan song for Detroit's pennant hopes.

Teddy Gray was matched up against Cleveland's 21-game winner Bob Lemon in an afternoon game that was played entirely under the lights—an eerie and ominous condition caused by a heavy dark haze from Canadian forest fires in the north. It turned out to be a classic pitching duel with a traumatic finish. Lemon gave himself a 1-0 lead in the fourth with a solo homer, but Johnny Lipon responded with a "dinger" in the seventh to tie the score. Some 35,000 fans, many of them Tiger followers who made the trip to root for the Bengals, were on the edge of their seats as the game went into the 10th inning tied 1-1. In the top half, Pat Mullin, who had singled, was left stranded by the heart of the batting order—suddenly an everyday occurrence by the now impotent Tiger wrecking crew.

Pitcher Lemon opened the home half of the tenth with a booming triple. Then Dale Mitchell and Bob Kennedy were intentionally passed to set up force plays at every base. Doby popped up to Don Kolloway for the first out, setting the stage for an inning-ending double play. Luke Easter played right into the Tiger strategy by bouncing to first baseman Don Kolloway, who stepped on the bag and fired a perfect strike to catcher Aaron Robinson in plenty of time to put the tag on Bob Lemon, who had bolted for home plate. Robinson stepped on the plate believing it was a force out, then walked away while Lemon crossed home with the winning run. A mental blunder had given the Indians a three-game sweep and virtually doomed the Detroit club's flag hopes, as the Yankees were once again dispatching the fading Red Sox 9-5.

That ill-fated ending would stick in the craw of Detroit fans for years afterwards as the Motor City's version of the "Merkle Boner." Poor Aaron Robinson played out the balance of his playing career with a double curse in the eyes of Detroit fans. First, he was the Bengals' compensation for the loss of promising pitcher Billy Pierce in late 1948—made more painful as the years went by, since Pierce proved to be a first-rate pitcher for the White Sox in the 1950s. And of course his unfortunate execution of what was called "Robinson's Rock" in that fateful game in Cleveland would never be forgiven in the Motor City. Robinson was "history" by mid-1951, although many teammates came to his defense, blaming the "night game" conditions of that afternoon and the fact that the catcher's vision down the line was blocked, preventing him from seeing Kolloway step on first. But with so much at stake, Tiger fans found him guilty of not instinctively making sure all avenues were closed to the enemy by putting an affirming tag on the sliding Lemon.

Now 2-1/2 games out with only seven left to play, Detroit's only hope was a last-minute slump by New York. It never happened. Stengel's men took five of seven, while the Bengals were only able to take four of the last seven contests with the hapless Browns and the cursed Indians. They captured the runner-up spot, three games out and a game up on third place Boston.

What happened?—Many alibis were presented to explain away the disappointing finish in the following months, but perhaps the unscientific explanation says it best—they simply ran out of gas. By September, they were leaving hordes of runners on base and losing gut-wrenching one-run games, one after another. Detroit writers insisted that key Tiger players were tired and demoralized by Labor Day, and that the weak bench was unable to spell the starters adequately—not a problem for Casey Stengel's deep Yankee roster.

In retrospect, the absence of a healthy Newhouser in the season's first month and the virtual absence of proven starter Virgil Trucks after April might have easily made the difference. On the other hand, Diz Trout contributed 13 victories after seeming to be on the brink of extinction after 1949. And marginal starters Ted Gray and Hal White made giant pitching contributions beyond all realistic expectations. Also, many of the Tiger position players had career years, notably Johnny Lipon with .293 BA and Hoot Evers with 21 homers and 103 RBIs. For so many regulars to have their best seasons in the same year is indeed a rarity, and maybe for that reason the Bengals were simply enjoying a lucky year and were actually playing over their heads.

But to the nearly two million Detroit fans who flocked to Briggs Stadium, their beloved Tigers were a team of destiny—cheated out of a championship by the fates. In Detroit, as it was nearly every year in Brooklyn, the cry was "wait 'til next year." But "next year" never came, as the 1951 Tigers stumbled into the second division and the following year finished in the cellar for the first time in the history of the franchise.

A concessionaire's dream

A team of fat Canadians, none to weigh less than 200 lbs., is being organized to take a trip through New York State this summer to play against the local fatmen's teams of Buffalo, Rochester, Troy, Albany, and New York. They will meet with a right royal welcome when they come. (The Toronto Globe, *1881.)*

—David McDonald